Catalog It!

A Guide to Cataloging School Library Materials,

Second Edition

Allison G. Kaplan
Ann Marlow Riedling

Linworth Books

**Professional Development Resources for
K-12 Library Media and Technology Specialists**

Dedication

This book is dedicated to all of the wonderful people who, out of the kindness of their hearts, donate uncataloged materials to school library media centers...and to the library media specialists who must do the cataloging.

And to our families:
David, Rebekah, and Hannah – AGK
Russ and Marlow – AMR

Library of Congress Cataloging-in-Publication Data

Kaplan, Allison G.
  Catalog it! : a guide to cataloging school library materials / Allison G.
Kaplan, Ann Marlow Riedling.-- 2nd ed.
      p. cm.
  Includes index.
  ISBN 1-58683-197-6 (pbk.)
  1. Cataloging--Handbooks, manuals, etc. 2. School libraries. 3.
Instructional materials centers. I. Riedling, Ann Marlow, 1952- II. Title.
Z693.K28 2006
025.3--dc22

                                    2005034165

Published by Linworth Publishing, Inc.
480 East Wilson Bridge Road, Suite L
Worthington, Ohio 43085

FSC
Mixed Sources
Product group from well-managed
forests and other controlled sources

Cert no. SW-COC-002283
www.fsc.org
© 1996 Forest Stewardship Council

ISBN: 1-58683-197-6

Table of Contents

PART I: THEORY & TOOLS

Table of Contents continued

PART II: APPLICATION

Table of Contents *continued*

Table of Contents *continued*

Table of Figures

Preface | *to the Second Edition*

"I don't know if this is kosher but ..."
"I hope the cataloging police don't catch me doing this!"

These are common statements found on electronic discussion lists accompanying cataloging questions. With *Catalog It,* we hope to address some of the burning issues that make school library media specialists squeamish about cataloging. It is not the intent of this book to make school library media specialists into professional catalogers. A book of this size and the very nature of most cataloging classes for school library media specialists cannot hope, nor is it necessary to hope, to accomplish that task. However, what we do hope to do with this text is to give school library media specialists the tools needed to be intelligent consumers of commercially available cataloging and the knowledge to edit or create new catalog records if necessary. We want to see a decrease in statements such as those above and help school library media specialists feel comfortable in dealing with knotty cataloging questions. If nothing else, we hope that the information in this text will help practitioners face the latest in library holdings, e.g. DVDs, graphic novels, and Web sites. We hope that the examples and descriptions presented here will alleviate the fear of organizing these materials and provide the library media specialist the tools with which to quickly and effectively catalog and provide access to *all* library materials.

We are excited to have the opportunity to write a second edition of this text and we hope the text will be as useful to those working alone, as for those taking a class. This is not to say that one should not take a cataloging class, we would never make such a suggestion. However, we are cognizant of the reality of some school library situations and so wanted to create a manual that would be helpful to all sorts of school library media specialists, be they veteran or new professionals. Readers of both editions will note that, while the main structure of the book remains the same as the first edition, there are some changes to the organization of the text. We have divided the text into two parts: *Theory and Tools* and *Application.* The meat of the matter is in Part II: *Application*; however, readers will also find Part I to be helpful in their day-to-day work.

Part I: Theory and Tools. In this section, the reader will find a brief history of cataloging, the cataloging environment today, and how cataloging standards work with the MARC format. *Chapter 1: A Brief History of Cataloging* presents the history part of the text to help explain why it is catalogers do what they do. *Chapter 2: Copy Cataloging and Cataloger's Resources* offers the reader some cataloging hints as well as links to resources that will expedite the cataloging process. *Chapter 3: Cataloging Theory and the MARC Record* presents background information transferring information about the item to an electronic library catalog using cataloging standards and the MARC format.

Part II: Application. As mentioned above, this is the meat of the matter. Under the heading of application, readers are provided with instructions and exercises for using MARC format to describe subject matter of book and non-book materials. *Chapter 4: Intellectual Access – Subject Headings* covers the theory and application of subject headings. Also included here is a discussion on the difference between subject and keyword retrieval. Both the *Sears List of Subject Headings* and the *Library of Congress Subject Headings* are discussed in terms of practical application in the school library environment. The Dewey Decimal Classification (DDC) system is reviewed in *Chapter 5: Intellectual Access – Classification.* Classification is a difficult topic to cover in a text of this size. However, we do investigate the principles and applications of DDC providing the reader with illustrations and exercises. Readers are also referred to the current edition of the *Abridged Dewey Decimal Classification* and to the *Abridged 13 Workbook* by Sydney W. Davis and Gregory R. New (Forest Press, 1997) for a more complete explanation of classification. *Chapter 6: Physical Access* covers the basics of standardized cataloging in the eight areas of description. Discussed in this chapter are each of the areas and the general rules of the *Anglo-American Cataloguing Rules* (2004 update) in terms of creating records using the MARC format.

The book concludes with chapters on future issues and processing items. Several appendices are also included: a MARC hint sheet, a template, information on library systems, answers to the exercises, and a glossary.

In writing this text, we tried to present realistic examples that can be used as templates for cataloging all types of school library materials. Our examples include books, books with tapes and on tapes, CDs, videotapes, DVDs, graphic novels, and Web sites. Following the examples, step-by-step, the new and the experienced library media specialist should be able to catalog anything in a school library media collection.

Before delving into the text, we would like to point out two things: first, we use the abbreviation *AACR* to refer to Anglo-American Cataloguing Rules in its most generic form as well as the current revision and update of the standards. In chapter one we describe the history of *AACR* and at that point will be specific as to which edition is being described. We use just the abbreviation *AACR* because the most recent version of *AACR* is the 2002 revision, 2004 update. This is a confusing description and difficult to abbreviate: AACR2R2002r2004u! The long abbreviation of the latest edition of *AACR* illustrates how much things change in an area that most people believe is rather static. Cataloging rules are changing with alarming frequency and, with remote access to catalogs, we no longer have the luxury of organizing materials the way we have always done. School library media specialists owe it to their students to keep current with changes in cataloging standards.

Second, we point out that learning about cataloging really requires the proper tools. Readers may find it helpful to have on hand a copy of the latest edition of *AACR, Abridged Dewey Decimal Classification,* and *Sears List of Subject Headings.*

As we said in the beginning, this is not a text to help create professional catalogers. But if the reader of this book can deal in a quick and efficient manner, with that box of uncataloged items so lovingly donated by well-meaning parents or teachers then we have done our job.

Happy cataloging!
Allison & Ann

Instructor's Preface | to the Second Edition

Creating a cataloging textbook is by nature self-limiting. It is virtually impossible to include all of the nuances of cataloging and maintain a text of manageable size. Therefore, for the instructor, there is no substitute for having and being familiar with the most current editions of *Anglo-American Cataloguing Rules*, *Sears List of Subject Headings*, *Library of Congress Subject Headings*, *Abridged Dewey Decimal Classification* (DDC), *Library of Congress Classification*, and MARC.

The authors have provided limited instruction for the application of DDC (abridged edition). It is difficult to teach this system without the use of DDC, therefore, instructors are encouraged to have their students working with copies of abridged DDC as they go through this part of the text. Additionally, there is an excellent workbook that covers this topic: *Dewey Decimal Classification Workbook* that can be used to supplement this textbook. Although the workbook is for the 13th edition of DDC abridged and the most current abridged edition is the 14th, the workbook still is a useful resource for an instructor.

This textbook includes examples specific to the school library media center collection. While the authors have attempted to include enough exercises to provide students with sufficient practice opportunities, instructors may feel the need to add to the exercises given. In teaching, the authors have found that providing students with "old cataloging" to update is an excellent method of testing student cataloging knowledge.

The examples in this book are taken from publications that should be readily available in any school or public library. The authors try to present an accurate picture of the information provided on the item; however, there is no substitute for having the item in hand. Instructors may find it helpful to have the items available for students to look at while working with this text. Many example texts are referred to in this book, however the most frequently used example items are as follows:

- *Accidents May Happen* written by Charlotte Foltz Jones, illustrated by John O'Brien. New York: Delacorte Press, 1996.

- *Bard of Avon: The Story of William Shakespeare* written by Diane Stanley and Peter Vennema, illustrated by Diane Stanley. New York: Morrow Junior Books, 1992.

- *Frog and Toad Are Friends* (book & cassette) by Arnold Lobel. New York: Harper Carousel, 1985.

- *Green Eggs and Ham* (computer software) by Dr. Seuss. Novato, CA: Living Books, 1996.

- *Harry Potter and the Order of the Phoenix* by J. K. Rowling. New York: Listening Library, 2003.

- *Noodlebug on the Move* (DVD & CD-ROM). Peru, IL: Carus Publishing, 2003.
- *Ohio* by Ron Knapp. Berkeley Heights, NJ: MyReportLinks.com Books (Enslow), 2002.
- *Persepolis* (graphic novel) by Marjane Satrapi. New York: Pantheon, 2003.
- *Strega Nona* (videotape in Spanish) by Tomie dePaola. Weston, Conn.: Weston Woods, 2000.

Acknowledgments

T In the summer of 1998, Ann and I had the good fortune of attending the annual conference of the International Association of School Librarianship in Tel Aviv, Israel. Part of the conference included bus transportation from the hotels to the conference site. Israel has some of the worst traffic in the entire world. Stuck on a bus in a horrendous traffic jam, I struck up a conversation with the person sitting next to me. While the bus moved at a snail's pace, I had the opportunity to discuss with my seatmate one of my favorite topics, which is teaching cataloging to school library media specialists. I mentioned that one semester I had a student who finally threw up her hands in frustration and said, "Isn't there a cataloging textbook that uses examples of something we would actually run into in our school libraries?" I told my seat partner that one day I would write such a book. My partner turned out to be Ann who said she would happily help me write such a book. The rest, as they say, is history.

There are many people who helped make this book possible. A thank you from Allison: First, I would like to thank that frustrated student, Denise Allen, who has since left the school library and is now Education Associate, Libraries/Technology/Media in the Delaware Department of Education. If she hadn't been so frustrated, I would never have thought of attempting this task. Second, I would like to acknowledge the technical support of Christine McBride and Debra Lloyd. Chris, my cataloging assistant in the Education Resource Center and star-cataloging student, read drafts of this book and provided much needed technical assistance. Debbie, Director of the Delaware Learning Resource System for Sussex County (Delaware), ran checks on *Sears* headings and checked for consistency in the area of subject headings. The second edition benefited from the helpful suggestions of my students at the University of Delaware and McDaniel College. I know I am a better teacher for their help and I hope this book is a better teaching tool.

I would also like to thank my supervisor, Peggy Dillner, who supported this endeavor with understanding and a great sense of humor and who encourages my participation in teaching classes and offering training sessions throughout the state of Delaware in an effort to improve the quality of Delaware school library catalogs. Third, I would like to thank my husband, David, and my two daughters, Rebekah and Hannah, who more than tolerated this project and who didn't cheer too loudly when I announced it was finished. Their love and support helped to keep me grounded during this process and reminded me there is life before, during, and after writing a book. I would also like to recognize my mother, sister, and late father who saw potential in me long before I saw it in myself. Finally, I express my gratitude to Annie as my co-author and dear friend who listened to my thoughts and helped to form them into cogent ideas. Her continuous suggestions and unwavering assistance are the things that made this book a reality.

A thank you from Ann: I am so thankful I met Allison on that steamy day in Israel! Not only have we shared a book, but also a deep friendship. In addition, I thank my husband, Russ, and my daughter, Marlow, for their constant support, guidance, patience, and love.

We could not have come this far without the help and comments of our reviewers and the patience of Cynthia Anderson and all the staff at Linworth. Of course Ann and I bear responsibility for any errors in the text.

About the Authors

Allison graduated from the University of California, Los Angeles with a Master of Arts in Dance and a Master's of Library and Information Science in 1986. Allison's interest in cataloging began at UCLA where she was fortunate enough to learn cataloging theory and practice from Elaine Svenonius, Elizabeth Baughman, and Marcia Bates. Moving to Delaware in 1987, Allison began teaching cataloging to school library media specialists in 1990. Through the years she has learned much from her students regarding the practice of cataloging while kids are climbing the bookshelves and asking for another book "just like this one." Allison is currently the coordinator of the School Library Media Specialist program and assistant director of the Education Resource Center at the University of Delaware. She does not keep her sound recordings or spices in alphabetical order.

Ann is a graduate of Indiana University with a B.S. in education; graduate of the University of Georgia with a Master's Degree and post-graduate work in Library Science and Educational Technology; and graduate of the University of Louisville with a Doctorate in Educational Administration and Information Technology/Distance Education. Ann has presented both in the United States and internationally on the following topics: information literacy, using young adult literature to address diversity, reference skills for school media specialists, online teaching, and course production.

PART ONE

Chapter *1*

A Brief History of Cataloging

Introduction

From the time knowledge became greater than one person could accurately store and recall mentally, humans have sought ways of organizing and storing information. Why do we have this need? For the most part, we do this so that we can easily and efficiently retrieve and access specific information. True, there are those of us who happily exist in cluttered and chaotic environments, but to make the best use of information it should be well organized and easily accessible. A simple definition of cataloging is: the organization of information so that it is easily accessible for anyone who needs it. The resource created in the process of cataloging will contain some kind of description that makes the item being described accessible to someone, other than the cataloger, through a variety of access points. In other words, to catalog is to organize and make retrievable information. The resulting record of this organization can take many forms: a book, a catalog card, or a computerized database. This chapter will explore the ideas and concepts of cataloging within a historical context.

Functions of the Library

Consider the services of a library: to collect, to disseminate, and to organize. In order to create a collection, one must select and collect materials; this is known as acquisitions. In larger libraries this is often a department unto itself. For school library media specialists, the act of acquiring materials consists of searching through the various books and media catalogs and reviews and, perhaps most importantly, by working with and obtaining recommendations from classroom teachers and students, thus ensuring that the library materials accurately reflect the academic and leisure reading needs of the learning community.

To disseminate information is to get the information to the user. In schools, we think of this as circulation. However, dissemination covers all aspects of the flow of information from checking out a book to teaching a person, class, or classroom teacher how to use the Internet. Instruction belongs in this category because the goal is to move information from the source to the user. When information moves from its source to the patron, that is information dissemination.

To access information efficiently, it must be organized. Organizing information means describing and classifying it; in other words, cataloging it. Typically library collections are too large for a single librarian to know the content and location of every item. Even if it were a small enough collection, the goal of making patrons independent users of the collection is thwarted if users must rely on the memory of a single person. Thus systematic and standardized organization of the library collection becomes the foundation of the library itself.

The Ancient Past

Even before the establishment of the great library of Alexandria, before Benjamin Franklin founded the Free Library of Philadelphia, and before Melvil Dewey divided knowledge into 10 classes, people were devising ways to organize and retrieve information; that is, they developed cataloging systems.

Ancient peoples organized tablets using the incipit, or the first lines, of the tablets. More than 5,000 years ago, in the ancient Mesopotamian city of Ur, catalogers used key words from the first two lines of the text and imprinted these words on the ends of the clay tablets. The tablets were stored in such a way that these ends could be browsed and the information (that is, the right tablet) retrieved (1).

As time passed and technology advanced, more elaborate ways of controlling information access were created. The ancient Chinese arranged materials according to literary quality. Those scrolls of the lowest quality were hung on lacquer rods and the highest quality scrolls on fine red-glazed rods (2). By the 15th and 16th centuries, private libraries grew to such extents that some nobles hired their own librarians. These librarians created catalogs of the private holdings and used the catalogs for collection purposes. They would also often travel great distances to purchase books for their masters (3). These early private libraries were a source of pride for their owners and a sign of vast wealth. The early librarians took immense pride in knowing not only the titles in the entire collection, but also much of the contents within those titles. As printed information became easier to produce and store and as libraries took on more and more important roles in society, it became critical to create efficient standardized systems for organizing and retrieving information.

Modern Times

The rules and ideas that guide catalogers today came from ideas expressed in the later part of the 19th century and formalized in the early part of the 20th century. In her book, *Introduction to Cataloging and Classification* (4), Lois Mai Chan offers a description and explanation of the development of cataloging standards that is summarized here.

In 1839, Sir Anthony Panizzi developed a cataloging code for the British Museum. "Panizzi's 91 Rules" formed the first of the modern-day cataloging codes. Charles C. Jewett of the Smithsonian Institution followed Panizzi's lead, and in 1853, he developed 33 rules based on Panizzi's 91 Rules. Jewett developed what is considered the first attempt to codify subject headings. He also proposed "stereotyped" cataloging entries in order to facilitate cooperative and centralized cataloging.

Charles Ammi Cutter published *Rules for a Printed Dictionary Catalog* in 1876. In this work, Cutter defined 369 rules for descriptive and subject cataloging and card filing. This became the basis for the dictionary or alphabetical catalog, that is, entries arranged alphabetically regardless of subject

---

Cutter's statement of objects of the catalog and means for attaining them. (5)

Objects
1. To enable a person to find a book of which either:
   - a) the author
   - b) the title   } is known
   - c) the subject
2. To show what the library has:
   - a) by a given author
   - b) on a given subject
   - c) in a given kind of literature
3. To assist in the choice of a book:
   - a) as to its edition (bibliographically)
   - b) as to its character (literary or topical)

Means
1. Author entry with the necessary references (for 1a and 2a)
2. Title entry or title reference (for 1b)
3. Subject entry, cross-references, and classed subject table (for 1c and 2b)
4. Form entry and language entry (for 2c)
5. Giving edition and imprint, with notes when necessary (for 3a)
6. Notes (for 3b)

---

relationship. (The other type of catalog is the classified catalog that is arranged by class number, i.e. subject, as in shelf list catalogs.) Cutter proposed three objectives of the catalog and the means to achieve the objectives (which he called "objects"). These objectives are still evidenced in *AACR* rules today.

Standards in cataloging blossomed in the 20th century despite complaints that changes in standards created havoc for librarians who would have to update older records in their catalogs to keep their records current and accurate. The first joint effort of creating standard cataloging rules between the United States and British librarians was published in 1908. Unfortunately, the two countries could not come to a complete agreement regarding the rules, and two versions of the rules, British and American, were published. Known in the United States as *Catalog Rules: Author and Title Entries*, the publication was 88 pages in length, omitted subject headings, and largely ignored the needs of smaller libraries. Agreements to revise the rules were preempted by the onset of World War II. Nevertheless, the American Library Association (ALA) produced a 408-page elaboration of the 1908 rules in 1941. Referred to as the "ALA Draft," these rules divided cataloging into two parts: 1) entry and headings and 2) description. The precise instructions for cataloging were criticized for being too legalistic (a complaint often echoed by beginning catalogers regarding the current rules). Paths diverged again; this time only in America, when, in 1949, the Library of Congress and ALA both published separate cataloging rules. These two works formed the basis of the Anglo-American Cataloguing Rules used today.

If Panizzi and Cutter laid the foundation, it was Seymour Lubetzky who built the framework for the current standardized cataloging rules. In *Cataloging Rules and Principles*, Lubetzky criticized the 1949 rules as long and confusing and offered instead a cataloging proposal based on two objectives:

The first objective is to enable the user of the catalog to determine readily whether or not the library has the book he wants ... the second objective is to reveal to the user of the catalog, under one form of the author's name, what works the library has by a given author and what editions or translations of a given work (6).

Anglo-American Cataloguing Rules

In 1961, 53 countries and 12 associations met in Paris for the International Conference on Cataloguing Principles. Basing their work on an unpublished manuscript of Lubetzky's, the result of the conference became known as "Paris Principles." Focusing on descriptions based on title page information and standardization of the concept of authorship, this report represented a breakthrough in international cataloging standards. In 1967, the first edition of *AACR* was published. It incorporated the Paris Principles (which dealt mostly with entry and authorship) and the 1949 Library of Congress standards for descriptive cataloging. However, this edition of *AACR* did not reach the international scope hoped for in Paris and, as with the 1908 rules, was published in two versions: North American and British. *AACR* chapter six (monographs) was revised in 1974 to incorporate (among other things) the standards established in 1971 as the *International Standard Bibliographic Description (for Single Volume and Multi-Volume Monographic Publications) (ISBD)*. ISBD standards were created to enhance international cataloging standardization with three basic principles in mind:

> First, that records produced in one country or by the users of one language can be easily understood in other countries and by the users of other languages; second, that the records produced in each country can be integrated into files or lists of various kinds containing also records from other countries; and third, that records in written or printed forms can be converted into machine-readable form with the minimum of editing (7).

ISBD is supported and revised by the International Federation of Library Associations & Institutions (IFLA). A full description of ISBD can be found on the IFLA Web site at: http://www.ifla.org/VII/s13/pubs/isbdg2004.pdf. The ISBD rules are responsible for the dashes, slashes, colons, semi-colons, and periods in today's bibliographic record. While troublesome at first for the new cataloger, it is just one aspect of the bibliographic record that makes it possible for library users to feel comfortable in using different types of libraries in their communities and around the world.

AACR has been revised periodically since its first publication in 1967. With each revision, catalogers complain about the repercussions of changes in the bibliographic record; however, each change has not been without merit. The incorporation of the "optional" rule in 1978 allowed catalogers the choice of following strict standards or adapting the standards to meet individual institutional needs. This was an important change in cataloging standards as it allowed smaller libraries the freedom to catalog with less detail than was required of large research-oriented libraries. The 1978 edition also included the much-needed updated rules for cataloging non-book materials. The 1988 revision is not considered a new edition (*AACR3*) because the basic premise and organization of the rules remains the same as the 1978 edition. That is, the basic code is the same, but merely updated to reflect current theory and technology. The 1988 revision was the first to consider machine-readable cataloging developments that might affect the *AACR* rules, although examples were still given in the style of the manual catalog card. The greatest number of changes of the code in the 1988 revision were with respect to entries under pseudonyms and description of computer files. This was the edition of *AACR* that is responsible for the change of entering a work under Seuss, Dr. instead of under Geisel, Theodor. Chapter nine (computer files) included revisions to better accommodate the cataloging of a new media, microcomputer software.

With surprisingly little fanfare, *Anglo-American Cataloguing Rules, 2nd edition, 1998 revision*, found its way into the cataloger's world. While jokes abounded regarding how catalogers should refer to this book (AACR2Rr?), like its 1988 predecessor, it too marked not a change in code, but a modification of the code. One aspect to note concerning its publication is that it appeared in three different formats. First, as a traditional book, second as a loose-leaf notebook, and third in an electronic format, fondly referred to as *AACR2-e* (the later two created for ease of updating between revisions).

In September 2002, another version of *AACR2* was released as *AACR2, 2002 revision*. No longer available in the traditional book format, this loose-leaf edition boasted the inclusion of all amendments and revisions of the rules since 1999. Digital information has long been a topic of heated discussion in cataloging circles and the changes in the 2002 revision reflect outcomes of these discussions. The 2002 revision is significant for changes in rules for cataloging cartographic materials, electronic resources, and "continuing resources." Continuing resources were referred to as serial publications in previous *AACR* editions. With the new revision of *AACR* the definition has been expanded to include, among other publications, Web sites—especially those related to serial publications published either formerly or simultaneously in paper format.

Probably because it is so easy to do, revisions to *AACR* seem to happen with increasing frequency. In September 2003, a new update was released. This update marks the beginning of annual updates. It contained some corrections plus updates of some rules particularly in the area of access (chapters 21 and 24). This update included the standardization in capitalizing the names of the planets. In the past, the planet Earth was only sometimes capitalized, but now the cataloger should always capitalize its name. (The dirt on the ground, however, is still "earth.") In terms of access, rules have been changed to reflect a relaxing of the rules for added title entries. Particularly bothersome, and the reason we refer to the work only as *AACR*, is the title page. One might expect that catalogers, in creating a work for other catalogers, would pay attention to the layout of the title page. Perhaps they did, and perhaps it is the nature of the beast, but the title pages for the 2002 revision and the 2003 update are different, but just similar enough, to be infuriatingly similar. (It would make a good final exam question to have cataloging students create a bibliographic record for both versions of *AACR*!)

Digital Information, FRBR, & AACR3

AACR3 is being revised as this book is being written. Information about the new edition can be found at the Web site for the Joint Steering Committee for Revision of *AACR*: http://www.collectionscanada.ca/jsc/aacr3draftpt1.html. This new work promises to be a bona fide new edition with changes to the organization of the standards reflecting a more integrated approach to cataloging all material types. It will even have a new title, tentatively set as "Resource Description and Access" (RDA). This new edition will be published no earlier than 2007. The structure of RDA will look drastically different from *AACR*, with much more emphasis on online access to the standards than ever before. The new standards do not disregard earlier rules of *AACR* and ISBD, but they do rely more heavily on the Functional Requirement for Bibliographic Records (FRBR).

FRBR relies on the concepts of "work," "expression," "manifestation," and "item" rather than "information package" and "surrogate record." FRBR began as a project under the Study Group on Functional Requirements for Bibliographic Records of IFLA, 1992-1995. The result of this study group was the publication of the FRBR report (8) and the subsequent adoption and studies by the Library of Congress and OCLC (9). The basis of FRBR is that description based on relationships is clearer than description based on information packages themselves:

- [W]hen we say "book" to describe a physical object that has paper pages and a binding …, FRBR calls this an "item."

- When we say "book" we also may mean a "publication" as when we go to a bookstore to purchase a book. We may know its ISBN but the particular copy does not matter as long as it's in good condition and not missing pages. FRBR calls this a "manifestation."

- When we say "book" as in 'who translated that book,' we may have a particular text in mind and a specific language. FRBR calls this an "expression."

- When we say "book" as in 'who wrote that book,' we could mean a higher level of abstraction, the conceptual content that underlies all of the linguistic versions, the story being told in the book, the ideas in a person's head for the book. FRBR calls this a "work" (10).

We see then that under FRBR there is much more emphasis on relationships between items rather than the isolation of individual items. While this seems to be foreign to part-time catalogers (such as school library media specialists), the terminology is critical in the revision of *AACR*. We hope that providers of cataloging programs for the schools are watching these developments very carefully so that school libraries are not, once again, left behind in the organization of information. For more information about FRBR, readers are encouraged to view the LC Web site at: http://www.loc.gov/cds/FRBR.html.

Changing AACR

Who is responsible for making changes to *AACR*? There are numerous people representing many organizations and associations who are responsible for the content of the changes to *AACR*. With the publication of the second edition of *AACR* in 1978, the body responsible for revisions was formally recognized in the name it is known as today, the *Joint Steering Committee (JSC) for Revision of AACR*. The JSC is comprised of members of The American Library Association, The Australian Committee on Cataloguing, The British Library, The Canadian Committee on Cataloguing, The Chartered Institute of Library and Information Professionals, and The Library of Congress. Many committees of professional library organizations meet to discuss concerns regarding *AACR* and provide suggestions to the JSC for consideration. Meetings at the ALA annual and midwinter conferences provide opportunities for non-committee members to hear about proposed changes and, on occasion, to comment on change proposals. Non-committee members can also keep track of changes from the Library of Congress Cataloging Policy and Support Office Web page: http://www.loc.gov/catdir/cpso/ and through the MARC Forum discussion list: http://www.loc.gov/marc/marcforum.html.

Bibliographic Record

The bibliographic record supplies the physical and intellectual description of the item and its location in the collection. Recording the physical description of the item (e.g. number of pages, timing of video) is referred to as descriptive cataloging. Describing the intellectual content of the item (i.e. what the item is about) is done through subject cataloging and classification. Figure 1.1 shows various types of bibliographic records.

The Book List: The book list is the oldest form of library catalogs. It was portable and could be copied and shared. The University of Delaware Project Coast list (see

Figure 1.1

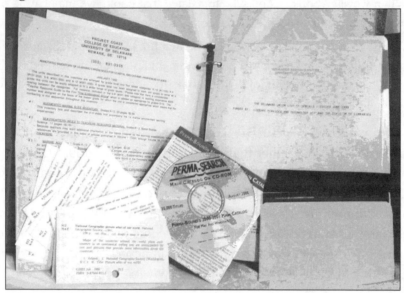

Samples of catalogs. Clockwise from top left: Book list from University of Delaware Project Coast, State of Delaware Union List of Serials, Library of Congress microfiche, CD-Rom compilation of books from PermaBound, catalog cards.

Figure 1.1) is one such example. Organization of the book list was difficult. If the organization was by date of accession, that is to say no real organization at all, then long lists became useless (who wants to search through page after page of text for a single item?). If organization was alphabetical (author or title), then it became costly to update because it had to be rewritten every time new items were added. Even worse, in order to not rewrite the list, new items might be added to the end of the list, thus compromising the organization of the list.

The popularity of lists declined with the development of the card catalog; however, as computers became more abundant in libraries, computer generated booklists (such as the Project Coast list) became popular once again. Computer generated lists were easier and less expensive to update than their manual predecessors, thus making different forms of arrangement (author, title, and accession date) more feasible. Union lists are often published this way. The State of Delaware Union List of Serials (see Figure 1.1) is an example of a computer generated union list.

The Card Catalog: In 1853, Charles Folsom created a card catalog for the Smithsonian library. This is considered the first card catalog in the United States. By 1893, a survey of 58 American libraries showed that 43 libraries were using the card catalog. In 1876, Melvil Dewey standardized the size of the catalog card to the 3x5 inch cards so ubiquitous in the recent past. He also published, anonymously, the first edition of the Dewey Decimal classification system. The publication was 44 pages and 100 copies were printed. Folsom's card catalog, using Dewey's card and classification system, would be the dominant form of information organization well into the 1960s.

The card catalog was not portable, but was easily updated. The problem was typing all of the separate cards for the various entries: title, author, subject (see Figure 1). If one considers that the manual typewriter of the late 1800s was clumsy and difficult to work with for extended lengths of time, then one can see the reasons behind some cataloging quirks and frustrations. The concepts of no more than three subject headings, of a single main entry card, and of not capitalizing words in the title, all stem from the problem of first, writing out each card by hand, and later by using the manual typewriter.

The Electronic Catalog: The integration of computer technology into the library completely revolutionized the cataloging process. Indeed, all library functions were affected by computerization. Computerized databases are terrific, not only because they arc casily updated, but also because they are portable. By copying records on to a disk, printing the records on paper, or accessing them via the Internet, the collection can be in the user's hands, regardless of where the user is in relation to the catalog or even the library itself. Another advantage of the computerized database is the increase in access to information in the bibliographic record. No longer does a clumsy typewriter limit the desires of the beleaguered librarian. With computerization, multiple subject headings, added titles, and notes can be created liberally and with ease. Once entered, data are easily accessed, and if cards do need to be printed, that, too, is done painlessly.

Computerized databases are flexible and current; however, they are also expensive. Ever-changing technologies demand large and frequent expenditures. Librarians are forced to spend money on newer computers, as well as service contracts, and are forced to spend time learning how to use the computers and programs. Furthermore, while libraries have long been heralded as the great equalizers in terms of providing information to all citizens, computer technology is a stumbling block to that credo. Libraries that do not have the resources to purchase and maintain good computer technologies are left behind. Even into the 21st century, there are libraries in the United States that do not utilize computerized cataloging programs. As the libraries suffer, so, too, do the users.

Sharing Bibliographic Records

Following Jewett's call for "stereotype" cataloging, the Library of Congress took the lead in the United States for providing authoritative cataloging to share. In 1901 the Library of Congress began its printed card service. The printed card service encouraged shared cataloging and standardization of cataloging rules. Two hundred and twelve libraries were subscribers to this service merely one year after it started. By the 1960s, Library of Congress cards became the symbol of cataloging with subscribers from Japan to the Vatican.

As library collections grew, librarians realized the usefulness of cooperating with each other through shared cataloging and the development of cataloging standards. There are numerous advantages to standardizing rules and sharing cataloging. The savings in time and money by sharing cataloging appears obvious. Users also benefit from standardized rules by knowing what to expect when walking into any library. A user familiar with the Dewey Decimal classification system can walk into any public library and know precisely where to look for a work on any discipline. Similarly, there is comfort in going to a catalog and knowing where the information on the card will be for author, title, and call number. Early programmers capitalized on this comfort level by creating the Online Public Access Catalog (OPAC) programs to display information exactly as it would look as if it were in a card catalog. Paramount to shared cataloging, however, is that catalogers must follow the same rules in order to share their records.

When the Library of Congress began distributing copies of its printed catalog cards in 1901, the cost was the cost of the card plus 10 percent. The idea of purchasing cataloging from the Library of Congress caught on quickly and soon the Library of Congress became *the* distributor of shared cataloging. Libraries could also purchase bibliographic records in the form of book lists to refer to when creating catalog records. Perhaps the best known of these lists in the United States is the *National Union Catalog* (NUC) published by the Library of Congress. An indispensable cataloging tool since the 1940s, no large academic library would have been without the omnipresent volumes of the NUC. Today, this publication has been replaced by Internet access to the Library of Congress database.

The Library of Congress began distributing cataloging in electronic form as early as 1969. These magnetic tapes contained LC cataloging of English language monographs. It would be several years before "MARC" (MAchine Readable Cataloging) would be a common term in other libraries. But common term it would be. Today, even neophyte librarians know of this phenomenon called "MARC" and expect it to do magical things. MARC was developed by and for the Library of Congress; it was not meant to supplant cataloging standards or become a standard unto itself. For better or for worse, MARC format has become not only a national, but also an international template for creating bibliographic records in an electronic environment. It must be emphasized, however, that all punctuation and input practices seen in MARC records come from the *AACR* and ISBD standards. There is no such thing as "MARC cataloging." The cataloging is set by cataloging standards, such as, but not limited to, *AACR* and ISBD. MARC is a program for taking cataloging and putting it into the automated environment. Starting as an in-house system in the late 1960s, MARC has become MARC 21; it now incorporates standards from many English-speaking countries and is published jointly by the Library of Congress and the National Library of Canada.

Another form of shared cataloging is the Library of Congress Cataloging in Publication (CIP) program. The CIP program began in 1971 and is heavily relied upon by numerous librarians, especially by those in smaller libraries. The bibliographic information commonly found on the verso of the title page is the CIP information. Prior to publication, catalogers in the Library of Congress receive galley proofs from publishers and create bibliographic records from these proofs. Helpful as it is, this system is not without its faults. Anyone who has experience with the publishing process knows that some things can alter from the time the galleys are printed to the time the actual book is printed. Some "errors" in CIP information are not due to problems in cataloging, but are due to changes that have been made between the time the cataloger saw the item and the time it was actually published. Besides perceived errors, "missing" information, such as the number of pages and the dimensions of the item, is also the result of cataloging from galleys rather than from the actual item.

But It Isn't Just about Books

When the MARC format was developed, it was based on descriptive formats for cataloging books because the majority of the items cataloged at that time were monographic in nature. In time, however, more and more items that were not books in any traditional sense were being cataloged. Digital images, Web sites, and so forth do not always conform well to the structure of the MARC record. Catalogers worldwide are concerned about the ability of the MARC format to handle these elusive material types that do not follow the monographic format.

The change in the nature of library items from books to "information packages" had an impact on all library functions. As schools of library science became schools of library and information science, cataloging courses became classes in knowledge or information management. *AACR*, MARC, and ISBD became only a portion of the array of tools taught for describing information for retrieval purposes. Items being cataloged became not books and non-books, but information packages; bibliographic records became surrogate records; and metadata became the information package that was the most troublesome to be described and organized. The future of cataloging is focused on the organization of metadata.

Recently, numerous articles have been published concerning ways of dealing with metadata. In 2003, an entire issue of *Cataloging and Classification Quarterly* was devoted to this topic and at the 2004 ALA midwinter meeting, a preconference was held regarding the topic of teaching the control of metadata. The most simplistic definition is that metadata is data about data. Arlene G. Taylor (8) defines metadata as, "an encoded description of an information package (e.g., an *AACR2* record encoded with MARC, a Dublin Core record, a GILS record, etc.); the purpose of metadata is to provide a level of data at which choices can be made as to which information packages one wishes to view or search, without having to search massive amounts of irrelevant full text" (pg. 371). When Taylor talks about an "information package," she is referring to the item that is being described, be it a book, videotape, or a Web site. It is practical to talk about an information package because in those two words one is discussing anything that is being cataloged without having to list out each type of item. Although the bulk of items being cataloged in a school library are still books, there is a phantom item that should be cataloged but often is not. That phantom is the Web site. When describing Web sites, one can discuss the entire site or merely parts of the site. The information package is that part (or whole) of the Web site that is being cataloged. People in the field of cataloging or information management assert that MARC is not an appropriate tool for dealing with the anomalous nature of Internet-based information packages.

Enter the Dublin Core Metadata Initiative (DCMI). The DCMI began in 1995 to address and advance the state of the art in the development and extension of methods, standards, and protocols to facilitate the description, organization, discovery, and access of network information resources. The Dublin Core Metadata Element Set is a set of 15 descriptive elements that can be recorded, stored, or transferred using HTML, XML, RDF, or relational databases. Details about DCMI can be found at the Web site: http://dublincore.org/.

An additional project of the future is the OCLC Cooperative Online Resource Catalog (CORC). CORC is a project from the OCLC Office of Research that has the goal of creating a system that will accept both MARC and DCMI data. While there are similarities between MARC, CORC, and DCMI, the systems are independent of one other. For now, announcements of the death of the MARC format are greatly exaggerated. However, even school library media specialists should be aware of these issues.

OPAC – The Result of All of This Trouble

The result of electronic organization of materials is that we are no longer limited to searching by author, title, series, or subject. Patrons today can search for an item based on nearly every part of the record. The curricular implications of this searching capacity are immense. Now we *must* teach our students how to be effective users of the online catalog because there are so many avenues from which to choose to get to the required information package.

In chapter four we will learn about keyword searching, but the OPAC is capable of much more retrieval than that. If a record has the information, and if the system indexes that part of the record, then your students can find information packages based on keywords, grade levels, reading levels, class assignments, reading programs, language, or media type. We repeat, the automated system must have the capacity to index this information, but if that is done, students will have almost limitless access to information. For that reason alone, it is vital that the catalog records are clean and conform to the most current cataloging standards. Information about some of the automated systems that cater to the school library environment is offered in Appendix III.

Most of the time, the school library media specialist has very little control over what part of the record is indexed for information retrieval purposes because indexing is defined by the system itself. Most OPACs are configured to allow for power, advanced, or limited searching. In this way, a student could search for the dog books on Mrs. Smith's reading list, or the dog books at the 4.5 reading grade level, or the dog books in Spanish. All of these searches are possible, but only if the information is in the record. The school library media specialist who is unaware of these capabilities in the system, who provides only minimal cataloging, or who does not keep up with current trends in cataloging, is cheating the student and classroom teacher population by not taking advantage of all the systems have to offer.

Similarly, it is the responsibility of the school faculty to work with the school library media specialist to decide which items should be noted as meeting school or district curriculum standards. Curriculum mapping can play an important role in cataloging. If the school library media specialist knows what is going on in the classrooms, then he or she can make curricular related notes in the records and students (and classroom teachers) will be able to retrieve materials based on the curriculum.

Implications for School Library Media Specialists

Despite all of the wonderful developments in cataloging, school and small libraries have been virtually ignored. Minor attempts have been made to create abridged standards; however, smaller libraries have existed by adapting rules when possible or simply creating their own rules. Earlier, when each library was a library unto itself, it was possible to exist in this fashion. In today's world of online catalogs and Internet access to catalogs, it is not only impossible but also unwise to ignore cataloging standards.

The history described in this chapter is important for a variety of reasons. It is important for little reasons, such as knowing that it was hard to constantly type capital letters on old manual typewriters and that led to the fact that only the first word of the title and proper nouns are capitalized in the title statement area. It is also important for larger reasons, such as knowing that punctuation is important because it helps users to move comfortably from one library to another. It is important for reasons even larger still, such as knowing that MARC was developed as an in-house tool and carries with it all of the idiosyncrasies of an in-house tool that the greater world population of catalogers has learned to accept. Most of all, it is hoped that the reader will come to understand that it is important to know how the standards developed and why one must follow these standards today.

Access to information does not happen by accident or by magic. Organization of information is paramount to access. When access to information through the Internet was just beginning, people likened it to a large library where all of the books were on the floor. Creators of electronic information now realize the importance of organizing that information. Large organizations, such as Google and Yahoo, are working to create organization for the information retrieved on those sites. Libraries are also working with electronic information providers to put more and more information online in an organized fashion. We sometimes look at these projects and think they have no impact on our individual school libraries, but we are wrong to think this. More and more often students are expecting to find information electronically. Therefore, we must understand at least the rudiments of information organization and apply that knowledge to our own collections. In the following chapters, we will explore information access as it applies to the contents of our collections.

References

1. Fred Lerner. *The Story of Libraries From the Invention of Writing to the Computer Age*. New York: Continuum, 1998. 15.

2. Ibid., 56.

3. Ibid., 100.

4. Lois Mai Chan. *Cataloging and Classification: An Introduction*. 2nd ed. New York: McGraw-Hill, 1994.

5. Ibid., 35.

6. Seymour Lubetzky. *Cataloging Rules and Principles*. Washington: Library of Congress, 1953. 36.

7. Chan, 42.

8. *Functional Requirements for Bibliographic Records, Final Report*. IFLA Study Group on the Functional Requirements for Bibliographic Records. Munchen : K.G. Saur, 1998. (UBCIM Publications, New Series ; v. 19). Accessed May 15, 2005. Available at http://www.ifla.org/VII/s13/frbr/frbr.htm.

9. Examples of work LC has conducted relating to FRBR can be found at: http://www.loc.gov/marc/marc-functional-analysis/ and examples of work conducted by OCLC can be found at: http://www.oclc.org/research/projects/frbr/default.htm.

10. Tillett, Barbara. *What is FRBR? A conceptual model for the bibliographic universe*. Library of Congress, Cataloging Distribution Service. Accessed May 15, 2005. Available at: http://www.loc.gov/cds/FRBR.html.

11. Taylor, Arlene G. *The Organization of Information*. 2nd ed. Westport, Conn.: Libraries Unlimited, 2004.

Chapter *2*

Copy Cataloging and Cataloger's Resources

Introduction

Along with understanding the mechanics of cataloging one should have the ability to take advantage of cataloging from other libraries. Using cataloging that has previously been created by another cataloger is called *copy cataloging*. The records themselves are referred to as *copy* or *copy cataloging*. In this chapter, various places to locate copy cataloging for items commonly found in school library collections are discussed. Should the school library media specialist find her/himself with miscellaneous information packages that need to be cataloged or with a collection that is not accessible on an automated system, a number of useful resources are listed to help with the organization of these items. This chapter is divided into four sections: *Copy Cataloging, Databases, Programs,* and *Online Tools.* The Copy Cataloging section provides a brief definition of the process of taking the records from one institution and putting them into your own database. In the section regarding Databases, Internet sites where one can obtain catalog records are discussed. The Programs section offers commercial fee-based programs that lead to catalog records or provide a cataloging template. The chapter concludes with a section on Internet sites that provide cataloging assistance should you need to fix downloaded records or create your own records.

Copy Cataloging

Before we can talk about useful tools for helping to organize a collection, we have to understand what goes into organization. Some of this will be discussed in more detail in the following chapters. For now, we present enough information so that one can understand how to use the tools described in the remainder of this chapter.

Recall from the previous chapter that the first librarians were responsible for knowing not only the titles of the books in their master's collections, but also the contents of each of those items. Working with a small collection, it would not be impossible to have that knowledge. Indeed, the experienced librarian is often able to recite summaries of at least 100 titles with alarming accuracy. However, it is not always feasible for the librarian to be called upon to recite this information (besides the fact that there should be more than 100 titles in any school library collection) and so we must create some kind of written record of each information package that includes data about the package regarding its physical and intellectual aspects. We call that record the bibliographic or surrogate record. Access to surrogate records from other libraries is critical in the copy cataloging process.

Because there is so much work to be done in a school library besides cataloging, we need to make use of resources outside of our library that will help us to make surrogate records for our uncataloged information packages quickly and accurately. Of course we can create our own surrogate records, but it makes much more sense to use the records others have already created. When we accept a record from another library, we accept it either as is or as it will be modified by us once we download it into our system. Most of the time the records we download will match our items in hand exactly; however, there will be times when the match is not exact. In accepting copy cataloging, we also accept that we may need to change some information on the record. By the time you are finished with this book, you should feel comfortable enough with the material that adapting copy to your own needs will not be a problem.

Databases

There are many sites on the Internet that supply, to varying degrees, quality cataloging at no cost. Some libraries supply cataloging unwittingly, simply because they have put their databases on the Web. Others maintain databases for the express purposes of providing information for copy cataloging. No one site is perfect for all needs, thus there may be a need to look at more than one database and there is always a need to examine the records for accuracy and completeness. Merely because a record is on the Internet does not mean that the record is without fault, even from the best cataloging institutions.

Databases are made available on the Internet through something called the *Z39.50 protocol,* a standard communications protocol developed by the *National Information Standards Organization (NISO).* This protocol allows one computer to ask questions of another computer without the user knowing a whole lot about the second computer. Just as a person can go from one library to another and expect the Dewey classification to be the same at each library, the Z39.50 protocol allows similar search strategies to be applicable from one library database to the other. It is not necessary for the school library media specialist to know how Z39.50 works, only to understand that because of this protocol, it is possible to not only search a library database using familiar commands, but also to retrieve and download the records belonging to that library. The following is a description of some of our favorite databases to use for copy cataloging purposes. This is by no means an exhaustive list and each librarian will soon find his or her own favorite places to go for copy cataloging purposes.

The Granddaddy of Them All

Library of Congress (LC) http://lcweb.loc.gov. One cannot say enough about the cataloging tools available for free provided by the Library of Congress. As we learned from the previous chapter, the Library of Congress has been assisting catalogers in creating authoritative bibliographic records since the beginning of the 20th century. Until the advent of electronic information sharing, many of the tools from the Library of Congress were fee-based and much too costly for smaller public and school libraries. Before there was free electronic access to the LC database, school library media specialists would often rely on the Cataloging in Publication (CIP) data for copy cataloging information. As mentioned in the previous chapter, this program was created to provide bibliographic information on the item itself, usually on the verso of the title page, to assist with the cataloging needs of other libraries. To date, some librarians still rely on CIP information for cataloging purposes, as it is one of the simplest forms of copy cataloging available. However, one must keep in mind that CIP is cataloging created before the items are actually published. This means that there may be errors in the cataloging simply because the item had been altered in some way(s) from the time the Library of Congress received the manuscript to the time it was actually published.

If a librarian has access to the Internet then he or she has access to the LC database. Searchable by nearly any aspect of the surrogate record, the user can have access to the MARC records of practically any Library of Congress item, all 130 million of them! But there is a caveat: LC is the library of the United States Congress; it is a national library only by default. Therefore, there are items in a school library collection that have not made their way into the Library of Congress collection or its database. Most school library media specialists complain that educational and children's media (videotapes, computer software, DVDs) are the types of materials least often found in the LC database. Additionally, children's and young adult books have been cataloged by the Library of Congress with varying degrees of specificity through the years. This means that even if the record is in the LC catalog, it may not be the most complete record available from the Internet. Thus the cataloger should be aware that the LC catalog, although authoritative, might not always be the best place to go for copy cataloging.

However, once a record is found it is possible to download the record into most school library automated systems. The site for the Library of Congress includes directions for downloading records. Additionally, there are several commercial programs (see the Programs section) that will search the LC database and include a seamless way of downloading the records.

Other Free Databases

While the Library of Congress is one of the larger of the databases to search, it is not the only database available for free on the Internet. When a number of libraries get together as a consortium and merge their separate databases into one, they are creating a *union catalog*. Union catalogs are useful places to search for copy cataloging due to the fact that one can view the collections of numerous libraries simultaneously. Here are several examples of union catalogs:

- **Amicus.** Amicus is the name of the database for the Canadian National Catalog. It includes more than 30 million records from more than 1,000 Canadian libraries including the Library and Archives Canada. It offers records in numerous languages and formats. Librarians often praise this database for its access to records for media (e.g. vhs, CD-ROM, DVD). In order to view MARC records, one must register to use the database. This registration is free. Records are easy to download and the system includes the feature of batching records, that is, to download multiple titles at once. We emphasize that this is a Canadian database. Until recently, cataloging practice in Canada varied slightly from that in the United States. Therefore, while there is much authority to this database, one may need to clean the records of cataloging discrepancies, including Canadian subject headings in both English and French.
    - Amicus: http://www.-catalog.cpl.org

- **Access Pennsylvania.** This database was established in 1986 and provides access to the surrogate records of more than 50 million items. It is a statewide consortium of nearly 3,000 school, public, academic, and special libraries, thus offering an excellent cross section of different types of information packages. The records can be searched by title, author, subject (including *Sears*), keyword, ISBN, and classification numbers. The search can be limited by library type or state location. Records are easily batched and downloaded using the export buttons. The caveat here is that not every record is created by a fully trained cataloger; therefore, one should be careful to review the records before downloading them, or at least understand that the records may need to be altered once downloaded.
    - Access Pennsylvania: http://www.accesspa.state.pa.us

- **Genesse Valley BOCES.** This consortium of school libraries in the Genesse Valley BOCES (Board of Cooperative Educational Services) in New York provides access to MARC records from 22 public and private K-12 schools. The nice feature of this database is the provision of book covers and the tables of contents for some of their items. Records are easily downloaded by clicking the "MARC Download" button. The site is graphically appealing, but note that only the records can be downloaded, not the accompanying book covers and tables of contents.
    - Genesse Valley BOCES: http://gvb.library.net/default.htm

- **Link+.** As a consortium of more than 40 public and academic libraries in California and Nevada, this database offers author, title, keyword, and subject searching. Records may be saved to a file either individually or in batches. This is not a very attractive site, but it can get the job done by providing access to MARC records and, for us, that's what counts.
  - Link+: http://csul.iii.com

Not all institutions provide the ability to download records, nevertheless, they still provide access to records than can be copied and pasted into a database. It's not as elegant or as easy as clicking a button, but if one is having a hard time finding a surrogate record for an information package, copy and paste is better than having no record at all from which to copy. The following databases are excellent resources even if their MARC records are not available for downloading.

- **Clevnet.** "Established in 1982, the CLEVNET Consortium is a cooperative partnership between the Cleveland Public Library and 30 library systems throughout nine counties in Northern Ohio … With combined holdings of over 2.6 million unique titles, over 10 million items … the CLEVNET system is one of the largest public library automation systems in the world." The default search is by keyword but within that first search page, one can specify material type, reading level, language, and publication date.
  - Clevnet: http://www-catalog.cpl.org

- **CowlNet.** This is the union catalog for Winfield Public Library, Southwestern College, and the Unified School District 465 (Kansas). One of the outstanding features of this site is the ability to search by *Sears* subject headings.
  - CowlNet: http://cowlnet.sckans.edu

- **Sunlink.** This is one of the better-known sites among school library media specialists. Sunlink is the union catalog of the K-12 public school libraries of the entire state of Florida. As the project is described, all contributors to the database have been carefully trained in the MARC format. Having said that, the contributors to the database may add holdings to existing records or create their own records. The consequence of this practice is that a search for a specific information package may result in multiple records for a single item. Due to the high likelihood of finding a school library item at Sunlink (there are more than 16 million records), this is an excellent resource for copy cataloging even though the records cannot be downloaded.
  - Sunlink: http://www.sunlink.ucf.edu/

There is one fee-based database that needs to be discussed here: the OCLC database.

- **OCLC.** It is doubtful if any of the 38,000 member libraries of OCLC are school libraries, but this non-profit, membership-based consortium is one of the best places to search for surrogate records. The program began in 1967 as a method of sharing resources between academic libraries in Ohio. This data-base has blossomed into an international shared database of more than 45 million records with new records being added every 15 seconds. With a database this large, there are drawbacks to the OCLC database; it is fee-based and most of the MARC records are accessible to members only. However, through such programs as First Search and World Cat, many school library media special-ists have access to the MARC records in this international database. Even if one cannot buy into the database or is not part of a consortium that allows access to the database, the Web site still provides access to the public access form of the records (some items also include access to the MARC form).

- OCLC: http://www.oclc.com/home

One last comment about accepting copy cataloging from any online resource: remember that cataloging rules have undergone extensive changes over the years. At the very least, be skeptical of records that were created before 1978. In accepting copy cataloging for non-book information packages, try to find a record created as recently as possible. If you must accept older records, be prepared to update them.

Programs

For catalogers with money to spend, there are several programs that are immensely helpful for facilitating the cataloging process.

- **BookWhere.** This is a software program that links the cataloger to online catalogs for ease of searching and downloading of catalog records. BookWhere links to Library of Congress and thousands of other library catalogs worldwide. A bit short on representing school libraries, there is an advantage of being able to search numerous library databases simultaneously. A click of the mouse creates a file for downloading to the home system. BookWhere requires Windows 95/98 or NT (no format for Macintosh systems), is compatible with many school library cataloging programs, and costs approximately $400 for a single user license.
  - BookWhere: http://www.webclarity.info/products/bookwhere.html

- **MARC Wizard.** This software program is a suite of modules that run from simple database clean up to retrospective conversion and copy cataloging. The configuration of the program depends on the needs of the library. School library media specialists often sing the praises of the MARC Magician that can run global changes, print spine labels, and clean up records. AccessMARC boasts of access to millions of library records with a special emphasis on nonprint materials such as video recordings, DVDs, and CD-ROMs (the types of information packages that few of us really like to cata-log). The price of the program, depending on the modules, the number of copies, and the number of subscription years being purchased, can range from $179 to $369. MARC Wizard products run on Windows operating systems.
  - MARC Wizard: http://www.mitinet.com

Additionally, most book companies (vendors), for a small fee, will provide cataloging for materials purchased from them. School library media specialists must know what to ask for in requesting cataloging from these companies. They must know how to define the subject headings and classification systems. They must also know how much cataloging the vendor will supply (full or minimal record) and the source of cataloging the vendor uses for the records (LC or in-house). Above all, school library media specialists must know if the cataloging supplied by the vendor meets the standards of MARC and *AACR*. Sometimes library media specialists, or their administrators, opt not to take on the added expense of purchasing cataloging from vendors. If the vendor is supplying inferior records, this might be a wise decision. However, if the vendor is supplying good surrogate records, then it is probably a good idea to spend the extra money (often less than $1 per item). It may seem like an added expense, but it is more likely than not less than the cost of you sitting at a terminal and adding original records or scanning databases to download (and edit) copy cataloging.

Online Tools

Even if you never have to create an original catalog record, the chances are that you will have to update or somehow enhance a record. Beyond this textbook, there are Internet sites that can assist in this process. Here one can find rules for creating MARC records, subject headings, and even Cutter numbers.

- **LC Cataloging Directorate:** This site is "the place to go" for cataloging assistance from the Library of Congress. Not to be missed is the link to the MARC homepage (http://lcweb.loc.gov/marc) that includes the entire list of MARC tags for all media formats. The Library of Congress also sells a program called *Cataloger's Desktop*. This program is linked to all of the LC tools and is a wonderful program for creating and updating records. It includes links to all of the LC databases including subject headings, classifications, and AC headings. Sadly, at an annual subscriptions rate of $690, it is well beyond the budget of most school libraries.
  - LC Cataloging Directorate: http://www.loc.gov/catdir

- **Cataloger's Reference Shelf:** First posted in 1997, this site has quickly become a favorite site for catalogers. It provides information on many aspects of cataloging including MARC format, Library of Congress subject headings structure, LC Cutter templates, and media cataloging.
  - Cataloger's Reference Shelf: http://www.tlcdelivers.com/tlc/crs

Many academic libraries have placed cataloging tools on the Web for their own cataloging departments. There are many such sites, including:

- **MIT (Massachusetts Institute of Technology)** (http://macfadden.mit.edu:9500/colserv/cat/),

- **Memorial University (Newfoundland)** (http://staff.library.mun.ca/staff/toolbox), and

- **Princeton University** (http://library.princeton.edu/departments/tsd/katmandu/catman.html).

These guides should be viewed carefully, as some information pertains only to the specific institution posting the cataloging hints. However, there is also much general information provided in these sites for those who are interested or in need of assistance.

- **OCLC** has many hint sheets and directives for their catalogers. As with the academic libraries, it should be noted that the directives pertain to OCLC catalog contributors and might vary slightly from the needs of the school library media center.
  - OCLC help: http://www.oclc.org/bibformats/default.htm

Finally, help is just a short e-mail message away with electronic discussion lists.

- **AUTOCAT:** This is the place to go for the discussions on the latest events affecting cataloging policy. It is a good idea for school librarians to take a look at this list every now and then. Caveat: This is a list of the very best in the cataloging world. Most members are very reasonable about answering questions; there have been times, however, when questions from neophytes have been met with less patience than would have been appreciated. Take a look at the archives (http://listserv.acsu.buffalo.edu/archives/autocat.html) before plunging into the fray. For those who are insecure about going to the membership of AUTOCAT, most school library automation programs have user group electronic discussion lists where one might feel more comfortable asking questions.
  - AUTOCAT: http://ublib.buffalo.edu/libraries/units/cts/autocat/subscribe.html

- **MARC Forum** provides discussion on the latest topics in MARC standards. Recently there has been much discussion on FRBR and the new *AACR*, making this a good place to go for keeping up with the latest in cataloging trends. The list members seem to be obliging in answering questions, although most questions are at a very high level.
  - MARC Forum: http://www.loc.gov/marc/marcforum.html

Conclusion

The variety of free and fee-based databases and programs available to help catalog items is demonstrative of the importance of the need librarians have for cataloging assistance. Even purchased records must be evaluated for inclusion of library specific information to the surrogate record. This chapter has presented information on Internet, free, and fee-based resources applicable to the copy cataloging process.

Even though there are many resources available to help in the cataloging process, knowledge of the construction of the surrogate record is vital in purchasing records from vendors and accepting copy cataloging from other institutions. The following chapters will provide information on the cataloging process from classification to physical description.

Chapter *3*

Cataloging Theory and the MARC Record

Introduction

Y ou have had a brief history of cataloging and an introduction to copy cataloging. It is now time to learn about the art of cataloging. In this chapter we are introduced to the standards of cataloging. Chapter three is designed to provide you with background information regarding cataloging theory so that you can make intelligent decisions about copy cataloging and any original cataloging you may have to do. In Part II we will put this theory into practice.

Material Types

The rules described in the *Anglo-American Cataloguing Rules (AACR)* cover a wide variety of material types. Some of these types are more common than others in the school library media collection. In order for this text to reflect a practical approach to cataloging, not every material type included in *AACR* will be discussed. The material types that will not be discussed are printed music, microforms, and manuscripts. There is one other material type that will only be discussed briefly: continuing resources. "*Continuing resources*" to *AACR* is synonymous with periodicals or serials to us. The title of the material type was changed with the 2002 revision of *AACR* because it needed to reflect cataloging practice of not only regular periodicals, such as *Seventeen Magazine* and *Sports*

Illustrated, but also publications that were continuously updated in the form of loose-leaf publications and electronic magazines. Since the practice of serials cataloging is so specialized, we will not be covering that topic in this chapter. However, in chapter six we will discuss some ways to keep track of serials.

This leaves us with books, cartographic materials, sound recordings, motion pictures and videorecordings, graphic materials, electronic resources, and three-dimensional artifacts and realia. Some of these terms may seem foreign to you because these are standard cataloging terms. To translate: Cartographic materials are maps and globes, but not atlases that are cataloged as books even though they are a compilation of maps. Sound recordings refer to music or non-music recordings regardless of recording medium (tape cassettes, CD-ROMs, or even the old LPs). The important thing to remember is that it is the medium that is important; therefore, a book on a tape is considered a sound recording, not a book. Motion pictures and videorecordings are the items we know as videotapes and DVDs. We can also include here 16mm films if those items can still be found in your school. Graphic materials are defined as two-dimensional objects such as posters, flash cards, and wall charts. Projected objects such as transparencies or slides are in this category as well. If you have a library that still has filmstrips, those too would be graphic materials but will not be discussed in this text as most are so dated that it is not worth spending time cataloging them.

Electronic resources are those items that require computer technology in order for the user to access the information. While not so long ago that seemed like a very clear definition, today it is less clear. There was a time when a CD-ROM worked only in a computer and was therefore easily identified as an electronic resource. However, a CD-ROM or a DVD no longer requires the use of a computer, so how do we catalog it? We suggest that the content be the guide for deciding what type of material one has. If a CD-ROM is a recording of music, then it should be cataloged as a sound recording and not as an electronic resource. If that same CD-ROM includes a bonus track that requires a computer to see the visual images, it is still a sound recording because that is the main function of the item (similar to the argument that one would use in deciding if a multi-part item is a kit or other material type, see below). Similarly, a DVD of *Gone with the Wind* is a motion picture, not an electronic resource. These definitions are still debated in cataloging circles but seem to make the most sense to us in the school library environment and, therefore, we stick by them.

Three-dimensional artifacts are treated in *AACR* chapter 10, "Three-dimensional Artifacts and Realia." This covers the "odd-ball" items in a school library media collection such as games, puzzles, or models, as well as media equipment such as computers, LCD projectors, screens, and so forth. Kits present an interesting dilemma in cataloging. Non-catalogers tend to attribute the term "kit" to more items than do catalogers. Theoretically, if multiple item types are sold together in one package and no single item type is dominant over the other parts, then that resulting package is a kit and should be cataloged as such. However, merely because multiple item types are packaged together, do not assume that the package is truly a "kit." Catalogers are careful to examine the items and decide if one part is more important than any other part. We believe that it is important to keep multipart items together, that is how they are sold and how they are meant to be used. Consider this example, a book with an accompanying tape cassette. Can either of these two items exist alone? Well, yes, the book is an item unto itself and more likely than not was published before the tape was released. Therefore, we would catalog the item under the rules for cataloging books with added information about the tape. (Just how we account for the tape will be discussed later in this chapter and in chapter six.) It can, of course, be argued that the tape can exist without the book and, therefore, it should be the item type under which these things are cataloged. We stand by the first decision, but you should feel free to make your own decision (as long as you keep the book and tape together). Looking at what other libraries have done for the same or similar items will help in making the decision (assuming you are uncomfortable with the one we posited).

Here is another example: a CD-ROM with a book and a user's guide. The book reflects the textual content of the CD-ROM and, as in the case of our first example, was published before the CD-ROM. However, the CD-ROM itself includes the text of the book plus the added feature of interactivity between the user and what is being shown on the screen. Thus, the CD-ROM proves to be the most important part of this multipart package; therefore, the package is cataloged as an electronic resource. From this discussion, you should see that defining a multipart package as a kit is a tricky decision to make. Using copy cataloging, as mentioned above, will help in the decision making process.

Chief Source of Information

Recall that the idea of cataloging is to describe an information package so that the library user can be matched with just the right package. We create surrogate (bibliographic) records to best reflect the physical description and intellectual content of the package. In creating these records, catalogers have defined for us reliable sources of information that we can use to describe the packages. For intellectual description, we use the entire information package and match its content to standardized classification systems (such as DDC) and subject schemes (such as *LCSH* or *Sears*). To describe the physical aspects of the information package, we use a *"chief source of information"* for that specific package. *AACR* (2005 update) defines the chief source of information as "the source of bibliographic data to be given preference as the source from which a bibliographic description (or portion thereof) is prepared" (p. Appendix D-2).[1] In other words, use that part of the package that has the best information about the package. For example, the chief source of information for a book is the title page and the information on the back (or verso) of the title page. Not all packages are as clearly marked, however. Take for example an information package that consists of a CD-ROM, trade book, and user's guide. Which part of this package has the "best" information about the package as a whole: the title page of the

---

[1] The loose-leaf edition of AACR (2002 revision, 2005 update) uses a combination of chapter and page numbers to number the pages in the book. As such, the fifth page from the first chapter will be numbered 1-5. In the citation page. Page 1: D-2 we are referred to the second page of the D appendix.

trade book, the title screen, or the title page of the user's guide? To deal with this and other conundrums, *AACR* provides us with a definition of the chief source of information for each material type. See the box for definitions of chief source of information for each material type discussed in this text.

Areas of Description

In the first edition of this book, we began our exploration into physical description by discussing the Eight Areas of Description. These areas are based on the structure of the 3-by-5 catalog card. In teaching cataloging using this text, we have found that this approach was not very successful. Most OPACs put the cataloging information into a format that resembles the old catalog card, but that process is transparent to the school library media specialist doing the cataloging. Instead, he or she has to deal with inputting the information into the MARC record. Therefore we will briefly discuss the eight areas just to provide some theoretical basis for the structure of the MARC record, but describing the eight areas will not be our main focus. It is important, however, to reinforce the concept that MARC is only a communications tool to get the information from the item itself to the library community in an electronic format. MARC is *not* a cataloging standard and one should not speak of MARC cataloging. The Anglo-American Cataloguing Rules together with the International Standard Bibliographic Description (ISBD) rules determine *how* the information should appear in the surrogate record. The MARC21 rules determine *where* the information should appear in the record.

Having said that, it is helpful to understand why we have the information we have in the surrogate record. If you had a copy of *AACR* in front of you, you would see that it is divided into two parts. Part I covers physical description and Part II covers the concept of "entry" ways of entering names and titles for retrieval purposes. In this text, we will focus our attention on Part I of *AACR*. With the exception of chapter one, which deals with generalities of description and chapter 13, which deals with analytical cataloging, each chapter in *AACR* is devoted to describing one type of

---

The Eight Areas of Description:

1. Title and Statement of Responsibility: corresponds to tags 1XX, 245, 246, and 7XX
    - Record here the title of the item, other title information, and name(s) of person(s) or corporate name(s) of those involved in the intellectual content of the package (e.g. author, illustrator).

2. Edition: corresponds to tag 250
    - Looking for words such as "edition," "revised," or "version," record here statements related to the edition of the package.

3. Material Specific Details: corresponds to tags 254, 255, and 256
    - Used only for cartographic materials, electronic resources, and printed music, record here a description of the type of package being cataloged (e.g. scale for a map).

4. Publication, Distribution, etc.: corresponds to tag 260
    - Record here information about the place of publication, the name of the publisher, and the date of publication.

5. Physical Description: corresponds to tag 300
    - Record here the physical aspects of the item including number of pages, running time of a videotape, and accompanying materials.

6. Series: corresponds to tags 4XX and 830
    - Record here information about series statements, such as New True Book, Nancy Drew Mysteries.

7. Notes: corresponds to tags 5XX
    - Record here additional information such as language of text if a translation or non-English text, a table of contents, or reading level; or explanations about other information found in the record taken from some place besides the chief source of information (unnumbered pages, or no title page).

8. Standard Numbers: corresponds to tags 01X – 09X
    - Record here standard numbers found on the item, most commonly the ISBN; also in this area will be found classification numbers.

Along with the Areas of Description, *AACR* follows the punctuation rules of *International Standard Bibliographic Description* (ISBD). Notice that the eight areas cover physical description of the information package only. Subject headings and classification (intellectual description) are not part of *AACR*.

item, e.g. books (chapter two), cartographic materials (chapter three), and so on. Each of those type-specific chapters is divided into sections beginning with general rules and ending with specific details. In chapters two through 12, all chapters include eight sections that correspond directly to the eight areas of description. Using a standard model for describing any type of item allows the cataloger to follow certain basic steps in creating the surrogate record. In the box, on page 27 you can see the areas of description and the rough correspondence to the MARC tag numbers. Not every MARC tag is described in this box, only those that are most commonly used in the school library environment and that corresponds to one of the areas.

The MARC Record

As mentioned in chapter one, MARC began as an in-house system at the Library of Congress to translate information about the information package to an electronic catalog for use by the patrons of the Library of Congress. Today, as MARC 21, this program is used worldwide despite complaints that it is an archaic way of organizing data, that is does not work well with non-English language materials, and that it does not work well for remote access data (metadata and Web sites). (For a good synthesis of the other types of formats available for information organization, see the Arlene Taylor book, *Organization of Information*, cited in chapter one.) Nevertheless, in school library media automation systems, it is the standard format being used and so we will describe its organization here.

The MARC record is divided into three parts: the leader, the directory, and variable fields. Each line within each of those parts is referred to as a tag or field. Note that the terms field and tag are interchangeable. Most people refer to the lines themselves as tag but to the specific information within the tags as subfields. To say "Leader tag" is just the same as saying "Leader field." Most of our discussion will focus on the variable fields; however, we will also touch upon the other parts of the record. *Remember, the content of the record is based on the rules of* AACR *and the punctuation is based on ISBD.* The typography is based on the American Standard Code for Information Interchange (ASCII) standards, some of which are not reproducible from the average computer keyboard. This accounts for the fact that an LC record may have characters that don't look like the characters you see in this book. The point is that once the structure of the MARC record is understood, small anomalies like that should not be problematic to you.

The surrogate record for the book *The Town Mouse and the Country Mouse* is reproduced in the box on page 29. Note that some of the information is easy to understand while other information is not. The information that is easy to understand is referred to as "eye-readable;" that is, one can look at it and, without any assistance, understand the information. The tags 100 through 900 are eye-readable. One can clearly see the title, the publication information, and so on. These tags correspond to the eight areas of description. The other tags, 000 through 082, are not as easily understood without some cataloging knowledge. Except for the 010 and 020 tags, these tags do not have any correspondence to the old-fashioned areas of description and were designed solely for electronic retrieval of information.

MARC record for the book The Town Mouse and the Country Mouse:

Leader	**000**	nam a
Control #	**001**	EA696ACB059711D4B71B006097338C03
Date & Time	**005**	20041222111028.0
Fixed Data	**008**	960923s1995 nyua 000 1 eng d
LCCN	**010**	$a 94009789 AC
ISBN	**020**	$a0553541838
Sys Control#	**035**	$aEA696ACB059711D4B71B006097338C03
Cat. Source	**040**	$aDLC
		$dERC
		$dICrlF
Dewey#	**082** 00	$a398.24/5293233
		$aE
		$220
MEPers Name	**100** 1	$aSchecter, Ellen.
Title	**245** 14	$aThe town mouse and the country mouse / $cretold by Ellen Schecter ; illustrated by Holly Hannon.
Edition	**250**	$a2nd ed.
Publication	**260**	$aNew York :
		$bBantam Books,
		$cc1995.
Phys Desc	**300**	$a47 p. :
		$bcol. ill. ;
		$c23 cm.
Series:Title	**440** 0	$aBank Street ready-to-read
Note:General	**500**	$a"A Byron Preiss book."
Note:Summary	**520**	$aWhen the town mouse and the country mouse visit each other, they find they prefer very different ways of life. An adaptation of the Aesop fable.
Note:Audience	**521**	$aFor reading grade levels 2-3.
Note:Audience	**521** 8	$aAD 600
		$bLexile.
Subj:Topical	**650** 1	$aFables.
Subj:Topical	**650** 1	$aMice
		$xFolklore.
AE:Pers Name	**700** 00	$aAesop.
AE:Pers Name	**700** 11	$aHannon, Holly,
		$eill.
Local Call #	**900**	$a398.24 SCH 1995

Leader

The Leader tag is a fixed-length tag of 24 character spaces. It tells the computer that this is the beginning of a new record, the type of package being cataloged (book, map, etc.), and the type of cataloging (full, partial, *AACR* or not). Most school library media specialists don't even know this tag exists because it is often not displayed in the MARC record. Perhaps it is an effort to simplify the cataloging process that vendors make the Leader a secretive part of the MARC record. One really has to know about it in order to access it. However, it is the information in this tag that leads to this question, "I cataloged a video tape but the record shows that this is a book. How do I change the icon to show it's really a tape?" To "change the icon" one has to get into the Leader tag. How that is achieved is system dependent; however, once it is achieved the librarian should easily see the place in the tag that needs to be changed in order for the "book" to become a "tape." If the system has the tag written out in one long line, it will look something like this:

00723cam 22002418a 450

Or

000 00994pam 2200253 a 450

The first example shows what the Leader looks like if there is no tag number in front of it. The second example shows the information in the 000 tag. Most school library systems do not display the Leader in this way but parse out each part of the tag into its component parts labeled in English. See Figure 3.1 to see an example of the Leader tag as presented in the Follett Catalog Plus (Ver. 5.10) program.

Figure 3.1 Example of the Leader Tag

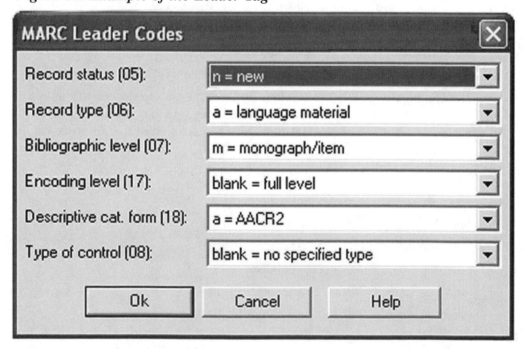

MARC Leader Codes

Record status (05):	n = new
Record type (06):	a = language material
Bibliographic level (07):	m = monograph/item
Encoding level (17):	blank = full level
Descriptive cat. form (18):	a = AACR2
Type of control (08):	blank = no specified type

Ok   Cancel   Help

[2]Unless otherwise noted, the MARC information presented here comes from the *MARC 21 Concise Bibliographic Format* Web site: http://www.loc.gov/marc/bibliographic/ecbdhome.html.

> *Definitions of material types to put in the 06 position of the Leader tag:*
>
> a – Language material (printed material)
>
> e – Cartographic material (maps, atlases, globes)
>
> g – Projected medium (videorecordings in any format (vhs or DVD), slides, anything projected)
>
> i – Nonmusical sound recording (book on tape)
>
> j – Musical sound recording (in any format)
>
> k – Two-dimensional nonprojectable graphic (posters, flash cards, etc.)
>
> m – Computer file (computer software)
>
> o – Kit (two or more types of items where one type is not predominant over the other types)
>
> r – Three-dimensional artifact or naturally occurring object (games, puzzles, three-dimensional art work, computers, LCD projectors)

The part of the Leader that most concerns us is the Type of record element (space 06 on the character line: line is numbered from 00 so we are looking at the seventh character in these strings). In our examples above, we see the letter "a" meaning "language material;" that's "books" to us. If what we really had was a videotape, we would need to change that letter "a" to a letter "g." Happily for us, most of the school library automation systems tell us the letter to choose. See the box above for the letters that match the types of materials we will be cataloging in this text. Note that we have to do a little bit of fudging. As we saw in our examples, the letter "a" is used for books. The true definition of that letter is "language material including printed, microform, and electronic language material." This means if you were cataloging a Web site, you would use the letter "a." Unfortunately, this means that our school library automated system will bring up the "book" icon, making the user think this is a book and not an online resource. This predicament forces us to select the letter "m" for computer file even though, technically speaking, a Web site does not fit in this category.

Directory

The directory is a stream of 12 character positions and is used to tell the computer about the fields being found in that specific MARC record. This area will not be modified by the school library media specialist; therefore, we will not discuss it in any further detail.

Variable Fields

Now we are into the meat of the record. Most of the variable fields consist of a three digit number, a space, a two space area for the field indicators, another space, and then the content of the field marked off by subfields if necessary as

Figure 3.2. Example of a Variable Field

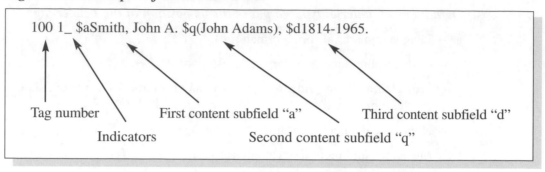

100 1_ $aSmith, John A. $q(John Adams), $d1814-1965.

Tag number   First content subfield "a"   Third content subfield "d"

Indicators   Second content subfield "q"

seen in Figure 3.2.

However, not all variable fields are structured in this way. The control fields (00X) do not have indicators or subfields. Most of these fields can be repeated; that is, there can be more than one of them in a surrogate record. As we go through each of the fields in the following chapters, we will point out those that can and cannot be repeated. Unless otherwise noted, the fields will all end with a full stop, or what we would call a period (.). Some fields have what is known as "display constants." Those are words or phrases that appear in the record automatically according to how the indicators are defined instead of having the cataloger type in the words or phrases. Display constants are most often found in the notes area or the 5XX tags. Again, we will discuss this in more detail in the following chapters. It should be pointed out, however, that some display constants are MARC defined and appear in the OPAC display according to the definitions of the system itself. For example, the word "Author" may show up in the OPAC in front of what would be our 100 tag. This happens automatically according to the system and has nothing to do with the person creating the record. Those constants cannot be changed by the building level school library media specialist. The example record we present in this chapter shows names for the tags that have been defined by the vendor. Another vendor may have different tag names, although they will be similar enough so as not to confuse the librarian or the user who moves from one system to another.

Let us again look at the MARC record, but this time we will take out the parts of the record that do not correspond to the eight areas of description. Remember, these areas were defined in the days of the 3-by-5 catalog card; therefore, there are parts of the MARC record not accounted for in these areas simply because they have to do with communicating with the computer rather than describing the physical composition of the information package. Additionally, these areas deal only with the physical description and not the intellectual content of the item.

MARC record for the book The Town Mouse and the Country Mouse:

LCCN	010	$a 94009789 AC
ISBN	020	$a0553541838
MEPers Nam	100 1	$aSchecter, Ellen.
Title	245 14	$aThe town mouse and the country mouse /
		$cretold by Ellen Schecter ; illustrated by Holly Hannon.
Edition	250	$a2nd ed.
Publication	260	$aNew York :
		$bBantam Books,
		$cc1995.
Phys Desc	300	$a47 p. :
		$bcol. ill. ;
		$c23 cm.
Series:Title	440 0	$aBank Street ready-to-read
Note:General	500	$a"A Byron Preiss book."
Note:Summary	520	$aWhen the town mouse and the country mouse visit each other, they find they prefer very different ways of life. An adaptation of the Aesop fable.
Note:Audience	521	$aFor reading grade levels 2-3.
Note:Audience	521 8	$aAD 600
		$bLexile.
AE:Pers Name	700 00	$aAesop.
AE:Pers Name	700 11	$aHannon, Holly,
		$eill.

Area 1: Title and statement of responsibility. This area is probably the most important part of the record as it tells the user the title and author of the information package. The Library of Congress took the title of this tag directly from the title of the area: "Title and statement of responsibility." In our sample MARC record, we can see the 245 tag:

Title	245 14	$aThe town mouse and the country mouse /
		$cretold by Ellen Schecter ; illustrated by Holly Hannon.

Notice the ISBD punctuation of the "/" before the name of the author and illustrator. But this is not the only tag that comes from Area 1. We also have:

MEPers Name	100 1	$aSchecter, Ellen. *and*
AE:Pers Name	700 11	$aHannon, Holly,
		$eill. But also,

AE:Pers Name   700 00 $aAesop.

AE:Ufm ttl   730 01 $aTown mouse and the country mouse.

$lEnglish.

Looking at the 245 tag, it's clear that we get the 100 tag for Schecter and the 700 tag for Hannon from that information. We have to go deeper into the record to find out from whence came the Aesop and other title tags. We get Aesop because the story is based on Aesop's original story and probably if we look at the item, we would see someplace, either on the title page or the verso, some reference to Aesop. So references to the entity responsible for the content of the item and the title of the item itself, Area 1 information, are found in the 1XX, 24X, and 7XX tags.

Area 2: Edition. If your item has some kind of statement that includes the word, edition, revision, version, or revised, then your item has an edition statement. This is the tag to use to record that information. If your item does not include this information, then leave this tag blank. In our sample MARC record, we see the 250 tag:

Edition   250 $a2nd ed.

Area 3: Material specific details. This refers to descriptions of the type of material being cataloged. For our purposes we will use it only for describing scale in cataloging cartographic materials. Since it does not apply to book cataloging, our sample MARC record does not include the appropriate tag. We'll see this tag in action in chapter six.

Area 4: Imprint. Record here information on the publisher, place of publication, and date of publication. In our sample MARC record we see the 260 tag:

Publication   260 $aNew York :

$bBantam Books,

$cc1995.

We notice here the ISBD punctuation before the $b and $c. Look at the line that has the date of publication, there are two letters "c," which is not a typographical error. The first letter "c" notes that this is the subfield "c" and in the 260 tag this tells the computer that the date information is coming up. The second letter "c" is entered because on the item the date is noted as a copyright date. If there is a copyright date then the date is preceded by the letter "c." If there was just a publication date, with no other distinction, then that subfield would look like this, $c1995.

Area 5: Physical description. In this area, record information about the physical aspects of the package. For a book, that includes page numbers, illustrations, and dimensions. Other material types would include running time, inclusion of sound, if the picture is in black and white or color, the number of pieces of a puzzle, the number of items in a kit. For multipart items, this area includes a description of the predominant part and then a brief description of the accompanying material. In our sample record, we see the following:

Phys Desc	300	$a47 p. :
		$bcol. ill. ;
		$c23 cm.

Again we see the ISBD punctuation. This is a simple example, if there was something, like a music CD-ROM, with the book, we would see this:

Phys Desc	300	$a47 p. :
		$bcol. ill. ;
		$c23 cm. +
		$e 1 sound disc ((20 min.) : digital, stereo ; $4^3/_4$ in.)

Notice how the information in the subfield e parallels the structure of the entire 300 tag. Again, other examples and more detail will be given in chapter 6.

Area 6: Series statement. Record here statements given on the item about the series of which the item is a part. The trick is in discerning between true series statements and other statements that look like series statements. Usually the look-alikes are really statements about a division of a publishing house. Take a look at our sample record:

Series:Title	440 0	$aBank Street ready-to-read
Note:General	500	$a"A Byron Preiss book."

On the item there is a clear statement that Bank Street Ready to Read is a series and this item belongs to that series. The other statement about being a Bryon Preiss book is a publishing statement and not uncommon in children's book publishing. We see lots of these kinds of statements such as "A Piper Paperback," "An Aladdin Paperback," or "A Reading Rainbow Book." These are not true series statements, and so the cataloger puts them in a general note rather than in the series area (notice the different tag numbers and the use of quotation marks around the publishing statement in our example). Notice in our series statement that there is no full stop at the end of the line. When this line shows up in the OPAC, it should be in parentheses; therefore, the closed parenthesis at the end of the line acts as the final punctuation for this line.

Area 7: Notes. This area is used to record a myriad of aspects of the item. If the cataloger supplies a title or takes the title from a place other than the chief source of information, that has to be recorded here. The language of the text, if not English or if bilingual, is recorded in this area. Information about the table of contents, a summary statement, reading or audience level, are also recorded in this area. Information about the material type (vhs, DVD) and special system requirements (Windows, Mac) are recorded here. Also recorded here is information about any awards or honors given to the item and location of reviews about the item. Each type of note is given separately as we see in our example:

Note:General	500	$a"A Byron Preiss book."

Note:Summary	520	$aWhen the town mouse and the country mouse visit each other, they find they prefer very different ways of life. An adaptation of the Aesop fable.
Note:Audience	521	$aFor reading grade levels 2-3.
Note:Audience	521 8	$aAD 600
		$bLexile.

Notice that some tags appear more than once, as in the case of the 521 tags. Most of the 5XX tags can be repeated, which is nice because sometimes there is so much to say about an item and it's important to keep the notes clear and organized. This is an important area and almost every type of note just described has its own tag number that will be discussed in detail in chapter six.

Area 8: Standard Numbers. Record in this area standard numbers associated with the item, such as ISBN, ISSN, and government document numbers. In our example, we have recorded the ISBN:

ISBN	020	$a0553541838

A frequently asked question for this area is what to do if there is more than one standard number given to an item. The question is usually referring to an item that has more than one ISBN associated with it, usually an ISBN for the hardbound, paperback, and library binding printings of the book. Most school children don't really care if they have the hardbound or paperback version of a book, but some do. Cataloging theory states that a different number warrants a different record, but is that really necessary for us? The answer depends on your population. If you have both the paperback and hardbound copies of a book and you know that your users prefer the paperback because it's easier to stuff into a backpack or take to the pool, then you might want a different record for the two different printings. However, this tag is repeatable so it might work just as well for you to have both ISBNs in the record and use the notes area to point out that you have both printings. You may even opt to add a suffix to the classification number to show that one copy is hardbound and the other is paperback. The point is that more than one ISBN can be in a record. Your decision on how to deal with different printings depends on you and your library community.

Other parts of the record: That takes care of the standard eight areas; what about the rest of the record? Continuing on our downward journey of our sample record we see the 6XX tags:

Subj:Topical	650 1	$aFables.
Subj:Topical	650 1	$aMice
		$xFolklore.

These tags are not part of the eight areas of description because they deal with the intellectual content of the item rather than the physical description of the item. In our sample, we also have a 900 tag:

Local Call #   900 $a398.24 SCH 1995

    Anytime you see a tag with a "9" in it, regardless of the position of the nine, you know you have a locally assigned tag. These tags are not defined by the Library of Congress, but are used as placeholders for times when librarians want to describe some aspect of the item in a non-standardized form. The information in the 900 tag looks like a standard Dewey number with additional Cutter information (SCH) and a publication date information. So what's the problem with this number that it has to be in a 900 tag? If it is a Dewey number, why isn't it in the 082 tag? Our record clearly has a Dewey number:

Dewey#   082 00 $a398.24/5293233

                                      $aE

                                      $220

    Why does this library need a different number? The answer is simple; the recording of the classification number in many school library automation programs was not standardized when these systems first appeared. Thus it was that the systems often did not recognize the 082 tag as the place to retrieve classification number information. Many systems provided to the school library media specialists something called a "holdings" area wherein the classification number and other copy specific information for each item was recorded. Although systems today can be set to accept the 082 as classification information, most of us still opt to use the holdings area for this. Our example library continues to use the 900 tag for classification information even though it no longer needs to do so. But beyond the mechanics of the system, compare the two numbers. The number in the 900 tag is much shorter than that found in the 082 tag. As we will see in our discussion of Dewey classification, the number given in the 082 tells us that the item may be classified in folklore under the number 398.245293233 or that it may be classified under the "E" area but in either case, the number is based on the 20th edition of the unabridged Dewey Decimal Classification system. Most school libraries will want to use the abridged edition. If you took a look at the 14th abridged edition of Dewey, you would see that 398.24 is as far as we can go. Because the number is displayed in the non-standard 900 tag, there is no way of telling which edition was used by this library to create that number. Regardless of the edition used, it is clear that this library prefers the shorter number to the longer one. We will get a clearer picture of the meaning and use of Dewey numbers in chapter five.

    Remember, any time you see a "9" in a tag number, be that 092, 590, 690, or 900, you are looking at information that has been created by the library and may not reflect standard practice.

Conclusion

We have taken a brief look at the mechanics of the MARC record and compared it to cataloging standards. In the next few chapters we will be applying theory to the practice of cataloging. In chapter four we will apply this to subject headings, followed by classification in chapter five. Chapter six will pull all of this information together as we learn about using the full MARC record.

PART TWO

Introduction to Part II – Application

We are now about to journey into the realm of the art of cataloging. We will discuss and show examples of subject headings, classification, and physical description. To do this we will refer to as many real-life examples as we can. Throughout these chapters, however, we will consistently refer to nine different publications given here:

- *Accidents May Happen* written by Charlotte Foltz Jones, illustrated by John O'Brien. New York: Delacorte Press, 1996.

- *Bard of Avon: The Story of William Shakespeare* written by Diane Stanley and Peter Vennema, illustrated by Diane Stanley. New York: Morrow Junior Books, 1992.

- *Frog and Toad Are Friends* (book & cassette) by Arnold Lobel. New York: Harper Carousel, 1985.

- *Green Eggs and Ham* (computer software) by Dr. Seuss. Novato, CA: Living Books, 1996.

- *Harry Potter and the Order of the Phoenix* by J. K. Rowling. New York: Listening Library, 2003.

- *Noodlebug on the Move* (DVD & CD-ROM). Peru, IL: Carus Publishing, 2003.

- *Ohio* by Ron Knapp. Berkeley Heights, NJ: MyReportLinks.com Books (Enslow), 2002.

- *Persepolis* (graphic novel) by Marjane Satrapi. New York: Pantheon, 2003.
- *Strega Nona* (videotape in Spanish) by Tomie dePaola. Weston, Conn.: Weston Woods, 2000.

We selected these examples because they cover different types of information packages with different types of cataloging problems and because it would make sense to see these titles in school library collections. If possible, you might want to see if you can get copies of these titles. While we will do our best to describe these items, there is no substitute for having the item in your hand when making cataloging decisions.

Chapter 4

Intellectual Access— Subject Headings

Introduction

*I*ntellectual Access refers to information retrieval based on the content of the item itself, rather than physical access via title or author. Subject access is provided to show the user the items a library has on a given *topic* as opposed to classification which is used to organize the collection according to the *discipline*. Applying subject headings means one is describing what the item is all about. This chapter will present information on: 1) the concept of subject headings vs. keyword access; 2) the principles and application of subject access including putting subject headings into the MARC record; and 3) the pros and cons of using either *Sears List of Subject Headings* or *Library of Congress Subject Headings*.

Subject Headings vs. Keyword Access

We begin this chapter by recalling that one of Cutter's objects and means was to find a book (or information package) according to its subject. In order to meet this need, controlled vocabularies of subject terms were established. These controlled vocabularies became known as subject headings. Subject headings reflect the intellectual content of the item; that is, the content or the topic of the item—what it is about. The Library of Congress Subject Headings (LCSH) and Sears List of Subject Headings (Sears) (the two most commonly used lists in school libraries) are examples of controlled vocabularies that are accepted worldwide. Inherent in the use of standard subject headings is a structure such that if a specific heading does not exist for a topic, a new heading may be developed by the cataloger following specific rules for assigning new subject headings.

One of the consequences of computerizing card catalogs was that the library patron was no longer bound by the confines of subject headings for retrieving information. Automated programs included the ability to look at each line of the surrogate record and pull out *"key words"* for retrieval purposes. For example, if the word "surfing" appeared anywhere in the record, in the title, subject heading, summary statement, anywhere at all, the user could search that word and pull up records with that word. This would apply to any meaning of the word "surfing" be it surfing the Internet or the ocean waves. It is important to emphasize that *content*, or the meaning of the word, is not taken into consideration in keyword searching. *Keyword* searching involves the retrieval of information based on the incidence of the word in the surrogate record and is *not necessarily reflective of the intellectual content of the item*. Since the introduction of keyword searching, researchers have been exploring the benefits of keyword searching over subject searching. Even from the earliest stages of electronic information retrieval, the question was not which one is better, but how to use both as effective methods of information retrieval. (There was a series of articles edited by Pauline A. Cochrane published in *American Libraries* from February 1984 through July/August 1984. Although some aspects of information retrieval no longer apply to these early arguments, there is still much to be learned from this series.)

The oft asked question is, "If the user can retrieve information from any part of the surrogate record, why should librarians bother with controlled vocabulary?"

A list of *controlled vocabulary* helps lead a user to the desired materials by ensuring that all *similar materials have been assigned the same subject headings*. An uncontrolled vocabulary (keyword) does not make that same assurance. In fact, a keyword search may result in a list of completely unrelated items. To illustrate, suppose we have a user who is interested in the kind of surfing that requires tidal motion and lots of sand. Now let's say we type in the keyword, "surfing," and get back these two titles: *Surfing the Ocean Waves of the Internet* and *Surfing the Great Ocean Waves*. The search has resulted in great retrieval. That means our user has been presented with two items from which to choose. However, the precision in the search is lacking because only one of the titles is on the topic about which the user is interested. It might not make that big of a difference if we're only talking about two titles, but let's see what happens in a real life example. If you go to the Library of Congress Web site (http://lcweb.loc.gov), click on "Library Catalogs," click on "Basic Search," type the word "surfing," and then click "keyword," you will get more than 500 titles in response to your search. A brief review of the results will illustrate for you right away that this is not an efficient search. Sure, there are items about gliding across ocean waves on a board, but there are also items about the solar system, punk rock musicians, and East Germany. And that's just the first screen of results! Now go back and click subject. The resulting list is the 25 headings that fit your surfing search. The first heading, "surfing," is connected to just 70 titles that will be on the topic of gliding across ocean waves on a board. Keyword searching often results in greater retrieval and less precision. It doesn't make keyword searching wrong; it's just a different way of accessing information.

Thinking about our example, we may come to the conclusion that keyword searching is a bad idea. It is not, but, it has to be approached with the knowledge that we're talking about the incidence of the word and not the intellectual content of that word. Keyword searching can be especially helpful when one is unsure of the subject heading to use. A good keyword search will often lead the user to just the right subject heading.

Consider the example given in Figure 4.1 of a real surrogate record for a book about the baseball player Jackie Robinson.

Figure 4.1. Example of a surrogate record for the book **Teammates.**

Title:	Teammates / written by Peter Golenbock ; designed and illustrated by Paul Bacon.
Author:	Golenbock, Peter, 1946-
Published:	San Diego : Harcourt Brace Jovanovich, c1990.
Description:	[32] p. : col. ill. ; 22 x 28 cm.
Notes:	"Voyager books."
Notes:	An NCSS-CBC Notable Children's Trade Book in the Field of Social Studies--Back cover.
Notes:	Redbook Children's Picturebook Award winner.
Notes:	Describes the racial prejudice experienced by Jackie Robinson when he joined the Brooklyn Dodgers and became the first black player in Major League baseball and depicts the acceptance and support he received from his white teammate Pee Wee Reese.
Notes:	Lexile Measure: 930
Subject:	Robinson, Jackie, 1919-1972.
Subject:	Reese, Pee Wee, 1919-1999.
Subject:	Baseball players--United States--Biography.
Subject:	Brooklyn Dodgers (Baseball team).
Subject:	African Americans--Biography.
Subject:	Race relations.
Subject:	Baseball.
Added Entry:	Bacon, Paul, 1923- ill.

Imagine a user is interested in items about baseball players. There is a subject heading for baseball players (the third subject line in our record); therefore, entering a subject search "baseball players" would result in the retrieval of this and other items with that subject heading included in the record. Now imagine that the user used a keyword search instead of the subject headings search. Along with this book and any other items about baseball players, included in the list would be items about basketball players, bridge players, even banjo players not to mention baseball rules, baseball history, and baseball teams!

There is a distinct efficiency in using a controlled vocabulary, but it doesn't always work for us the way we would like it to. For example, if our user didn't know the right subject heading and instead used "baseball biographies" for the subject search, then the list would be short indeed. In fact, unless the cataloging was incorrect, the user would get no titles at all as a result of that subject search and come to the conclusion that the library has no biographies about baseball players. Here is where the keyword search "baseball biography" would come in handy. In our example, we see that a controlled vocabulary assumes that the user knows the words that are on the subject list. Thus the user must know that the subject is "baseball players" and not "baseball biographies." Keywords do not make this heroic assumption. A keyword search of "baseball biography" would at least result in some retrieval of relevant materials if not pulling up this specific title. Once related items are retrieved, the user can then click on the proper subject heading and have access to just the right items.

Some automated systems are created with the understanding that K-12 students may not know the right words to use in their subject searches. To help the students, instead of responding with zero hits to a "wrong" subject search, the system will display subjects that are alphabetically close to the student's search term(s). In our case of "baseball players" versus "baseball biographies," our user may luck out if the display is long enough to give the hint on the correct heading. The user might not be so lucky if the "right" subject term is not alphabetically close to the "wrong" search. In a recent article, Hatcher (2005) described the results of a subject search when the word she used was "kamikazes." She typed in the word, but the item she knew she had about kamikaze pilots was not displayed. In fact no titles were retrieved given her search. It turned out that, according to *LCSH*, she had the wrong subject heading. The correct subject heading was "World War, 1939-1945 – Aerial operations, Japanese" (2). In this case it would be impossible for an alphabetical list to bring the two terms close together.

Electronic retrieval programs take keywords from certain areas of the surrogate record. Which part of the record is used for retrieval purposes is dependent on the design of the database. Minimally, these words are taken from the author, title, subject, and notes fields of the surrogate record. The more fields the program searches, the longer the search will take. Until recently, vendors severely restricted the fields searched because the technology was slow and users did not like waiting for search results. Faster technology, however, has allowed for more extensive use of the surrogate record. The result is that the user now has access to nearly the entire record for keyword searching purposes.

Keyword access is a tremendous boon to library users and information retrieval. The benefit is especially noticeable in searching for aspects of the item that are not related to the subject of the item. The abundance of reading programs such as Accelerated Reader and Reading Counts have made searching by reading, Lexile, and target level a must in school library settings. Students often get assignments to read books only from a reading program list, and so it is helpful for them to use keyword searching to retrieve titles based on the name of the list and reading levels. In the case of our baseball book, a keyword search might include "accelerated reader baseball" to find a book about baseball that is also on the Accelerated Reader list. This combined search is not possible using only a subject headings search.

Lexile searching is a little bit trickier than searching for the name of a reading program. Theoretically a student should be able to type in the area of interest (in our case, we'll stick with baseball) and the Lexile level to which he or she has been restricted and come up with an item (assuming the library has an item at exactly that Lexile level on baseball). However, for many school library systems, that kind of keyword search is too sophisticated. Usually a keyword search on just the Lexile number, for example 660, should yield a list of information packages. However, the mix of the number and the topic is not always as successful. If all the student needs is a book at a certain level only, then a number and keyword search will work fine. However, if a topic is important, then students will need to learn more advanced searching techniques to combine reading levels with topical searches. How this is done is dependent on the system itself, but it is a technique that should be taught to students especially if the school emphasizes reading level over topic.

Teaching your students about the differences between retrieving information via keywords or subject headings is crucial. It is also important for the librarian to understand this difference when deciding what type of information to include in the surrogate record. Remember, the essence of cataloging is organization for the purpose of retrieval. Use keywords in the record to supplement the controlled vocabulary of the existing subject headings.

Sears List of Subject Headings and Library of Congress Subject Headings

The two standard subject headings lists used in school library media centers are the *Sears List of Subject Headings* and the *Library of Congress Subject Headings*. Before we discuss the use of these headings, we offer a little background on the development of these lists.

A Little Historical Background

In 1923, with small public and, by extension, school libraries, as the focus of the work, Minnie Earl Sears created a work that was easy for librarians to use and users to understand. Sears eliminated scientific terminology found in *LCSH* in favor of more vernacular terms with the express purpose of making retrieval easier for the non-academic library user. Sears knew that her list was anything but exhaustive and comprehensive. Instead of attempting to include all possible headings and ending up with a multivolume work like *LCSH*, Sears included explicit yet simple directions to librarians regarding how to create subject headings that are necessary for the specific needs of the library but that have not been included in her text. There was no attempt to codify these added headings, but to simply allow librarians to create lists that were specific to the needs of their users. In the earlier editions of her work, there was space in the margins of the book for librarians to write down their added subject headings. (An unfortunate aspect of the newer editions is the omission of that space.)

The Library of Congress, on the other hand, created a subject authority list to best serve its clientele, members of the United States Congress. To be fair, the Library of Congress has certainly recognized that not every library user is a member of Congress or even an academician; nevertheless, terms used in LCSH tend towards the scientific and scholarly. In recent years, LC has moved from unnatural language (scientific nomenclature and inverted headings) to more natural language. Also, to meet the needs of cataloging children's materials, LC created the Library of Congress Annotated Card Subject Headings list (LC/AC). Devised and first implemented in the mid-1960s, the LC/AC headings were designed as exceptions to the LC subject headings to replace technical terms with words more easily understood by a younger group of users. The LC/AC headings enhance rather than replace the LC headings. Thus, it takes both lists to assign subject headings to children's materials. LC/AC headings tend to be more general than LC headings. For example, while LCSH uses the heading "Teenage marriage," LC/AC is limited to the broader term "Marriage." In an upper elementary school, the LC/AC term "Marriage" may be sufficient for retrieval purposed. In a senior high school situation, however, it might be more useful to differentiate between those items that are about marriage in general from those specifically about teen marriage. Therefore, the elementary school librarian might use the LC/AC heading while the senior high school librarian will want to use the LC heading.

The Comparison

Although in the greater world of cataloging there are a variety of standardized subject headings lists, there are basically two lists used in schools: *Sears* and *LCSH* (including *LC/AC*). Before the advent of automated cataloging, most school library media specialists depended on the *Sears List of Subject Headings* (*Sears*) for assigning subject access to the library materials. Librarians appreciated the easy, natural language of the *Sears* headings and were comfortable with adding their own headings when required. Besides that, the one volume of *Sears* is more compact and more affordable than the multiple volumes of *LCSH*. However, as library catalogs entered the automation age and reliance on copy cataloging increased, school library media specialists began to accept the subject headings provided on the records regardless of the origin of the headings. It is probably safe to say that most school library catalogs are now conglomerates of *Sears* and *LCSH*. Today, many vendors offer school library media specialists the choice of adding *Sears, LCSH*, or both subject headings terms to their records.

At face value, there seems to be little problem with the use of LCSH in a school library. It is so easy to accept the cataloging provided by vendors and most vendors do supply LCSH in their cataloging. However, the problem is not in accepting that which is provided by the vendor, but how to deal with assigning subject headings to items not cataloged by a vendor. If one must apply subject headings, and this might be done even with vendor supplied cataloging, then it is a good idea to have a current copy of an authoritative subject headings list.

Another important issue to address is that of making up headings if they are not provided for in either Sears or LCSH. Sears anticipated that librarians would need to make up headings and included instructions on how to add headings to her list. The new headings would be constructed according to her guidelines but would not be "standardized" in that they may be used in only the library adding the heading. LC, on the other hand, is much stricter about the addition of new headings or the adaptation of existing ones.

Although it is true that new headings are constantly being added to LCSH, these headings are not added without careful (and often lengthy) consideration. Catalogers may fill out reports to LC recommending the addition of new headings. Acceptance of new terms is predicated on literary warrant. That is, the determination that there are enough publications on the subject to warrant the creation of a new heading. Suggestions for adding or changing headings are submitted to the Subject Authority Component of the Program for Cooperative Cataloging through a Subject Authority Proposal form available on the Internet: http://www.loc.gov/catdir/pcc/prop/proposal.html. Weekly subject headings lists are posted on the Library of Congress site for the Cataloging Directorate, Cataloging Policy and Support Office: http://www.loc.gov/catdir/cpso/cpso.html#subjects. Few school library media specialists will have the time to check this list on a weekly basis; however, there are some headings for which it would be wise to check for revisions and updates.

Some areas such as sports, current events, and biographies are particularly sensitive to popular trends and are some of the hardest areas to keep current. For example, the passion for extreme sports has existed for many years; however, the subject heading for items on that topic has only existed since 1996. Prior to that time, subject headings for the specific equipment (e.g. skateboards) or venue (e.g. mountain climbing) have been the only viable subject headings available. Today the subject term "extreme sports," which is much more descriptive of the intellectual content, is used to guide the user to the exact items desired. However, without being aware of changes in LC headings, school library media specialists may continue to apply and accept the older headings. It might take some time for new headings to show up in vendor databases and copy cataloging resources. If the librarian is aware of the changes she/he can enhance the records to reflect the newer heading.

Just as the catalogers in the Library of Congress do not go back and update subject headings with each subject heading change, it would be unreasonable to assume that the school library media specialist would go back and update the school catalog. What the school library media specialist does need to be aware of is that subject headings do change. They change and are added on a weekly basis. The school library media specialist must know if the vendor is keeping up with and providing authority records for subject heading changes. For those school library media specialists in districts with centralized cataloging, there must be assurance from the cataloging department that current subject headings are being applied to the library materials with proper cross-references when required.

The benefit of using *Sears* headings is that it allows for each library to add and change headings as best suits the needs of that library. Between *Sears* and *LCSH*, *Sears* is certainly the easiest and least expensive of the two. Because *Sears* is designed for the small and school library, it presents subject headings with Dewey classification numbers attached to the headings. This is a very useful aspect of the list that does not exist with *LCSH*. *Sears* is also known for using much more natural language than *LCSH*, although this is beginning to change. Being designed specifically for schools and smaller libraries, one may find that *Sears* is the resource to have. The benefit of using *LCSH* is that those headings are more commonly seen in copy cataloging than are *Sears* headings. It is easier merely to download an LC heading than it is to create a *Sears* heading. Finally, LC has now made its subject headings authority list available for searching, online and for free, to the general public. This feature will probably outweigh the benefit of connecting headings to Dewey classification numbers. Realistically speaking, there probably will be very

The school library media specialist should consider having a hard copy of a standardized subject headings list. Provided here is a chart of the advantages and disadvantages of *Sears* and *LCSH*.

Sears List of Subject Headings	*Library of Congress List of Subject Headings*
Pro: List created expressly for school and small collections; relatively inexpensive to keep current edition in collection; organized for in-house addition of headings; links headings to specific abridged Dewey classification numbers; includes prefatory information on the theory and application of subject headings.	**Pro:** Extensive, widely used list; authority of headings may be checked online for free; includes special subject headings just for children's materials (*LCSH/AC* headings).
Con: Not readily available for authority checking online; not often found in resources offering copy cataloging; not updated annually (approximately every three to four years).	**Con:** Unnatural academic language (*LC/AC* excluded) difficult for school aged children to use; expensive; five large volumes.
Updated: 18th ed., 2004; updated approximately every three to four years by H.W. Wilson Publishing Company.	**Updated:** annually (28th ed., 2005); updated headings posted weekly on LC Web site: http://lcweb.loc.gov/catdir/cpso/cpso.html#subjects
Cost: $110 (North American price)	**Cost:** $295 (North American price)

few school library media specialists in the years to come who will rely completely on *Sears*. This also means that school library media specialists must be vigilant about the headings that they are accepting from vendors and online databases.

The Electronic LCSH

Recently, the Library of Congress made its authority files available to the general public. What this means is that one can now look up the LC files for authorized subject headings *online and free of charge*. Therefore, if one wasn't sure if the videotape about spiders should get the subject heading "spiders" or "arachnida," a quick trip to the LC authorities database (http://authorities.loc.gov) would prove that either is acceptable, but that spiders is the preferred heading for assigning headings to children's materials.

If we were to go to the LC authority records Web page (http://authorities. loc.gov), we would click on the highlighted "Search Authorities" link and be taken to a search page wherein we could search for subject, name, title, or name/title authority headings. Both the name and the subject authority searches are of interest to us in terms of subject headings. Names would be applied to creating biographical headings and subjects for topical and geographic subject headings. When we enter a search and look at the results, we will find that our term is in a center column with the type of heading on the right side and a special button, "Authorized & References" on the left side. We want to see that special button as it will lead us to making sure we have an authorized heading. In the right column under "Type of Heading" we want to make sure we have "LC subject headings" or "LC subject headings for children." We may also see other types of headings listed, but we are only interested in LC or *LC/AC* headings. Let us look at an example for "spiders" in Figure 4.2.

Figure 4.2. Results of the Subject Search "Spiders" on the LC Authorities Database

LIBRARY OF CONGRESS AUTHORITIES

| Help ① | New Search | Search History | Headings List | Start Over |

SOURCE OF HEADINGS: Library of Congress Online Catalog
YOU SEARCHED: Subject Authority Headings = Spiders
SEARCH RESULTS: Displaying 1 through 25 of 25.

◀ Previous   Next ▶

#	Bib Records	select icon in first column to... View Authority Headings/References	Type of Heading
Authorized & References 1	68	Spiders	LC subject headings
2	216	Spiders.	LC subject headings for children
3	3	Spiders 1910-1920.	Thesaurus for graphic materials: TGM I, sub. terms

Screen shot of the Library of Congress Web page after searching "spiders" in the LC Authority Files database (captured August 15, 2005).

Figure 4.3.

SOURCE OF HEADINGS: Library of Congress Online Catalog
INFORMATION FOR: Spiders

Please note: Broader Terms are not currently available

Select a Link Below to Continue...
Authority Record
See: Gerholdt, James E., 1943- Spiders
Narrower Term: Actinopodidae
Narrower Term: Agelenidae
Narrower Term: Amaurobiidae
Narrower Term: Anapidae
Narrower Term: Antrodiaetidae
Narrower Term: Anyphaenidae

Screen shot of the Library of Congress Web page showing LC subject headings related to the subject "spiders" (captured August 15, 2005).

If we click on the red button, "Authorized & References," we will see a link to the proper heading, the authority record, along with references to narrower terms (names of specific types of spiders) as we see in Figure 4.3.

And clicking on the "Authority Record" will lead us to a reference to the heading and then eventually to the heading itself (see Figure 4.4).

In the authority record we see something that looks like a MARC record, but it is also different. The definitions of these tags are different in the authority record than they are for the bibliographic or surrogate record. What we need to know from this record is that if our term is in the 1XX tag of the authority record,

Figure 4.4. MARC Authority Record for the LCSH Term "Spiders"

LC Control Number: sh 85126625
    HEADING: Spiders
        000 00418nz a2200181n 450
        001 4775544
        005 19950421135230.3
        008 860211il anannbabn |a ana
        035 __ |a (DLC)sh 85126625
        906 __ |t 8751 |u fk03 |v 0
        010 __ |a sh 85126625
        040 __ |a DLC |c DLC |d DLC
        053 _0 |a QL458.4 |b QL458.42
        150 __ |a Spiders
        450 __ |a Araneae
        450 __ |w nne |a Araneida
        550 __ |w g |a Arachnida
        953 __ |a xx00 |b ta25

Screen shot of the authority record for the LCSH term "spiders" (captured August 15, 2005).

then it is a term we can use. If for example, our search had been "araneae" which is in the 450 tag, then we would know that we have selected a term that is not used and we should use "spiders" instead. We can also see this example in a "Labelled Display" that helps us to understand the reference without needing to understand the MARC structure of the record, thus:

Figure 4.5. Labelled Display for the LCSH Term "Spiders"

Figure 4.5. Labelled (or eye-readable) display of the authority record for the LCSH term "spiders" (captured August 15, 2005).

What this database does not do for the cataloger is to show *how* subject headings are constructed or which subdivisions are viable with specific subject headings. While having access to these files, especially for free, is a great asset to the school library media specialist cataloger, it may not be sufficient for cataloging needs in creating enhanced or original records. Therefore, it might still be helpful to have a current list handy. Because *Sears* and *LCSH* headings are created following similar rules, the *Sears* book will help in creating new headings and has the additional feature of suggesting abridged Dewey classification numbers to the subject headings. Therefore, even though libraries may drift from using only *Sears* headings, there will still be a use for that resource in original cataloging and in enhancing existing records.

Authority or authority control refers to the linking of various forms of a name or subject heading. The links are made in terms of "see" and "see also" references. In computer programs, these links are transparent to the user. It is usually up to the librarian, however, to establish these links. Thus the librarian must create what is known as *authority records* to cross-reference name changes (e.g. Geisel, Theodor S. see Seuss, Dr.) and subject changes and additions (e.g. Skateboarding see also Extreme sports). Access to the Library of Congress authority records helps us in making sure that the names of the people, places, and corporate bodies, and the subject headings we want to add to our records are correctly constructed and are viable headings. Creating an authority record is not the same as creating a surrogate record. The surrogate record represents an information package. The authority record represents links to synonymous terms or names, such as Geisel and Seuss.

Basic Structure of Sears and LCSH

We have already discussed using the online version of *LCSH*; we shall now focus on the use of the print version. While *Sears* and *LCSH* are not identical, they share enough common structure so that they can be discussed together.

Both *Sears* and *LCSH* are arranged in alphabetical order with boldfaced entries marking valid subject headings and references from non-valid headings (those that are not in bold print) to the valid headings. References to similar headings are made using the navigational abbreviations: USE, UF, BT, NT, RT, and SA. Use (USE) directs the user from a term that is not accepted to a different term that is. Use for, or UF, is the opposite of USE and shows the user the term that is not used. Broader and narrower terms, noted as BT and NT respectively, lead the user to just that, terms that are broader or narrower in scope to the one in question. A related term, or RT, is a term that is on the same level as the term in question. The see also (SA) reference helps the cataloger create new or more specific headings. Both *LCSH* and *Sears* use notes under some of the more nebulous headings to clarify proper usage. At the beginning of both *LCSH* and *Sears* is a list of words that can be used as subdivisions for nearly every subject heading. These are called "free-floating subdivision" in *LCSH* and "commonly used subdivisions" in *Sears*. Also, each list establishes "key" (*Sears*) or "pattern" (*LCSH*) headings as models for using subdivisions. Directions for use of these headings and subdivisions are given in the introductory parts of each text.

Headings and Subdivisions

Subject headings typically are single word entries used to convey a concept or topic (e.g. baseball). On occasion, it may take more than one word to adequately convey the meaning of the topic (e.g. baseball players). Sometimes the subject headings can be further subdivided to bring out specific topics. Imagine what a catalog would look like if all works on United States history were entered only under United States! Further dividing of the subject heading can help lead the user to more specific works. These words are called subdivisions or subheadings. In the manual format, subject headings are divided into subheadings by the use of the double dash (—). In the MARC record, the dashes become transparent to the cataloger even though there may be some form of the dashes in the display of the record in the public catalog. Using a different subfield for each aspect of the subject heading tells the computer to insert dashes on its own. Let us take as an example a book about football coaching.

- In the print version of *LCSH* we would see:

  Football (May Subd Geog)
  — Coaching

- In *Sears* we would see:

  Football – Coaching   **796.33207**

- In the MARC record we would see:
  - 650 _0 $aFootball $xCoaching. (*LCSH*) OR
  - 650 _1 $aFootball $xCoaching. (*LC/AC*) OR
  - 650 _7 $aFootball $xCoaching. $2sears (*Sears*)

- In the OPAC we would see:
  - Subjects: Football – Coaching

Both the *LCSH* and *Sears* listings of the subject heading include the double dash but in *LCSH* the subdivision is on a different line and in *Sears* it is on the same line. Both headings are in bold print so we know they are legal headings to use. In our example, we see that *Sears* has provided us with a hint as to where to classify this item by supplying the appropriate Abridged Dewey Decimal Classification number (a *very* nice added feature). As we list subject headings in the MARC record, we place the information following the dash into a new subfield. In the MARC record, the double dashes will be inserted automatically in the OPAC by the computer because the subdivision is entered in a different subfield (in this case $x). Notice how the subject heading is displayed on the public catalog with the double dashes to separate the main subject heading from the subdivision. We will go over the structure of the MARC tag with more specificity later in this chapter. For now we will focus on the structure of the subject headings themselves.

> *Try this:* Take a look at subject headings by going to an online catalog. Many catalogs will allow you the option of looking at the public (OPAC) record as well as the MARC record. Flip back and forth and note how the MARC record information is translated by the computer into a format that is easy for the user to understand. Try this with a local database and the LC database.

LCSH headings and subdivisions:

Let's take a closer look at our football example. We see the following (the full subject heading as printed in the *LCSH* is abbreviated here for the sake of illustration):

Football (May Subd Geog)
[GV937-GV960]
Here are entered general works on football games as well as works on American football.
　　UF American football
　　　Foot-ball *[Former heading]*
　　BT Ball games
　　SA *subdivision* Football *under individual educational institutions, e.g.*
Harvard University--Football
　　　NT Flag football
　　　　Rugby football
　　　　Soccer
　　　　Touch football
　　　　— Accidents and injuries

— Attendance
>>USE Football attendance
— **Betting**
— **Clubs**
>>— Collective labor agreements
>>>USE Collective labor agreements – Football clubs
— **Coaching**

Look at the term "Football" and note that it is in bold print. This means that it is a valid subject heading. In the MARC record it can be used in one of the 6XX tags. "Football" is immediately followed by "(May Subd Geog)." This means that the cataloger can add a geographic subdivision after the term "Football," e.g. Football – United States. On the next line we see "[GV937-GV960]" which are hints to the cataloger that these are the classification numbers associated with this subject area. The classification system referred to here is the Library of Congress classification system and not the Dewey Decimal classification. It is not much help for us in the school library environment. This line is followed by a scope note about how the subject heading may be applied. Next we see a "use for" (UF) notation telling use that the terms "American football" and "Foot-ball" are not valid headings and we should us "Football" instead. Next we see the broader term reference (BT) to "Ball games." Following that is a list of narrower terms (NT), e.g. Flag football, and then the subdivisions. Note under the subdivisions there are some valid ones (in bold) and invalid ones (not in bold). The invalid headings have references to the alternative headings.

Sears **headings and subdivisions:** Now let's see how *Sears* handles the subject of football:

>**Football** (May subdiv. geog.)   **796.332**
>>BT **Ball games**
>>>**Sports**
>>NT **Soccer**
>**Football – Coaching**   **796.33207**
>>BT **Coaching (Athletics)**

Immediately, one can see a similar structure but much less detail. We still see that one may add a geographic subdivision for the subject heading and broader and narrower terms with the single subdivision for Coaching. What we do not see is the detailed scope note, the reference to invalid terms, and a long list of subdivisions. Remember that *Sears* is meant for smaller library collections and so there is probably less need for the detail included in *LCSH*. We also see a classification number here, but it is for Dewey and not for LC as Dewey is more commonly found in the smaller and school library environments than is LC. This is the *Abridged Dewey Decimal Classification* number and, for us in the school libraries, this number is much more helpful to use than is the LC classification number found with the *LCSH* heading.

The MARC Format: 6XX Tags

We will explore here in some detail the way to include *LCSH* and *Sears* subject headings in the MARC record. Subject headings occupy the 6XX fields of the MARC record. The fields are usually referred to by the number preceding the Xs. So this area is referred to as "six-x-x." They may also be referred to by the number of the first field in the area, as in "600" field. There are 12 different kinds of 6XX fields that are used to define different kinds of subject access. In general, school library media specialists will be most concerned with personal (600), topical (650), geographic (651), corporate (610), genre (655), and curriculum (658) headings. We will include a brief discussion on the meeting (611) and local (690) tags at the end of this section.

There are several types of 6XX fields. These are the common tags used with school library materials:

- Personal names (as in biographies) = 600.

- Topical headings (general subjects) = 650.

- Geographic headings (places as subjects) = 651.

- Corporate headings (as in theme parks) = 610.

- Genre headings (type of literature) = 655.

- Curriculum objective (link to state or district standards) = 658.

All 6XX tags are repeatable which means that more than one of any given 6XX field may be seen in a record.

Recall from chapter three that each MARC field is comprised of a field (or tag) number, two indicator spots, and the various subfields (designated for our purposes with the dollar sign "$" and the letter of the subfield, as in "$a"). Also recall that the indicators are codes that either tell the computer program to do something or define for the computer information included in the tag. In the 6XX tags, the first indicator is used to indicate a number of different meanings that will be made clear in the discussion of the individual tags below. The second indicator has the same definition for all 6XX tags that we will be discussing. It is used to show from whence the heading has come, that is, which controlled vocabulary list was used to create the subject heading. *Library of Congress Subject Headings* will have a second indicator value of "0." For subjects established in the LC Annotate Card (children's) headings, we see the value of "1." For *Sears* headings, the second indicator code is "7" with an added subfield "2" at the end of the heading and the word "sears" in that subfield. The value of "7" tells us that this is a heading from a controlled list and the subfield "2" is the place where we will explain which list was used (in our case the list is *Sears*). Again, these values for the second indicator hold true for all 6XX tags discussed. A good cataloger will know immediately the origin of the subject heading by just looking at the second indicator. Using the book, *Accidents May Happen*, we find these subject headings:

650 _0 $aDiscoveries in science $xHistory $vJuvenile literature.
650 _1 $aDiscoveries in science.
650 _7 $aScience. $2sears

Note first that all three headings are included in a single record telling us that this library makes use of all three controlled vocabulary lists. This is an important aspect of the record to understand. If the Library of Congress catalogs an item, it is possible to see both *LCSH* and *LC/AC* headings in a single record. LC would do this for children's materials in order to satisfy the needs of an institution that may make use of both types of subject headings (such as a public library) as well as an institution that may want only the *LC/AC* headings (such as a school library). If another institution catalogs an item (as is the case with our example), it is realistic to see the LC headings as well as *Sears* headings. Herein lies a big reason for understanding how subject headings are assigned and being able to make the decision to keep or delete subject headings as needed. Notice in our example that the first indicator space in all three lines has an underscore mark, "_" which tells us that this space is undefined, or blank. Although the 650 tag will be discussed in more detail below, one should notice in this example the difference in the headings themselves. The *LCSH* heading shows much more detail than either the *LC/AC* heading or the *Sears* heading. The meaning of the subfields will be described in more detail below.

We see in our example that the first subdivision is $a. This is the case for almost every tag in the MARC record. The other subject heading information, the subdivisions, is given in other subfields. The most commonly seen subfields in the 6XX tags are $x and $v. The $x is used for noting other topical information. In the case of our example we see "History" as a subdivision for the main subject heading. This tells the user that the information package is about the history of science discoveries. The $v is used for the form of the information package. In our case, we see that the item is a nonfiction work for children. We know this because in $v we see the phrase "Juvenile literature." Notice that neither the *LC/AC* nor the *Sears* headings make use of "$vJuvenile literature." The reason for this is very simple, since *LC/AC* and *Sears* headings are mostly used for children's materials, it is assumed that the item is for children and therefore any reference to juvenile work is redundant. Get used to seeing "juvenile literature" and "juvenile fiction" as one sees this a great deal in *LCSH* subject headings. Note that "juvenile literature" is used for works of nonfiction and "juvenile fiction" is used for works of fiction. School library media specialists often ask if they should use those phrases to differentiate the works for younger readers from those for older readers. It has been our experience that students, especially in high school, will shy away from an item marked "juvenile" as something for kids or at any rate for someone from 1950. We therefore recommend not using the "juvenile" designation at all. But do not discount the use of the $v, as it is also used to designate works that are dictionaries, bibliographies, and other formats.

600 Tag: Personal Name Heading

The 600 tag is used for items *about* specific people. Here the names of those people are entered as subject headings. *Bard of Avon*, for example, is a biographical work about William Shakespeare, thus we know that Shakespeare is a personal name subject heading that needs to be assigned and included in the surrogate record. Thus:

600 10 $aShakespeare, William, $d1564-1616 $xBiography $vJuvenile literature.
600 11 $aShakespeare, William, $d1564-1616.
600 17 $aShakespeare, William, $d1564-1616. $2sears

The construction of these tags is basically the same because they are making note of the same type of information, that is, entry under a person's name. For the 600 tag the first indicator has a value of 0, 1, or 3. A "0" value tells us that the name in $a is a first, or forename, as is used for identifying royalty, e.g. Elizabeth or Diana. A value of "3" tells us that the name in $a is a family name, as is used for works about an entire family, e.g. Du Pont Family. By far the most common value in the first indicator for 600 tags is the value "1," which is used to note a last or surname, as in Smith, Jones, or Clinton.

As stated previously, the second indicator is used to note the source of the heading: 0, 1, or 7 for *LCSH*, *LC/AC*, or *Sears* headings. Notice in the example, one again sees the difference in specificity between the *LC*, *LC/AC*, and *Sears* headings. Take a moment to identify for yourself the different headings. Remember, it is quite possible that all three headings would be included in a single record; however, in your own school, you may decide to use just one of them. If you are being zealous about using only one subject headings list, then you will have only one 600 tag in your record. If you were copying this record from a database (such as LC) or if you purchased the record from a vendor, you might have to look at the record and delete any unwanted 600 tag.

Note, however, that if the name is the same, that is, if there are three 600 tags for Shakespeare that are identical, then retrieval of the item will not be affected. This means that if the student enters a subject name search for Shakespeare, only one record will be retrieved. The system will not, or at least *should* not, bring up what would look like three separate records that, in reality, are the same information package. In other words, it is all right if there is more than one 600 tag for the same person in a single record. In our example, the *LC/AC* and *Sears* headings are exactly the same (the $2 is not considered part of the subject heading for retrieval purposes). If the record had only those two 600 tags, then only one record would be retrieved. The *LSCH* information, however, is slightly different. If the record is left unchanged, the search will result in what will look like two records even though there is only one item. This is the consequence of having more than one controlled vocabulary in use in a single database.

Information for personal names as subject headings usually comes from the item itself in the CIP information or from another copy cataloging source. In the past, before the days of easy access to other library databases, if name information was not on the item (in the form of CIP or other data) the librarian would make up the name entry as best as he/she could. Today, there are so many databases to look at and to use for this decision that it is no longer a matter of making something up. Here is where having access to the LC authority files really comes in handy. If we didn't have any idea of how to create a subject heading for Mr. Shakespeare, we could go to the LC authorities file (http://authorities.loc.gov/), look up his name, and find the correct tagging information.

There are 29 valid subfields under the 600 tag. In general, however, one typically sees three to eight of these subfields. They are:

- $a - personal name,
- $b - numeration (as in II),
- $c - titles (as in Sir),
- $d - birth and death dates,
- $q - fuller form of the name,
- $t - title of a work,
- $v - form subdivision,
- $x - general subdivision.

Of these eight subfields, one most often sees $a, $d, $v, and $x. Remember that the subfields are not necessarily used in alphabetical order. Going back to the Shakespeare example we see the following:

600 10 $aShakespeare, William, $d1564-1616 $xBiography $vJuvenile literature.
600 11 $aShakespeare, William, $d1564-1616.
600 17 $aShakespeare, William, $d1564-1616. $2sears

Note that the first indicator has a value of 1, so we know that Shakespeare is a surname. The second indicators show that the first example is from *LCSH*; the second from *LC/AC*, and the third is from *Sears*. All of the examples start with the $a and include the $d for Shakespeare's birth and death

---

Problems with the $x and the $v; or, why are so many LC records "wrong"?

We have to take a moment to discuss a little history about the form subdivision ($v). In looking at copy cataloging, one will see many subject headings tags with a $x to note the form of an item (e.g. Fiction, Juvenile literature). This is not a mistake, but an example of the fact that school librarians are not the only ones who are too busy to go back and fix records. In the late 1990s, the Library of Congress defined the $v as a way to differentiate items that were *about* a type of publication and items that *were* that type of publication. The decision to do this, to create the "form" subdivision, was not without controversy and many months were spent discussing just exactly when a "form" was a form and not a subject. School library media specialists are most likely going to run into this issue in looking at items with a "fiction," "juvenile fiction," or "juvenile literature" designation. Until very recently, those designations were entered under the $x, but today they are entered under the $v. As records are downloaded, the information should be updated and the subfields corrected. We should not think of records being "wrong" just simply in need of updating.

Summary for the 600 tag:

- Repeatable tag used for subject access under a person's name.

- The first indicator has the following values:
  - Value 0 means $a contains a forename, as in 600 00 $aJohn, $cthe Baptist.
  - Value 1 means $a contains a surname, as in 600 10 $aSmith, John. (This is the most common form of name.)
  - Value 2 means $a contains a family name, as in 600 20 $aDunlop family. (This is by far the rarest of cases and it is doubtful that a school library media specialist would ever be in the situation to use or create such a heading.)

- The second indicator 0, 1, or 7 notes the use of *LCSH*, *LC/AC*, or *Sears* headings (a tag with a 7 indicator must include a "$2sears").

- The most commonly used subfields are $a - name, $d - dates, $v - form, $x - general subdivision.

- Ends in full stop (for *Sears* headings, the full stop is before the $2).

- *LC/AC* and *Sears* headings usually do not include additional subfields beyond the person's name and dates.

Examples:
> 600 00 $aMadonna, $d 1958-
> 600 00 $a50 Cent, $c (Musician)
> (Note the use of the $c needs to show this is the name of a person, a musician in fact, and that there is no full stop as the close parenthesis acts as the final punctuation.)
> 600 11 $aKennedy, John F. $q(John Fitzgerald), $d1917-1963.
> 600 10 $a Balanchine, George.

Exercises:
Try to create personal name subject headings and then use a copy cataloging source or the LC authorities file to find personal name subject headings for the following (watch out for information that is important to know but may not be entered into the tag itself):

4.1. Eleanor Roosevelt, former first lady and human rights advocate who lived from 1884 to 1962.

4.2. Bill Clinton, 42nd president of the United States, born 1946 as William Jefferson Clinton, to most of the world he is just plain Bill.

4.3. Dale Earnhardt, American racecar driver, born 1951, died in an accident during a race on February 18, 2001.

4.4. Queen Elizabeth II, born 1926. Royalty presents all kinds of problems when setting up a personal name entry. Take a look at the entry established by the Library of Congress. Also, take a look at the entry for her husband, Prince Philip, and her son Prince Charles. Note that royalty is *not* entered under the person's last name, but under the first name (note the use of the 0 in the first indicator space). This sometimes creates some confusion but it is the answer to the question, "Why is the biography of Princess Diana filed between the biography of Johnny Depp and the biography of Celene Dion?"

dates. The first example from *LCSH* has a general subdivision ($x) to show the work is biographical in nature and a form subdivision ($v) to show it is a nonfiction work for children. (LC uses "juvenile literature" for children's nonfiction and "juvenile fiction" for children's fiction.) The *LC/AC* heading has only Mr. Shakespeare's name and dates. The reason there are no other subdivisions in the *LC/AC* heading is that children's collections tend not to need the detail necessary in larger adult collections. The heading is coded for children's headings so the addition of the form subdivision in $v would be redundant. *Sears* follows the *LC/AC* suit and also drops the extra subdivisions.

The 600 tag is most commonly found in records of biographical works. This is not, however, the only time one might use a 600 tag. There are times when a person is mentioned in an information package that is not, strictly speaking, biographical in nature. Historical works are typical of this situation. For example, a work on the history of public libraries in the United States that describes the contributions of Andrew Carnegie may very well have a 600 entry for Andrew Carnegie simply because he was so integral to the development of public libraries and is mentioned throughout the work even though the work does not cover detailed biographical information about him.

650 Tag: Topical Heading

Subject headings for specific topics, what we call topical subject headings, are entered in the 650 tag. Catalogers use as many 650 tags as are needed to convey what the item is about. This is the tag wherein the controlled vocabularies of LC and *Sears* really come into play, bringing together varied terms, such as cows and bovines but not cash cows, into a single term or phrase. Let us look at the topical headings for the example book *Accidents May Happen*:

650 _0 $aDiscoveries in science $xHistory $vJuvenile literature.
650 _0 $aTechnological innovations $xHistory $vJuvenile literature.
650 _1 $aTechnological innovations.
650 _1 $aDiscoveries in science.
650 _1 $aHistory, Modern $xMiscellanea.
650 _7 $aScience. $2sears
650 _7 $aInventions. $2sears

Notice that seven subject headings have been entered for this one item and that each entry is in its own 650 tag. The tags that look like they are repeating information (e.g. the second and third tags) are just the *LCSH* and *LC/AC* headings. As with the 600 tag entries, each individual library would decide if it wanted to use only *LCSH* or only *LC/AC* headings or both. Take a good look at the indicators and subfields; they should look familiar. As with the 600 tag, there are two indicators and a variety of subfields. The first indicator in the 650 tag technically has four values: blank (_), 0, 1, or 2. In practice however, most 650 tags will have a blank for the first indicator. The second indicators are the same in the 650 tags as found in the 600 tag, that is, 0 for *LCSH*, 1 for *LC/AC*, and 7 with a $2 for a *Sears* heading. The subfields also have the same meaning in the 650 tag as they do in the 600 tag. There are 13 valid subfields in the 650 tag of which only five are used with regularity (not including the $2 that goes with the second indicator 7). In the previous examples one sees the familiar $a, $x, and $v. The other common subfield is $z for geographic subdivisions. Consider this example sound recording *Civil War Songs*:

650 _0 $aFolk songs, English $zUnited States.
650 _0 $aPopular music $zUnited States.
650 _7 $aAmerican songs. $2sears
650 _7 $aWar songs. $2sears
650 _7 $aFolk songs $zUnited States. $2sears

The $z is used to show that the content of this item is focused on the subject in the United States. Catalogers add geographic subdivisions to topical subject headings when directed by the vocabulary list. In *LCSH* and *Sears*, the directive "May subdiv geog" following a subject heading, tells the cataloger that this heading may be followed by a geographic subdivision. If that directive, "May subdiv geog," does not appear after a subject heading then the cataloger does not add a geographic subdivision. Usually the $z will follow directly after the $a information and then is followed by additional subfields if necessary. Notice that the *LCSH* heading uses the phrase "Folk songs, English" while the *Sears* heading does not make a language distinction, relying instead on the geographic subdivision to say it all. It doesn't of course, as folk songs from the United States could be in any language, but it serves the purpose of a smaller collection as is commonly found in school libraries.

Topical subject headings generally are comprised of one or two words or phrases in natural or inverted order. The Library of Congress is working hard to update inverted headings, such as Peas, Frozen, and putting them into natural order, thus: Frozen peas. *Sears* does not make use of inverted headings. Note in our example that subject headings always begin with a capital letter. Subject headings that include more than one word, such as "Popular music," include a capitalized first word but the second word is not capitalized. Proper nouns, such as "English," will be capitalized. The words in inverted headings, such as History, Modern, are both capitalized. Each subfield begins with a capital letter, as we see in these examples:

- 650 _1 $aHistory, Modern $xMiscellanea.

- 650 _0 $aDiscoveries in science $xHistory $vJuvenile literature.

651 Tag: Geographic Heading

There are times when a work is about a geographic location, in which case the cataloger uses the 651 tag. The 651 tag can be repeated to cover as many areas as necessary. For example, a work about the United States and France would have two 651 tags, one tag for the United States and one for France. The first indicator in 651 is blank; it is undefined and will always be blank (until such time that the rules change!). The second indicator holds the same values as those in 600 and 650; 0, 1, and 7 with the accompanying $2. There are only nine valid subfields in the 651 tag. Of those nine, $a – geographic name, $v – form subdivision, $x – general subdivision, and $y – chronological subdivision are the most common.

Let's take the example of the book, *An American Plague: The True and Terrifying Story of the Yellow Fever Epidemic of 1793*, by Jim Murphy. This book is about a specific topic (Yellow fever), a specific place (Pennsylvania), and a specific time (1793). We can bring out this geographic heading using the 651 tag, thus:

651 _0 $aPhiladelphia (Pa.) $xHistory.
651 _1 $aPennsylvania $xHistory $y1775-1865.
651 _7 $aPhiladelphia (Pa.) $xHistory. $2sears

We have a very interesting example here because the *LC/AC* heading is more detailed than the *LCSH* heading in that it includes a date and yet it is more general because the heading is for the state rather than for the city. It is also interesting that the *Sears* heading is exactly the same as the *LCSH* heading. Notice the date given in the *LC/AC* heading. Dates are not to be invented by the cataloger. This means that we are not free to create a heading that looks like this:

651 _1 $aPennsylvania $xHistory $y1793.

Sears and *LC/AC* are very clear about the use of time periods or chronological subdivisions. If a time period is not provided in the list and the cataloger believes the learning community would be best served by adding a chronological subdivision, then this must be done by consulting the *LC Period Subdivision Under Names of Places* (3).

Recall that *Sears* allows for the addition of subject headings as needed. If one were to look for Philadelphia in the *Sears* book, one would be disappointed and perhaps a little confused because it is not there. How then do we make a heading if it is not there? *Sears* uses "key" headings as models for adding other headings. In the prefatory part of the book, there are instructions to use "Chicago (Ill.)" as a model for creating other headings about cities. Following that model, we can easily make up a heading for Philadelphia. Similarly, if we wanted to include the broader heading of Pennsylvania, we would use the model entry "Ohio" and come up with:

651 _7 $aPennsylvania $xHistory. $2sears

If you are going to use *Sears* as a subject headings list, you must take a good look at the prefatory material.

Summary for 651 tag:

- Repeatable tag used for subject access under a place.
- The first indicator is blank.
- The second indicator 0, 1, or 7 notes the use of *LCSH, LC/AC,* or *Sears* headings and a 7 indicator must include a $2 sears.
- The most commonly used subfields are $a - place, $v - form, $x - general subdivision, and $y – chronological subdivision.
- *LC/AC* and *Sears* headings usually do not include additional subfields beyond the first topic unless a time period is involved or the subject is historical in nature.
- Typically, time periods are predefined by the list and are not made up by the cataloger.
- Ends in full stop (for *Sears* headings, the full stop is before the $2).

Examples:
651 _7 $aUnited States $xPolitics and government $y1961-1974. $2sears
651 _0 $aIran $xHistory $y20th century.
651 _1 $aYosemite National Park (Calif.) $vFiction.

Exercises:
Create geographic subject headings for the following. Use copy cataloging resources to check your answers (try to find both *LCSH* and *Sears* subject headings).

4.9. Item about the American revolutionary war

4.10. Item about the Russian revolution

4.11. Item about China in the 1920s

4.12. World War I and World War II present some interesting cataloging questions because neither *Sears* nor *LCSH* use those phrases as headings.

How would you assign headings for a book about World War II in general?

What about an item that focused on the impact of the war in Germany only?

610 Tag: Corporate Name Heading

According to AACR, a corporate body is:

"an organization or a group of persons that is identified by a particular name and that acts, or may act, as an entity … Typical examples of corporate bodies are associations, institutions, business firms, nonprofit enterprises, governments, government agencies, projects and programmes, religious bodies, local church groups identified by the name of the church, and conferences …" (*AACR* 21-6-21-7).

If one has a work about the National Zoological Park in Washington, D.C., the Titanic, or Enron, then one has a work that needs a corporate subject heading. Sometimes subject headings can fool the cataloger by looking like they are geographic headings, but in reality they are not. The Library of Congress refers to these entities as ambiguous headings. For example, the names of airports, concentration camps, and theme parks are subjects under the corporate headings (610). Monuments and towers are topical subjects (650), and battlefields are geographic headings (651). A full list of ambiguous headings is available from the Library of Congress at: http://www.loc.gov/marc/ambiguous-headings.html.

The first indicator in the 610 tag has a value of 1 or 2. Indicator 1 means that the entity is named under the place first and then the name for the corporate body, for example, Delaware, Department of Education. A value of 2 means that the entity is listed in the direct order, for example, Los Angeles International Airport. The second indicators have the same values as in the other 6XX tags: 0, 1, and 7. There are 27 defined subfields for the 610 tag, but the ones most commonly used by the school library media specialist are $a – name or jurisdiction (place) and $b – subordinate unit (the rest of the name). One will also see $v – form, $z – geographic, and $t – title of document. For the most part, the school library media specialist will not need to be concerned with entering names using the first indicator 1 (jurisdiction order). The use of this tag for entries in jurisdiction order usually is the result of needing to catalog a local government item such as one would find for education standards from the state department of education. In cases like these, the 610 entry begins with the name of the state in $a and ends with the name of the state department in $b. Additionally, one uses the 610 tag for the purpose of referring to state and national documents. In this case, the name of the state or nation is listed first in $a and is followed by the name of the official document in $t. Consider these examples:

- 610 20 $aBluenose (Schooner).
- 610 20 $aEmpire State Building (New York, N.Y.).
- 610 10 $aUnited States. $tConstitution $vJuvenile literature.
- 610 11 $aUnited States. $tConstitution.
- 610 10 $aDelaware. $bDept. of Education.
- 610 20 $aUnited Nations $zAfrica.

Notice the use of the 610 tag for the US Constitution in both the LC and *LC/AC* formats. Note too that "department" is abbreviated "dept." Also note the last example that refers to the United Nations offices or activities in Africa. Notice the use of the $z in the last example to specify geographic subdivision just as it is used in the 650 tag.

611 Tag: Meeting Name Heading

Meetings are listed in the 611 tag. For our purposes, we might consider types of meetings commonly written about for student populations such as the Olympic Games, certain expeditions like those to the North Pole, and gatherings of historical importance such as Woodstock or a world's fair. Technically these are considered under the same rubric as corporate bodies in *AACR*. But in the MARC format, they have a separate tag and so are discussed separately from their corporate brethren.

    The 611 tag is repeatable and is constructed exactly the same as the 610 tag. Therefore, we have the first indicator with the values 1 for jurisdiction and 2 for name in direct order. The second is used, as with the other 6XX tags, to show the source of the heading (0 for LC, 1 for *LC/AC*, and 7 for *Sears*). Parenthetical information is often included in the 611 tag. Consider these three examples:

- 611 20 $aLewis and Clark Expedition $d(1804-1806) $vJuvenile literature.

- 611 20 $aByrd Antarctic Expedition $n(4th : $d1946-1947)

- 611 21 $aOlympic Games $n(27th : $d2000 : $cSydney, N.S.W.) $vFiction.

    There is much here that should look familiar to you; the tag number, the indicators, the first subfield, $a, and the $v to note a work of fiction. Because this can be a confusing tag, we won't go into too much detail, but we feel it is important for you to understand the construction of this tag. The information recorded in this tag deals with an event, like an expedition, and the time. For some events, like an Olympic competition, the place is also of importance. If it is important to note the time and place of an event, then you can be pretty sure you have meeting information, and in subject cataloging using the MARC format, that means the 611 tag. We feel that these examples can be used as models for most of the common meetings needing description in a school library media collection; however, don't forget that the Library of Congress can help out in this matter. Try a subject or keyword search for the meeting you need to catalog and chances are pretty good that you'll find the help you need.

655 Tag: Genre Heading

One type of heading that is appearing with more and more frequency in the school library media catalog is the genre heading (655). This heading is particularly useful for describing specific types of fiction such as science fiction, historical fiction, love stories, and graphic novels. The guide for deciding how to use this tag is *Guidelines on Subject Access to Individual Works of Fiction* (4). This tag can also be used to show the form of the item, for example, Dictionaries. The Library of Congress defines the use of genre terms as:

> Terms indicating the genre, form, and/or physical characteristics of the materials being described. A genre term designates the style or technique of the intellectual content of textual materials or, for graphic materials, aspects such as vantage point, intended purpose, or method of representation. A form term designates historically and functionally specific kinds of materials distinguished by their physical character, the subject of their intellectual content, or the order of information within them. Physical characteristic terms designate historically and functionally specific kinds of materials as distinguished by an examination of their physical character, subject of their intellectual content, or the order of information with them. (http://www.loc.gov/marc/bibliographic/ecbdsubj.html#mrcb655)

Summary for 655 tag:

- Repeatable tag used for defining genre of the item (not the subject of the item).

- The first indicator, more likely than not, will be blank. (There is another option of 0 to mark a faceted heading but it is doubtful a school library media specialist would use or even see this genre type.)

- The second indicator 0, 1, or 7 notes the use of *LCSH, LC/AC,* or *Sears* headings and a 7 indicator must include a $2 sears.

- The most commonly used subfields are $a – genre term, $v – form, $z – geographic, and $y – chronological.

- Ends in full stop (for *Sears* headings, the full stop is before the $2).

Example: 655 _0 $aGraphic novels.

It is important to note the use of genre for the *type* of work the item is rather than what the item is *about*. A work *about* graphic novels would have "Graphic novels" as a topical subject heading (650). On the other hand, a work that *is* a graphic novel would have "Graphic novels" as a genre heading (655).

658 Tag: Curriculum Objectives

This tag is not commonly found in school library media catalogs but it should be. It is through this tag that one can link directly to school, district, state, or other curriculum standards (but not informal classroom standards). It is this tag that will make the school librarian really indispensable when the classroom teacher comes in and says, "I'm looking for materials to help me meet the fourth grade standard number one for geography." Then the librarian can enter a subject search for that curriculum standard and up will pop all the materials that will help the classroom teacher meet that standard. Most of the time it will be a matter of the school library media specialist entering that information. Thus we immediately see why this tag is under used; it is time consuming. Certainly there is no time in the school library media specialist's schedule to go through the entire catalog and input this kind of information. However, this information can be added to new materials as they come in (especially if the materials have been requested by the classroom teachers) and as materials are identified as being useful in planning collaborative units with classroom teachers. Here then is the description of the 658 tag.

As we mentioned, the 658 tag is used to identify curriculum standards. We shall see in chapter six how to use notes fields to add classroom curriculum information as well. However, the 658 tag is used for standardized curriculum such as district and state standards. Both indicators are blank and the tag is repeatable. In $a, we enter the standard itself. In $b, we add secondary objectives. In $c, we create an abbreviation for the standard. In $d, we state the correlation of the item to the standard. In $2, we enter the source of the standard. Except for $a and $2, all other subfields are optional. There is no punctuation between the subfields. The subfield immediately preceding $2 ends in a full stop or a parenthesis. There is no closing punctuation after the $2.

Our first example shows the subject heading for a Delaware state standard in social studies.

- 658 __ $aCivics standard #1$b7compare and contrast various forms of government$cCS1PI1$dhighly correlated.$2local
    - $a tells us that this item is related to the Delaware Social Studies Civics Standard number 1.
    - $b tells us that the performance indicator met for this standard is the one in which students will be able to compare and contrast various forms of government in the seventh grade.
    - $c is the abbreviation of all of that: CS1 = Civics Standard 1, PI1 = performance indicator 1.
    - $d tells us that this item is highly correlated to the standard. Other terms seen here include: slightly correlated and moderately correlated.

- $2 tells us that this is a local standard. The Library of Congress has a list of standards for which they have provided abbreviations that is available on their Web site: http://www.loc.gov/marc/relators/relasour.html#rela658b. There are only four states that have been codified by LC, they are: Missouri (moss), Ohio (ohco), Virginia (slvps), and Texas (teks and txac). Any other state that wishes to have its standards recognized would have to apply to LC for an abbreviation (ndmso@loc.gov.).

Our second example shows the connection between the resource and the information literacy standards from the American Association of School Librarians (AASL) and the Association for Educational Communications and Technology (AECT).

- 658 __ $aSocial responsibility$bimportance of information to a democratic society$cAASLAECTIL7.$2local
  - $a tells us that this item relates to the standard on social responsibility.
  - $b tells us that it is standard #7 on understanding the relationship of information to a democratic society.
  - $c gives us the abbreviation: AASLAECT = the two associations responsible for the standards, IL = information literacy, 7 = the standard number.
  - Notice we did not include a $d. Remember, all subfields are optional except for $a and $2.
  - $2 tells us this is a local standard. Because this standard has not been coded by LC, we are forced to use the "local" designation, however unsatisfying that may be to us.

Our last example shows a notation for a standard for problem solving from the National Council of Teachers of Mathematics.

- 658 __ $aProblem solving 3-5$cNCTMPS3-5.$2local
  - $a tells us this is the problem solving standard for grades three through five.
  - $c gives us the abbreviation for the National Council of Teachers of Mathematics as NCTM, "PS" is for "problem solving" and "3-5" is the grade level of the standard.
  - $2 tells us only that this is a local standard. Because NCTM is not authorized by LC, we say that this is a local standard even though NCTM is at the national level.

Some vendors have selection tools that allow one to select books and media based on state or national standards. Unfortunately, the 658 tag is usually not included in the purchased cataloging of those materials. Now that you have knowledge of the usefulness of this tag, you might talk to your sales representatives about the advantages of including this tag in purchased cataloging. Until then, it is a good idea to try to include this tag whenever possible, especially if you have established a collaborative relationship with the classroom teachers and you know of resources that are used in connection to district or state standards.

690 Tag: Local Headings

There are a number of other tags in the 6XX field, but the ones described previously are the most commonly seen in the school library catalog. Catalogers can always look up specific tags from the LC Cataloging Directorate at http://lcweb.loc.gov/marc.

One 6XX tag that may appear occasionally in a surrogate record is the 690 tag. The cataloging library, i.e. the individual school, uses this tag to list subject headings that it has created without following any sort of schema. One should be very careful about creating subject headings (other than creating headings as directed in *Sears*). While it might be tempting, try not to do this. If you must, be sure there is a method established to keep track of these invented headings and be certain that the library system will index, or search on, the 690 tag. Not all library systems do this. It would be unwise to create a heading that the patrons can't use for retrieval purposes.

How Do I Know How Many Subject Headings to Add?

One may ask how many subject headings should be assigned to each work. We have alluded to this question elsewhere in the text, but it bears repeating. In the old days of cards that were handwritten or created on manual typewriters, the rule of thumb was no more than three headings per item. This rule makes sense if one imagines the poor librarian banging away on an old typewriter creating cards for the card catalog. No mechanical reproductions were available and it was an arduous and tedious task to type or handwrite each and every card.

Today, without the manual labor of dealing with leaky pens or sticky shift keys, the librarian is free to add as many headings as he or she desires.

One should be careful, however, of adding too many (or too few) headings. If, for example, in a biographical work about a scientist, the scientist is described as an avid surfer and no other mention of surfing is given, then it would be pointless to add "surfing" as a subject heading. It is pointless to do so because anyone looking for works on surfing would be led to this item that really has nothing to do with surfing at all. The fact that the scientist is a surfer may be interesting, but it is not what the item is about. This seems like a fairly obvious example, but it serves to illustrate the point that too many subject headings can adversely affect precision in the retrieval process. While in theory one can create an unlimited number of subject headings, one should always ask the question, "Is this heading really what the work is *about*?" The more headings assigned, the greater the probability the user will be erroneously led to a work.

On the other hand, too few headings can have an equally adverse effect. Users can be unaware of a potentially useful item because a heading was not assigned when it should have been. For example, a work about Andrew Carnegie may not be specifically about libraries but if there is significant information about his contribution to the growth of public libraries in the United States, then it would be a mistake not to assign a subject heading for libraries to the item.

The question of how many subject headings to assign should center on the "aboutness" of the information package. If the item is about 10 different things, then add ten different subject headings. If, on the other hand, the item is about one thing, then there is no need to pad the record with useless headings.

To know which subject headings to assign may take a thorough investigation of the information package or it may be a matter of reading the title. Young adult fiction is perhaps the most difficult type of information package for assigning subject headings. Often times the title is not indicative of the subject matter. In nonfiction works, a review of a table of contents, index, or manual is enough to get an idea of the subject matter. In children's fiction, it is easy to browse through the item to get an idea of the subject matter. However, young adult fiction may require looking at book jacket descriptions or even reading at least bits and pieces of the work. While it may really be a perk of the job to "have" to read the book, we often don't have time to read everything that needs cataloging. Relying on copy cataloging helps us to make subject headings decisions.

Conclusion

Intellectual access of information refers to retrieval based on the topic of the item rather than its physical description. This kind of access can be achieved through a keyword or subject heading search. Keyword searching will result in information retrieved based on the appearance of a word in the record. Subject headings are created using controlled vocabularies and result in information retrieved based on the context of the word. There are two lists of controlled vocabulary used in the schools: *Sears* and *LCSH* (including *LC/AC*). Regardless of whether the school library media specialist chooses to use Library of Congress or *Sears* headings, it is important to understand the nature of the differences of the headings and how to apply them. As copy cataloging and purchased cataloging take the place of original cataloging, and because LC headings and authority files are available online free of charge, *Sears* headings will probably fall into disuse. This is unfortunate as it is so well suited to the school library collection.

The most commonly used headings in the subject area are 600 (personal name), 650 (topical headings), and 651 (geographic heading). Some headings are ambiguous in nature and may also fall under the 610 corporate heading field. Be aware of a more frequent application of the 655 genre heading tag.

References

1. Cochrane, Pauline. "Modern subject access in the online age." A series of articles under this title published in *American Libraries* from February 1984 – July/August 1984 including responsive articles from others in the cataloging field.

2. Hatcher, April M. "The practice: Standardized subject headings and school curricula," *Knowledge Quest*, v. 33(4) March/April 2005: 38-39.

3. Library of Congress. *LC period subdivisions under names of places.* Washington, D.C., 1994.

4. *Guidelines on subject access to individual works of fiction, drama, etc.* 2nd ed. Chicago, IL: American Library Association, 2000.

Chapter 5

Intellectual Access – Classification

Introduction

This chapter focuses on the basic structure of the Dewey classification system and explores various nuances peculiar to the school library environment. This is not a chapter about creating Dewey numbers in any detail. Explaining the directions for applying DDC numbers to an item is difficult at best and nearly impossible without having DDC in hand. Therefore, we highly recommend that you have a copy of the *Abridged Dewey Decimal Classification and Relative Index*, 14th edition (*DDC14*) on hand to follow along with the descriptions in this chapter. For complete instructions on using Dewey classification system, please see *Abridged 13 Workbook: For Small Libraries Using Dewey Decimal Classification Abridged Edition 13* (1). Although it was written for use with the 13th edition of the abridged Dewey, it is still useful in understanding the basic DDC structure. Unlike subject headings that are assigned to show the topic of the information package, DDC is used to show the discipline or area of study to which the information package belongs.

Organization of Information

Before we discuss the structure of the Dewey classification system, it is helpful to understand the concept of organization of information. Recall that Cutter suggests we help patrons find information according to title, author, literature, and topic. All of these avenues to information retrieval reflect some kind of organization. Organization by topic is the focus of the chapter on subject headings. Organization by discipline is the focus of this chapter on classification. Things are organized all around us. For example, going to the store we see things organized by type of food and we get confused when the store rearranges things. Restaurants organize their menus according to what people eat for breakfast, lunch, or dinner. Museums organize their collections by time period. There is no one single way to organize information. Let's consider the list below and consider how you might organize it:

Apples	Fruit	Tomatoes	Cucumbers
Strawberries	Tubers	Potatoes	Radishes
Carrots	Oranges	Lettuce	Peanuts
Vegetables	Olive Oil	Vinegar	

There are a couple of ways we might arrange this list. Perhaps we would use fruit, vegetables, and tubers as our main headings and put the other items under the main headings. Of course that doesn't account for the olive oil and the vinegar. We could organize everything alphabetically, but that doesn't do much for bringing together like items. There are several other ways of bringing these terms together into groups; that's the point!

There is no *one* correct way of organizing information. Even within organizational schemes, there is room for controversy and decision making. Dewey wasn't the only one to propose a classification scheme; however, for many of us, his system works extremely well. One consideration that must be paramount in making classification decisions is the use of the collection. It may be that the Dewey number assigned to an item is correct but it doesn't fit the way your students approach your collection. You must be familiar enough with the Dewey system to know when a change in a number is necessary.

Dewey Decimal Classification Structure

Melvil Dewey published this system in 1876 after numerous years of research regarding other forms of classification systems suggested by various library luminaries, including Charles C. Jewett, William T. Harris, Charles Ami Cutter, Nathaniel B. Shurtleff, and Jacob Schwartz. Fifty years after its original publication, Dewey wrote this about the discovery of his system: "One Sunday during a long sermon by Pres. Sterans, the solution flasht (sic) over me so that I jumpt (sic) in my seat and came very near shouting 'Eureka!' Use *decimals* to number a classification of all human knowledge in print" (2). Thus was born the system known today as the Dewey Decimal Classification (DDC) system. The schedules were originally published anonymously in only 44 pages. Over the years, the system has grown into a system for classification that is used in libraries around the world.

As the name implies, DDC (both the full and abridged versions) is designed around the classification of all knowledge into 10 categories.

The 10 Main Classes of the Dewey Decimal Classification

000   Generalities
100   Philosophy, paranormal phenomena, psychology
200   Religion
300   Social sciences
400   Language
500   Natural sciences & mathematics
600   Technology (Applied sciences)
700   The arts   Fine & decorative arts
800   Literature (Belles-lettres) & rhetoric
900   Geography, history, and auxiliary disciplines

The 10 main classes are referred to as the First Summary. This table is again subdivided by 10 in the Second Summary, or Hundreds Divisions, and again by 10 in the Third summary, or Thousand Sections. The box below shows an example of the 300 section being divided into hundreds with one section showing the thousands divisions. Following the numbers from 300 to 390 to 392, we can see that the structure is hierarchical in nature, moving from the broadest classification to the narrowest.

Second Summary – Hundreds Division (example of the 300s classification) (3)

300   Social sciences
310   Collections of general statistics
320   Political science
330   Economics
340   Law
350   Public administration & military science
360   Social problems & services; associations
370   Education
380   Commerce, communications, transportation
390   Customs, etiquette, folklore

The description and instructions for using DDC are found in two forms: abridged and full. The full DDC is a multivolume set with directions for creating classification numbers in minute detail. Now in its 22nd edition (2003), the full edition is revised on a regular basis, approximately every six years. The CD-ROM version is updated annually and the Web-based version is updated quarterly. The abridged DDC is a single-volume work that is broader in nature and thus, like *Sears* to *LCSH*, fits better in the school library environment. The abridged version of DDC (referred to in this text as *DDC14*) is now in its 14th edition (2004); it, too, is revised approximately every six years with an online version, *Abridged WebDewey*, updated quarterly. In this latest edition the changes to note have been in the area of technology and computer science along with significant changes in the area of religion in order to correct the Christian bias of the original scheme.

DDC14 is arranged in seven sections: Introduction, Glossary, Manual, Tables, Summaries, Schedules, and Relative Index. Each section guides the cataloger to the creation of the correct classification number. The publisher, OCLC, recommends the abridged edition for libraries with collections of fewer than 20,000 titles. A tutorial for the *Abridged WebDewey* is available at: http://www.oclc.org/dewey/resources/tutorial/. It is worth taking a look at this tutorial because it depicts an excellent representation of the hierarchical structure and provides a superb introduction to this classification system. *Abridged WebDewey* has the advantage of allowing the user to connect to Cutter tables and to *Sears, LCSH,* and *LC/AC* subject headings lists. *Abridged WebDewey* is available at a cost of $65-$249 per year, depending on the number of sites needed and OCLC membership. The disadvantage of *Abridged WebDewey* is that it is somewhat vague about the process of building the numbers. It works well if one has an idea of a number or is very familiar with the structure of Dewey numbers, but not very well if one has no idea of the number or is new to using the Dewey system. A really good use of *WebDewey* is for checking the validity of numbers. It can be used to check numbers printed in the CIP data or other numbers found in copy cataloging. This can be especially helpful in translating a full Dewey number to an abridged number.

As mentioned previously, DDC is not the only classification system available for organizing information. In the United States, many public and academic libraries make use of the Library of Congress Classification (LCC) scheme. The LCC scheme is expansive (more than 40 volumes), expensive (more than $2,000), and not a very good fit for use in the school environment. It consists of multiple volumes of highly detailed divisions of information, much more than is needed for school collections. Fortunately for school libraries, the move from Dewey classification to LCC has not been as successful as the move from *Sears* to *LCSH* was. Most school libraries still maintain the use of DDC as its classification system of choice. Unfortunately, schools often work with older editions of either the abridged or full DDC and, as with the older editions of *Sears*, changes in numbering cause conflict in the catalog. The new editions have been updated to remove much of the Western bias of the original scheme and to accommodate changes in our lives based on technological innovations. Under no circumstances should a librarian rely on these older editions. With the print copy of the abridged edition priced at approximately $100, in addition to the fact that new editions are usable for approximately six to seven years, there should be no excuse for using the dated editions.

Many copy cataloging databases have Dewey numbers in their bibliographic records; however, these numbers are often for the full-format of DDC. In using these records, care should be taken to make sure of the format of DDC being used. We will see later in this chapter how to tell if a number is a full or abridged Dewey number and which edition was used to create the number. *Sears* makes reference to abridged DDC numbers in the list of subject headings but these, too, should be used as a guide rather than as a substitute for using the actual DDC. The current edition of *Sears* (18th) matches the numbers of the current abridged Dewey (14th).

Application

All Dewey numbers (except for biography) consist of at least three numerals. The first number specifies the general main class. The second number denotes the division, and the third number indicates the section. After the first three numbers, more numbers are added, if necessary, to specify such aspects of the item as form, historical coverage, language, or geography. These numbers are added to by following directions for using the four tables for: standard subdivisions (Table 1), geographic areas and persons (Table 2), individual literatures (Table 3), and individual languages (Table 4). With the exception of Table 1, no table is used without directions from the main number schedules.

Numbers are built hierarchically from broader to narrower fields of study. Note that we mentioned "field of study" and not "subject." Dewey is quite clear regarding that concept. We bring together like items that can exist anywhere in the library by subject headings. But we classify, that is, place the item on the shelf, according to the discipline or field of study. This is not a notion of "aboutness," as is the case with subject headings, but of *use* of the item. For example, a book *about* horses (with a subject heading "Horses") can be located in the discipline of zoology (study of the anatomy of the horse) or under the discipline of animal husbandry (breeding horses) depending on the purpose of the item according to the author. Finally, one must make a decision and stick to it remembering that two copies of an item *cannot* be located in two different places in the library. Let subject headings pull like items together in the catalog and let the physical structure of the library pull together the areas of study.

Let us look at these example items:

Visual Dictionary of the Universe	520.3
Sing a Song of Popcorn	808.81
Bard of Avon	822.3 or 92(0)

Our first example is straightforward, the book is a dictionary of things in the universe and fits nicely in the 520 classification for Astronomy and allied sciences with the addition of the .3 to designate that the item is a dictionary. Our next example is equally easy as a collection of poems under no particular subject. The number 808 is for collections of literatures and .81 designates a collection of poetry. Our last example shows two number choices, which is not at all uncommon in CIP data, but not seen in copy cataloging. As with many other aspects of cataloging, the cataloger is called upon to make decisions regarding the classification number to assign. The problem here is deciding how one will classify biographical works. This question will be addressed in more detail later in this chapter. For now, we see that this work is a biography of the English playwright William Shakespeare. The number 822.3 places the work with other works by and about Shakespeare. The alternate number, 92(0) places the work with other biographies. As the man said, "Aye, there's the rub." We shall explore this "rub" later on in this chapter.

Building a Number

Besides the summary tables previously illustrated in the boxes, *DDC14* is comprised of Schedules (further division of the summary numbers) and Tables. Schedules provide even more information about the field of study. Let us again look at the 300 summaries in the boxes. Let's take one of the numbers, 392, Customs of life cycle and domestic life, and see what it looks like in the *DDC14* schedule. From the information in the box on page 79, we can see that there are lots of options to bring out more specific aspects of domestic life than just the one number.

References that begin, "Standard subdivisions are added…" refer to the use of Table 1, which will be described next. Interestingly, divorce is not part of this number. Although divorce is certainly a part of domestic life, if we look closely at these headings we might come to the conclusion that divorce is not mentioned here because, at least in the United States, divorce is more of a legal action than a customary action. However, should you have an item about a culture for which there are customary activities related to a divorce, it would be difficult to place it under the 392 classification.

The Tables are used to add more specificity to the number in terms of geographic, form, and cultural focus. With few exceptions, Table numbers can only be added to the Schedule numbers when directed in the Schedules. As we mentioned, directions that begin with "Standard subdivisions…" are referring to the application of the division in Table 1. Table 1 is a nice table because it brings out the following aspects of an information package:

—**01 Philosophy and theory**: The information package approaches the field of study according to methodology or schools of thought. Example, philosophy of education: 370.1

—**02 Miscellany**: The information package approaches the field of study in a way not specific to any of the other Table 1 subdivisions. Example, interdisciplinary work on commercial trade: 381.02

—**03 Dictionaries, encyclopedias, concordances**: refers to the form of the information package and also includes thesauri, but not acronym dictionaries or biographical dictionaries. Example, dictionary of the solar system: 520.3

—**04 Special topics**: are used only when directed to be used in the Schedules; covers specific topics not covered elsewhere in Table (but specific so it doesn't go into "Miscellany" area). Example, special topics in applied physics: 621.04

—**05 Serial publications**: Information package is published serially, as in a magazine, newsletter, etc. Example, a magazine on motocross: 796.705

—**06 Organizations and management**: Information package approaches topic in terms of associations related to the topic. Example, astronomy associations and clubs: 520.6

—07 Education, research, related topics: Information package approaches topic in terms of study programs or education related topics. Example, summer dance programs: 792.807

—08 History and description with respect to kinds of persons: Information package approaches topic in terms of gender, cultural, or racial groups. Example, women doctors: 610.92082

—09 Historical, geographic, persons treatment: Information package is specific to a location or is biographical in nature. Example, swimming in China: 797.200951

In looking at these numbers, one might get confused thinking, "Well if the Table 1 number is 09, why does the classification number have two 0's? Similarly, if the Table 1 number is 03, why does the classification number have only 3? Or, if the Table 1 number is 08, why does the classification number read 082?" These are good questions. *DDC14* is full of directions requiring the cataloger to drop some zeroes and add others. There are also directions to give even more detail than is presented in the first line of directions. The other Tables in the classification scheme are used only if instructed to do so in the Schedules.

Following the Schedule numbers and directions allows one to build a number that is more specific than any number given in the Summaries. Building a number is like creating an addition problem. With a few exceptions, following the directions helps one progress from a general number to a specific number. Let us take the *Strega Nona* example. First, school librarians try very hard to create a separate section for non-book materials. That is fine if it is really necessary to keep non-book items out of the hands of the students, but we do not advocate letting accession numbers stand in place of classification numbers. It may be all right to simply number the tapes one through 10, but what happens if you get a grant that allows you to purchase 100 new tapes and DVDs? Now you have items numbered one through 100 and skimming the shelf to find the right tape is not easy or efficient. It is far better to organize even the non-book items in some logical fashion for easy retrieval because it is so difficult to predict future use or size of the special collection. We suggest treating non-book items the same way one would treat book items in all aspects of cataloging and that includes classification. So it doesn't matter if your copy of *Strega Nona* is a book, a videotape, or some electronic format, it still gets a classification number based on the content of the information package. See the box for a discussion on how to distinguish the book from the media in the classification number.

Strega Nona is a folktale from Italy. If we look at the Summaries, we can see that folktales belong in the classification number 398.2. We could, in fact, stop there. It is a perfectly legal number, but let's say we want to bring out the fact that this is a folktale from Italy. To do that, we must go into the Schedules. The instructions in the Schedule (pages 475-477 in the *DDC14*) tell us that we have a choice of classifying this folktale by country of origin (in this case Italy) or by the type of folktale: paranatural humans (.21), mythological persons (.22), quasi-historical tales (.23), plant or animal tales (.24), ghost stories (.25), physical phenomena (.26), or tales about everyday life (.27). From this list we can see that fables (stories using animals to prove a point) would be classified in 398.24 and a general collection of ghost stories would be classified in 398.25. But we don't really see how to bring out Italy. Before the Schedule goes into the smaller numbers, it tells us that we can use Table 1 to show the geographic nature of the story. This means that we can add –09 to 398.2 to get 398.209. But what happened to Italy? In Table 1 at –09, we are told we can go to Table 2 and get a more specific place number. The number for Italy is –45 so we add that to our number and get 398.20945! The process of adding a number as directed is fairly simple as long as the directions are crystal clear. Sometimes the directions are not so clear and even seasoned catalogers have to read the directions several times in order to understand them. Notice that there is only one decimal point in the number. The decimal point comes after the third digit and all other numbers are added behind it.

Hierarchical structure of Dewey Decimal Classification Numbers

We can see the hierarchical structure of our folktale example by parsing out each element:

398.20945
300   Social sciences
390   Customs, etiquette, folklore
398   Folklore
398.**2**   Folk literature
398.2**09**   Historical, geographic, persons treatment (Table 1)
398.209**45**   Italy (Table 2, as directed from Table 1)

In CIP data, you might see the number written thus: 398.2'09'45 or 398.2 09 45 or 3989.2/09/45. Those commas, spaces, and slashes tell you where you can stop the number if you think it is too long for your collection. We work backwards to shorten the number by first dropping the 45 then the 09. You cannot go beyond that to make a shorter number. So in classifying a work of folklore, the shortest number you can use is 398.2.

Identifying non-book information packages in classification numbers

We have advocated for classifying all information packages, regardless of format, by following the DDC rules. We recognize, however, that sometimes the librarian wants to show in the classification number that the item is not a book. To do this, we recommend adding prefixes or suffixes to the number. Thus, in cataloging the videotape of the folktale, we might add "vhs" to the end of the number "398.20945 vhs" to show that this is a videotape. Similarly, a DVD can be classed as 398.20945 dvd; a kit as 398.20945 kit. Or we may want to use the designation as a prefix to the number, thus: DVD 398.20945. In either case, there are ways of noting non-book materials that still allow the librarian to follow the classification rules.

So far we have been dealing with information packages that cover only one discipline. We know from experience that this is often not the case; Dewey accounts for that with four rules:

1. **Rule of Application**: If one discipline is acting on another, class the information package under the discipline being acted upon.

   Example: Effects of industrialization (338.9) on indigenous people of Australia (994), classify under 994.

2. **Subject Receiving Fuller Treatment**: If one subject is treated more fully than any of the other subjects, assign number to the fuller subject.

   Example: information mostly about dogs (636.7) but has a little bit of information on cats (636.8) and horses (636.1), classify under 636.7.

3. **First-of-Two Rule**: Two disciplines being treated with equal coverage use the number that comes first in the Schedule.

   Example: Information package on word games (793.734) and magic tricks (793.8), classify under 793.734.

4. **Rule of Three**: Three disparate disciplines under one broader heading, classify under the first higher number that encompasses them all.

   Example: Information package about ballet (792.8), vaudeville (792.7), and musical comedies (792.6) is classed under stage presentations (792).

On Famous People, Folklore, Fiction, and Other Classification Conundrums

As if things weren't bad enough, there are several areas in classification that never cease to create problems for school library media specialists. We discuss some of them here.

Biographies

DDC14 instructs catalogers to deal with biographical works in this way:

> 920 Biography, genealogy, insignia
> > Class here autobiographies, diaries, reminiscences, correspondence
> > Class biography of persons associated with a specific discipline or subject with the discipline or subject, plus notation 092 from Table 1, e.g., biography of chemists 540.92
> > > (Option: Class individual biography in 92 or B, collected biography in 92 or 920 undivided) (*DDC 14* p. 608)

Under these guidelines, the library would have two places for classifying biographical works; either within a given discipline area or with all other biographies.

Librarians constantly argue over the benefits of where to place a biographical work. There are those who argue that putting biographical works in a separate area means that students will read biographies only when the assignment is given to read a biographical work. They add that putting biographical works within a discipline area will allow students to reach for a biographical work perhaps unwittingly and will be opened to a new world of biography. The opposing argument is that keeping all biographical works together opens students to reading biographies of people other than the latest popular stars, because scientists and stars are placed together on the biography shelf. *DDC14* is explicit in the options available to the cataloger when dealing with biographical works; however, the choice is still the cataloger's.

One more point, Dewey offers the choice of using the number 92 or 920. Assigning the 92 number keeps the biographies clearly in a separate section from the rest of the nonfiction information packages. Using 920 has the biography section squarely in the middle of the history materials. This makes a certain amount of sense, as biographical works are sort of historical in nature, but most librarians who use this classification like to keep biographies in a separate section regardless of using the 92 or 920 classification number. Will Mr. Shakespeare reside next to works by and about the man (822.3) or between the scientist Carl Sagan and musician Paul Simon? The choice is yours!

Folklore

We saw how a work of folklore is classified under the 300 classification area. School children almost never miss the opportunity to ask the librarian why this is so, when they know very well that a number on a book means that it is nonfiction and clearly folklore is far from being nonfiction. The answer is in the number itself. Recalling that this system was created in the late 1800s, we have to think like a person from that time period. There were not a whole lot of children's books out there and recorded folklore, that which has been written down and published, was only around since about that time. (We take this from the publications of the Grimm brothers that started appearing in the early to mid-1800s.) Folklore at that time was not for entertaining children, but rather for teaching lessons. The stories were part of the customs and oral traditions of the cultures; therefore, Dewey placed them in with cultural customs, 398.

Recently we have had some problems with using 398 for folklore. It's all right for a "true" retelling of the story, but should James Marshall's version of *Little Red Riding Hood* sit side-by-side with the Grimm brother's version? Retellings with new settings and liberal interpretations are resulting in the splitting of these classic stories; some in 398 and others with the rest of the fiction collection. It is a dicey issue and there is no set answer at this point.

Fiction

Fiction has experienced a similar fate as folklore. Again, there was not very much fiction, certainly not very much children's fiction in the late 1800s. As such, works of light fiction were largely ignored. This is why most fiction is located in a separate section of the library under various headings, most often as F, FIC, or E (everybody books). "Serious" literature, such as classic works of Charles Dickens and Leo Tolstoy, are located in the 800 classification area. But is a work by John Steinbeck less "serious" than one by Charles Dickens? This has become a growing dilemma for librarians. Some catalogers decide that individual works will be classified in the fiction area while collections will be classified in the 800 section. The problem with this solution, of course, is the separation of collected works from individual works. A careful reading of the directions in Dewey is warranted, as this is again an area where the librarian makes the final call.

Story Collections

Another genre type that is often off by itself is the anthology, or story collection. Well meaning publishers take short stories and pull them together into one great volume sure to please any English language arts classroom teacher at nearly any grade level (although mostly middle and secondary grade levels). We will see how important table of contents notes in a record are to the retrieval of the titles in these collections later on in this text. For now, let us focus only on classification. Many libraries use the "SC" classification for these material types. As we've seen from previous discussions of odd-ball materials, there really is nothing wrong with this kind of classification. If it works, that is, if the students can find what they need by browsing this section, then there really is no reason to change things. Consider, however, how retrieval might be affected if these collections were classified differently.

DDC14 very clearly gives us instructions for collections of literature stating, "Class collections of works limited to a specific literary form ... in 808.81-808.88 ... class collections of texts from more than two literatures [e.g. poetry, fiction, and drama] in the same language with the literature of that language, e.g., collections of works from English, American, and Australian literatures in English (more than one literary form) 820.8..." (p. 747). What this means is that instead of putting these works into a separate section and hoping against hope that we remember each story within each volume, we can use the 800 classification area and our surrogate record to help us with information retrieval. We recognize, however, that using the 800 classification for collections of literatures may be confusing to our students who have been repeatedly told that Dewey numbers are for works of nonfiction. To cut down on the confusion, we use "SC," but is this fair to our students? By using "SC" we do not prepare them for academic collections that do make use of the literature classification. Nor do we prepare our students to use larger public libraries that also have substantial literature collections.

Realizing that we would be asking for the reclassification of a large number of materials if we were to advocate the use of the 800 classification for collected works, we simply lay the information before you and let you, the practitioner, make the decision. Regardless of your decision, please pay close attention to the notes and added entries discussions in chapter six to help you augment your surrogate records for collective works so that you will no longer have to remember which collection includes Louise Erdrich's story, "The Red Convertible."

Graphic Novels

The Library of Congress usually applies a 700 number to a graphic novel. To be exact, the number usually is 741.5, for "Cartoons, caricatures, comics" (p. 683). Here is our problem; do we have a collection of graphic novels in one section under comic books, or, rather, do we classify these items under the discipline for which they were originally conceived? Take our example of *Persepolis*. Here we have a graphic novel about the religious revolution in Iran in the 1970s. The Library of Congress has classified the book under 741.5. Recall that the basis for assigning a classification number is to bring out the discipline, or field of study, for which the item has been produced. We haven't talked to the author, but we can guess that she did not write this book with the idea of it being a comic book. More probably, the author wanted to write a book about this time period in Iranian history and simply chose the graphic novel format as the method of conveying the message. Thus, we would prefer to classify the book under 955 (Iran) to bring out the discipline and add a genre heading to bring out the format.

When graphic novels first started finding their way into school library collections, there appeared to be an inclination to keeping all graphic novels together in one place on the shelf. It was a new format of information and the general sense may have been that it was easier to point to the area for graphic novels than it was to have students look them up. Now that there are more and more of these titles in collections, we hope to see a change in that trend. As we advocate for the interfiling of media with books, we see no reason to separate graphic novels from other books. One could just as easily say that there should also be a section for historical fiction or science fiction. This simply is not an efficient way to organize a collection. Therefore, we advocate for changing all of those 741.5 classification numbers and to classify graphic novels according to their discipline.

The difficulty in assigning numbers to graphic novels is in deciding when an item is fiction and when it is nonfiction. *Maus I* and *Maus II* (graphic novels about World War II) are presented as nonfiction even though the characters (talking mice and cats) are most decidedly fiction. Interestingly, the Library of Congress has classified these titles as both fiction and nonfiction. According to the Library of Congress Classification, the item is nonfiction, having been given a "D" or "history" classification. On the other hand, the Dewey Decimal Classification number is 741.5 for comic books. Knowledge of the use of the item and classification systems will help the librarian to decide if he or she is going to apply the 741.5, 940, or fiction classifications to these books. On the other hand, a fantasy book such as *Batman, the Dark Knight Returns*, is easily classified in the fiction area. We again emphasize the philosophy of classifying according to discipline and letting genre headings pull together like formats.

Equipment

School library media specialists often find themselves in charge of equipment. Cataloging this equipment can be very important for keeping track of expensive television monitors, DVD players, computers, and the like. Like our unruly collection of media, we know now that these items need some kind of classification number. It is probably not the case that we will want to assign a DDC number to the item, after all, it is difficult to think into which discipline we should place a DVD player. However, we do need some kind of control over the items. We suggest the following formula for classifying equipment. Please note that this formula is based on our own experiences and has nothing whatsoever to do with DDC.

1. Begin with a prefix, such as "EQUIP."

2. Follow the prefix with an item type, such as "LCD," "DVD," or "DELLLT."

3. Follow the item type with a time keeper, either the year of purchase or the year of production (helpful in dividing the Dell computers received in 2004 and those received in 2005).

4. Follow the full number with a copy number.

Using this formula, a classification number for a Dell laptop computer might look like this: EQUIP DELLLT 2005 c.10, while a Dell desktop computer number might look like this: EQUIP DELL 2003 c. 50. We will find out more about the physical description of these items in chapter six.

It's OK to Change a Number

Let us examine the example item *Accidents May Happen*. The Library of Congress has assigned the number 124. A brief examination of cataloging from Sunlink finds that this item has also been classified under the number 608 and 609. Who is right? Our impulse is to follow the assignment given to us by the Library of Congress and so we look up the number 124. This is the assignment for works on teleology. Roughly speaking, teleology is the philosophical study of the purpose of natural processes. This book is about the history of things that have been developed or invented by accident. It would be extremely easy to classify if all the discoveries discussed in the book were scientific in nature but, alas, this is not the case. Included among the description of the invention of matches and dynamite, one also finds out how the United States national anthem was written and the meaning behind several nursery rhymes. Thus, one makes the assignment to a number that covers invention by natural process. So, while technically correct, one must decide if this item should be included in the philosophy section of the library (124) or the science section (608 and 609). This is where knowledge of library usage comes into play. Despite the philosophical classification, the subject headings point to a book about scientific discoveries. Even the subtitle on the cover, *Fifty Inventions Discovered By Mistake*, conveys a leaning to science over philosophy. The Library of Congress may prefer to class this book under philosophy, but our users will more likely browse the science section for books about inventions. Now let us examine the other two numbers found in association with this item on Sunlink: 608 and 609. The number 608 is used for items on inventions and patents. The number 609 is used for items on the historical treatment of inventions and patents. This book is about inventions, but with a focus on the history of the inventions. Therefore, 609 seems to be the preferable number between the two. The purpose of this example is to demonstrate two things: First, that numbers assigned by LC may not necessarily fit the school library usage and may, with justification, be ignored for better fitting classifications. Second, that classification numbers must be examined carefully before assignment and that it is helpful to look at neighboring numbers to make certain of a good classification fit.

Application of DDC14 in the MARC Format

Now that we have covered the structure of Dewey numbers, it is time to see what that number looks like in the MARC record. Information for classification is found in fields 050 to 086. The tag we are interested in is 082, Dewey Decimal classification number. The first indicator in this tag is used to note which version of DDC was used—0 for the full or 1 for the abridged. The second indicator is used to denote which library assigned the number; a blank (_) indicates that no information was provided, 0 means LC assigned the number, and 4 means some other library besides LC assigned the number. The number itself is entered in $a with the use of slashes if necessary (although using the slashes is optional). The $2 is used to record which edition of the DDC was used in creating the number. We already know if it is the full or abridged Dewey, but we need to know which full or abridged Dewey was used. This is very important, especially in cataloging older materials. If you have a record that used the abridged Dewey but it was the 12th edition, you know that you will need to check the number to see if it has changed at all. Here are some examples:

- **082 _1 $a398.20945 $213**
  - From the first indicator we cannot tell who created this number except that we know it was not the Library of Congress. From the second indicator we know the abridged Dewey was used. From the $2 we know it was the 13th abridged Dewey that was used to create the number.

- **082 00 $a614.5/41/097481109033 $221**
  - This horrendously long number was created by the Library of Congress using the 21st edition of the full Dewey scheme. There are two places where we can break down this number should we decide that it is too long for our purposes:
  - 614.541 OR
  - 614.5
  - A comparison of that number to the Abridged Dewey reveals the matching abridged number: 614.5
    - In the MARC format it would look like this: 082 41 $a614.5 $214
  - Having said that, because this book is dealing with a historical time period, we might want to go the route of Table 1 and add a geographic location: 614.509748. (Can you see that part of the number in the LC assigned number?) If that number is too long, we can break it after 09, thus: 614.509.

Some automated systems do not take the classification number from the 082 tag. Sometimes it is in the 092, 852, or 900 tags. You will need to find out where you should put that number from the program vendor.

Conclusion

The Dewey numbers are based on fields of disciplines. When beginning to assign a classification number, one should first ask, "In what field of study will this item be used and for whom was this work created?" In classification, one decides on the single most important discipline under which the item should be placed. While an item may have many subject headings, it can reside in only one place on the library shelves. Never, ever classify two copies of the same item in two different places. That's what subject headings are for! The introduction to DDC provides detailed directions to the cataloger regarding materials that cover more than one discipline. The Relative Index, Summaries, Schedules, and Manual help the cataloger decide on the area number to assign to an item. That is why it is so crucial to have some form of DDC in your hands when you are cataloging an information package. In this text, we can only briefly describe how to build a number. In theory, a small library collection could probably get along quite well without applying the Tables or even going beyond the third Summary. We do not advocate this, but it is a viable option.

Electronic discussion lists often have questions about classification. School library media specialists are nervous about changing classification numbers or adding prefixes to the numbers to separate non-book from book materials. These questions are often accompanied with concerns about "cataloging police" coming after them. The point to classification is putting like discipline materials together. If it works for a library collection to separate out specific materials by adding a prefix to a number (such as vhs for videotapes) then by all means, the librarian should feel free to do so. Likewise, if there are some items classed in history and some classed in geography, as is often the case with books about states and countries, then the librarian should feel free to bring these books together. A caveat in changing classification numbers: If we are trying to make independent library users of our students, before messing with assigned numbers, we should ask, "What is more important, information literacy skills or quick access?" We do no favors to our students by putting historical works together with geographical works as far as information literacy is concerned. On the other hand, sometimes having the books together is more important to us than obeying the strict rules of classification. There are no "cataloging police" lurking about waiting for an unsuspecting school library media specialist to change a classification number. However, with more and more school library collections becoming accessible through the Internet, following the rules becomes more important, if only for the sake of standardization.

References

1. Davis, Sydney W. & Gregory R. New. *Abridged 13 workbook: For small libraries using Dewey Decimal Classification Abridged Edition 13.* Forest Press: Albany, New York, 1997.

2. Weigand, Wayne A. *Irrepressible reformer: A biography of Melvil Dewey.* American Library Association: Chicago, 1996. 21-16.

3. *Abridged Dewey Decimal Classification and Relative Index.* Dublin, OH: OCLC, 2004.

Chapter *6*

Physical Access

Introduction

In previous chapters, we discussed the theory behind physical description and the practice of copy cataloging. In this chapter we will present the actual practical use of the MARC format as applied to physical description. Recall that the surrogate record is divided into eight areas and that the punctuation for each area is defined by the rules of the International Standard Bibliographic Description (ISBD). Physical description describes the physical characteristics of the item in hand. The tags of the MARC format correspond to particular aspects of the item. The *Anglo-American Cataloging Rules* together with the ISBD rules determine how the information should appear in the record. The MARC 21 rules determine where the information should appear in the electronic record. Although this chapter focuses on physical description, the exercises here will continue to include practice on subject headings and classification. We do this because intellectual access is tricky and it behooves the student librarian to get as much practice in this area as possible. Within the following discussions, we have tried to present realistic problems as graphically accurate as possible without creating a very thick text. In our examples we will try to show how the information would look in real life (noted with the phrase "On the item as" and then how it will look in the MARC format (noted with the phrase "Typed into the record as"). Additionally we have provided a help sheet template with which to refer as we work our way through the MARC format. We hope this is clear and helpful. Let us now explore the art of cataloging incorporating the MARC format.

Variable Control Fields – Tags 001-007

The MARC record has the capability to have an item described in aspects beyond those of *AACR*. Using codes understood by the computer, catalogers are able to note the language of an item, the cataloging agency, and other aspects of the item. Most of the time, school library media specialists accept any coded information in the tags about to be described simply because they do not understand the codes for the information being supplied. In some school library media automated programs, many of these tags are not even visible in the MARC record. This section will provide a very brief description of just a few of the tags involved in this part of the MARC record. After working through this section, one should at least feel comfortable with accepting the information in these tags in copy cataloging, if not feeling comfortable in assigning them. In this case and for all of the MARC tags, the reader is referred to the MARC Standards Web site for more detailed descriptions: http://www.loc.gov/marc/.

Tags 001, 003, and 005 are not usually modifiable in school library media automation programs. However, in looking at copy cataloging, it is possible that one will see these tags. Do not panic if you see them. Tags 001 and 003 represent control numbers and codes that do not apply to the school setting. Tag 005 represents the time and date a record has been modified. This is applied automatically in school library media automation programs, and is of no consequence to us at this point. These tags are mentioned here simply because you may see them and we don't want you to panic when you do see them! Here are some examples of what the 001, 003, and 005 tags may look like in a MARC record:

- 001 4ADB6E406AAD11D781DD00E0B816ADF5

- 003 DLC

- 005 20030409170435.0

*Help Sheet - Template for Cataloging Book Materials**

020	__	$a	(enter ISBN, no hyphens)
		^:$c	(optional to add price of item)
040	__	$a	(institution that originally cataloged item)
		$c	(institution that input the item in MARC format)
		$d	(institution that modified the record; your initials here)
082	14	$a	(Dewey # from abridged schedule)
		$2	(edition # of Dewey used)
100	1_	$a	(name of author of item)
		$q	(fuller form of name, if available and necessary)
		,$d	(birth/death dates)
245	XX	$a	(title, indicators show 100 tag and filing characters)
		^:$b	(subtitle if needed)
		^/$c	(statement of responsibility)
246	3_	$i	(type of title, if needed)
		$a	(added title to trace for numbers, abbreviations, and so forth)
250	__	$a	(edition statement using ordinal number, e.g. 1st , 2nd)
260	__	$a	(place of publication, additional places use ;$a)
		^:$b	(name of publisher, additional names use :$b)
		,$c	(date of publication)
300	__	$a	(number of units, i.e. pages)
		^:$b	(illustrative matter)
		^;$c	(dimensions)
		^+$e	(accompanying materials)
440	_0	$a	(series title)
		.$n	(number of part/section)
		.$p	(name of part/section)
		;$v	(volume number—this is the subfield to use in most cases)
5XX	__	$a	(Notes to explain cataloging decisions and emphasize other aspects of the item. Common tags are 500-general, 520-summary, 521-audience level.)
600	17	$a	(personal name as subject heading)
650	_7	$a	(topical subject headings)
		$y	(order of subfields varies according to subject heading)
		$x	
		$z	
		$2	sears
651	_7	$a	(geographical subject headings; add other subfields as 650)
700	1_	$a	(added name entries, e.g. illustrator, editor)
		,$e	(subfields are same as those for 100 tag)

* Note the following punctuation is used: ^ is to mark a space before the subfield punctuation; _ is to mark a blank indicator place; X is to mark placeholder in tag number.

Tags 006 and 007 are far more interesting and are worth some discussion here. In an irony of fate, tag 007 pertains to the *major* characteristics of the item while the 006 tag pertains to *additional* characteristics. Thus we have our first example of how number order of fields and alphabetical order of subfields really has nothing to do with importance or the content of the field. The information in both of these tags is specific to the type of item being described, so a letter "j" in cataloging a map means something completely different than the same letter in cataloging an electronic resource or a non-projected graphic.

The purpose of the 006 tag is to use computer codes for other parts of an item. For example, if you have a book and a tape cassette you can catalog for the book (described in code in 007 and also throughout the rest of the record) and use the 006 tag to code for the tape. The advantage of this is that some day in the future, you will be able to retrieve library items based on the codes in this tag. Like the 006 tag, the 007 tag also is a description of the item, this time the item itself. It's kind of a coded summary of most of the rest of the MARC tag. It's a very handy tag, but it too is seldom seen in a school library media automation program and is almost never altered by the school library media specialist. There is no real disadvantage in the lack of these tags in school libraries, as they are not yet used for retrieval purposes. One cannot help but wonder what will happen when the time comes that the systems become sophisticated enough to retrieve by these codes. We'll have to wait and see. For now it is enough to know that copy cataloging, especially from large institutions like the Library of Congress, will show those tags. Now that you have an idea of what they are about, you might be less inclined to delete them in adding the record to your own catalog. Here are examples of these two tags:

- 006 aa j 000 1
  - The information presented here tells us that this item includes a book (a); it has illustrations (a); it is for kids (j); it is not a conference program (0); it is not a festschrift (0); and has no index (0).

- 007 sdubsmennmplu
  - The information presented here tells us that the item is a sound recording (s), it is a record (d), it has no value (u); it runs at 33 1/3 rpm (b), stereophonic sound (s), with microgroove width (m); it measures 12 inches (e); it is not a tape so it has no tape speed (n); it is not a tape so it has no tape configuration (n); it is defined by OCLC (mpl), the last space is blank (u).

We're lucky that only the computer has to worry about deciphering this information and that we can simply accept it from copy cataloging and ignore it in original cataloging. (Although, technically speaking, we should enter this information, but, practically speaking, we probably won't.) If the mood should strike you, most school library automated programs have help screens to walk you through the process should you decide to enter this information yourself.

Fixed-Length Data Elements – Tag 008

This tag too may one day be used for retrieval purposes. It is a non-repeatable tag (created automatically by the computer) that records the date the record was created, the type of publication, date of publication, place of publication, language of publication, and other physical characteristics of the item being cataloged. The difference between the 007 and 008 is that the 008 tag includes less information about the physical characteristics and more information about content of the information package. There are 40 character positions in this tag, the first 18 and last five characters are the same regardless of the material type being cataloged. Character positions 18-34 vary depending on material type. If you have an item that is showing up improperly in your catalog (a book that is really a video tape), you have to correct the Leader (see chapter three) to fix that problem, not the 008 tag. Some automated programs use this tag from which to get publication dates in

---

008 Tag – Character positions and meanings common to all material types

- 00-005: date record was created, entered automatically by the system using yymmdd.

- 06: type of date; most often coded s for single date. Other common codes are m for multiple dates, c for continuing dates (as for serials), and n for unknown dates.

- 07-10: date 1; the year of publication.

- 11-14: date 2; if more than one year (e.g. publication plus copyright, multiple years), the second date is entered here.

- 15-17: place of publication; a two or three letter abbreviation for the U.S. state or country of publication. For a list of abbreviations, see the MARC Code List for Countries Web site: http://www.loc.gov/marc/countries/cou_home.html.

- 35-37: language; three letter code for language of the item, common languages are English (eng), Spanish (spa), German (ger), and French (fre); for other languages, see the MARC Code List for Languages Web site: http://www.loc.gov/marc/languages/langhome.html.

- 38: modified record; if you have accepted a record for copy cataloging accept whatever code is in this space. Likewise, accept any code that your system inserts here as a default; a blank means the record has not been modified, meaning it has been cataloged according to the standard rules and no information has been included that does not belong in the record.

- 39: cataloging source; if cataloging was originally created by the Library of Congress, this space will be blank. If another authoritative institution has created the original record, the space will be filled with the letter c; if you are creating your own original record, you might want to put in the letter d here, meaning some other institution created the record; it is a good idea to check this space to get an idea of how authoritative a record may be when accepting copy cataloging.

- Example of what a typical 008 tag would look like minus the information for material specific data:

  008   041007s2004   nyu   eng d

  - From this information we see that the record was created on Oct. 7, 2004; it has a single publication date, which is 2004; it was published in New York; it is in English; the record has not been modified; and the record was created by an institution other than LC or another authoritative institution. We still don't know what kind of publication this is because we are missing the characters between space 18 and 34, but there is much we do know.

order to print out age of collection statistics so it's nice if this tag is correct at least in the first 18 characters. In the future, some programs may also have the ability to search for a work according to language and that makes the end part of this tag useful. In the box on page 95 is a summary of the codes for this tag.

This is the minimal amount of information that should be included in this tag. Again, we refer the reader to the LC MARC Web site (http://www.loc.gov/marc) for coding for specific material type, although at this point most school library automation programs do not make it imperative that this information is included.

Number and Coded Fields – Tags 01X-04X

The next set of tags in the MARC record is used for recording standard numbers associated with the information package, as well as codes about the cataloging agency and more content codes. There are 30 tags associated with this part of the surrogate record. We will only concern ourselves with five of those tags: 020, 010, 040, 041, and 043.

We will tackle the 020 tag first because it actually belongs to one of our areas: area 8, standard numbers. This area is used to record standard numbers, such as the ISBN, ISSN, and other numbers associated with the item being cataloged. In the manual cataloging environment, standard numbers, which were developed after the standardization of cataloging rules, were entered at the bottom of that 3-by-5 card, hence its place as area 8. However, in the electronic environment, the numbers come first. The ISBN is recorded in the 020 tag. There is another tag associated with this area, the 022 tag for recording the International Standard Serial Number. The 022 tag is structured similarly to the 020; however, in this tag, the number retains the hyphens. Because we are not covering serials cataloging, we will not explore the 022 tag in any detail. The 024 tag is used to record government document numbers. Again, we are not covering that material type; it is only brought up here because it is part of area 8 for description.

Tag 020 – International Standard Book Number. This tag is used to record the ISBN only. This tag is repeatable, both indicators are blank, and there is no closing punctuation at the end of the tag. This information is entered in $a and the number is entered without the internal hyphens. The $c is used to record "terms of availability," that is, the price of the item. It is a good idea to have the price of the item listed some place in the surrogate record. Deciding where to record the price of the item will depend on how the 020 tag is displayed in the public record. In some systems, only $a is displayed, in others the 020 is not part of the display at all, and in still others, the entire 020 tag information is displayed. The problem arises in determining how public the item cost should be. Some libraries have a policy of charging a flat rate for a lost item. If the flat rate is, for example $10, and the user can see on the public record that the actual cost of the item was only $5, then there may be a problem in getting the patron to pay the $10. Vendors understand library reluctance to publicly list item prices and so often have other places in the record for recording this and other sensitive item information. Find out how the 020 tag is displayed in your system and then decide if the price will be listed in the 020 $c or elsewhere in the record.

Tag 010: Library of Congress Control Number (LCCN): Most of us have heard of the LCCN, and many use this number to search for an item. In the MARC record this number (always assigned by LC, never by a school library media specialist) is recorded in the 010 tag. This is a non-repeatable tag, both indicators are blank, and there is no closing punctuation at the end of the tag. The 010 tag consists of 12 spaces, although they may not all be used in a given instance. One usually just accepts the information in a copy cataloging situation, but in creating original records, one may very well need to enter the LCCN into the 010 tag. Usually this information is found on the verso of the title page in a book and is so noted by the abbreviation "LCCN," by the words "Library of Congress Control Number," or by the words "Library of Congress Catalog Card Number." In some items there is just a number such as "90-27237," with no designation as to what that number may be. Now you know what that number is and where it belongs in the MARC record.

Most systems start the entry of the number in the correct placeholder automatically. The LCCN structure is based on the year of publication plus a unique item number. The first LCCN was created around 1898 and the basic structure has not changed in all that time. The number begins with two digits defining the year of publication followed by a hyphen and five to six unique numbers, e.g. 98-23143. Note that the pre-2000 publication LCCNs have the two last digits of the year of publication and then a hyphen before the rest of the number. However, as of the year 2001, LCCNs were defined using the full four characters to note the year of publication, e.g. 2003111688. With the addition of the full four-digit number for the year, the hyphen has disappeared. When entering older numbers with hyphens into the 010 tag, that hyphen is ignored.

Examples:

- LCCN printed in the item: 76-4811; notice this number contains only six numbers, LC uses blanks (shown below as the letter b) and zeros (0) to create a number in the 010 that is 12 characters long. The zeros (0) are added between the year and the rest of the number. *Usually the system you are using will take care of this automatically.*
  - 010 __ $abbb76004811b

- LCCN printed in the item: 90-46564; again this number contains fewer than 12 characters:
  - 010 __ $abbb90046564

- LCCN printed in the item: 2001-45944; notice this is a publication from the year 2001 and includes a hyphen:
  - 010 __ $abb2001045944

- LCCN printed in the item: 2003111688; notice this is a publication from the year 2003 and does not include a hyphen:
  - 010 __ $abb2003011688

---

010 Tag: Library of Congress *Control* Number

- Record here the number as given on the item without hyphens.
  - The 010 tag is not repeatable, both indicators are blank, and there is no closing punctuation at the end of this tag.

Examples:

- On the item as: 99-16419
  - Typed into record as: 010 __ $a9916419

- On the item as: 2002075427
  - Typed into record as: 010 __ $a2002075427

Note in both examples, we have accepted the information on the item and will allow our system to put it into the correct format for us.

Tag 040: Cataloging Source: The 040 tag uses a three-letter code to identify the cataloging agency, which is the library or company that has created the original catalog record for the item in hand. The most recognizable code one sees is DLC, meaning the Library of Congress created the original catalog record for the item in hand. This tag is not repeatable, both indicators are blank, and there is no closing punctuation. Any library can apply to the Library of Congress to get a three-letter code; however, most school libraries will not want to do this as they seldom create original records that will be included in national databases. This tag can be useful in a school library if the school library media specialist has other people cataloging the collection. The tag information for the original cataloging agency is entered in the $a. There is also $d for the "modifying agency," which is the library that makes changes to the record. One may find it useful to add a $d to copy cataloging records to help identify the person within the library who made the changes to the record. By using a person's initials, the school library media specialist can keep track of who is adding to the library database and can follow up on record corrections thus:

Let us take this example:

040 __ $aDLC $dagk

Looking at this 040 tag, we can see in $a that the Library of Congress created the original record for this item. Looking at the $d, we can also see that the record was updated by the library volunteer with the initials "agk." The school library media specialist knows that "agk" is the volunteer, Mrs. Kaplan, who comes in on Monday afternoons. So the next Monday, the school library media specialist can ask Mrs. Kaplan to go back and take a look at that record she added because she forgot to add the 500 usage note.

Tag 041: Language Code: The 041 tag is used to note items that are translations, bilingual, or non-English language materials. For school libraries, this is the tag of the future. Someday, school library automated systems will be able to search the 041 tag and one will be able to retrieve materials by some aspect of language. Imagine being able to group together all bilingual Spanish-English items simply be searching on one tag!

The 041 tag is not repeatable and has no closing punctuation. The first indicator is coded 0 or 1. A 0 code means the item is not and does not include a translation. Use the code 0 for items that are in a language other than English but are not translations of an English work, for example, *Les Miserables* in French. Use the code 1 for items that include or are translations of works in other languages, for example, *Les Miserables* in English. The second indicator is blank. As ethnocentric as it may be, works in English do not get entries in the 041 tag. Use this tag only if some other language is involved. The language code is a three-letter code. Search the LC Code List for Languages Web site: http://www.loc.gov/marc/languages/. The codes most commonly seen in school libraries would probably include the following:

eng = English
fre = French
gre = German
sgn = Sign Language (American, Australasian, or British)
spa = Spanish

There are nine subfields associated with this tag; however, we will focus on just four; subfields a, b, d, and h. Let us examine the 041 tag first using a 1 in the first indicator place. Recall that first indicator value of 1 refers to an item that is or includes a translation. In this case we code for the language of the translation, as well as the language of the original work. *Do not apply this indicator value for bilingual texts.*

Examples:

- 041 1_ $aeng$hger
  - This work is in English, translated from the German. Notice there are no spaces between the subfields. The $a is used to enter the language of the item in hand, and $h is used to enter the language of the original publication.

- 041 1_ $aeng$hmul
  - This work is in English, translated from works of many (more than six) other languages.

Now let us look at items with the 0 in the first indicator position. Bilingual texts are included here. Although it could be said that there is some translation going on when a text is in two languages, the point usually is to present both (or more) languages; therefore, it is considered a multilingual text rather than a translation. When dealing with items with more than one language, it is important to tease out the exceptions to the rules. Audiovisual materials containing multiple soundtracks of different languages are not considered translations, and all languages are noted in $a. Audiovisual materials with overprinted titles, such as subtitles in a language different from the soundtrack, have the language of the subtitles recorded in $b. Finally, the language of audio materials, such as a tape cassette, is recorded in $d rather than in $a. If that recording includes textual materials in a language different from the recorded language, that information is recorded in $a.

Examples:

- 041 0_ $aengspa
  - This CD-ROM has two sound tracks, one in English and one in Spanish. Notice the language codes are written together with no spaces. Remember this is computer stuff and not meant for human eyes.

- 041 0_ $aenggerspa
  - This trilingual item has equal amounts of text in English, German, and Spanish.

- 041 0_ $aeng$bsgn
  - This videotape is in English with an open window of an interpreter signing in American Sign Language.

- 041 0_ $aengfre$dfre
  - This sound cassette is a collection of French folksongs in their original language but includes a booklet in both English and French.

041 Tag – Language Code

- Record here information about the language of the information package unless it is in English and is not a translation.
- This tag is repeatable, there is no closing punctuation at the end of the tag.
- The first indicator is coded 0 if not a translation, and 1 if it is or includes a translation; bi- or multilingual texts are coded 0.
- The second indicator is blank.
- Use $a for the language of the text or recording.
- Use $b for the language of subtitles.
- Use $d for the language of audio materials.
- Use $h for the code for the original language.

Exercises
6.1. Bilingual dictionary in English and Spanish
6.2. Work in English, translated from the French
6.3. Spanish language film with English subtitles

Tag 043: Geographic Area Code

Last on our list of our coded fields is the 043 tag. This tag is used to record the geographic area related to the item, if applicable. This is not to be confused with place of publication; rather, this tag is used to describe the geographic context of the item. For example, a book about French history would warrant a 043 tag, as would a collection of French folksongs. The 043 tag is not repeatable, both indicators are undefined, and there is no closing punctuation. The $a is used to record the geographic information. While the tag itself is not repeatable, the $a is. Therefore, an item that includes reference to the United States and Germany would have one 043 tag with two "a" subfields. The geographic codes are listed on the Library of

043 Tag – Geographic Area Code

- Record here the place of action of a story, or origination of the information.
- 043 tag is not repeatable, both indicators are blank.
- There is no closing punctuation at the end of the tag.
- Information is recorded in $a, which may be repeated.
- The codes can be found on the MARC Web page: http://www.loc.gov/marc/geoareas/

Examples:

- 043 __ $an-ca—-$ae-fr—-
    This item is about Canadian and French relations, thus it is coded for both countries. Notice there are no spaces between the two subfields.
- 043 __ $aa-ja—-
    This item is about Japan.
- 043 __ $afw———-
    This item is about West Africa, but not a specific country in that region.

Congress Web site at: http://lcweb.loc.gov/marc/geoareas/. The code is comprised of seven character spaces. The first character defines the continental location followed by a hyphen and then the country. For example, an item about the United States would be coded: n-us—, meaning North America, United States.

Classification and Call Number Fields – Tags 05X-08X

In this section of the MARC record, we see numbers pertaining to the classification of the information package. The 050 tag includes Library of Congress classification information, looking something like this: 050 _0 $aD804.3. Most school libraries use the Dewey system for classification so this is not a tag that usually holds much importance to us, nor will we discuss in any detail the construction of the tag. On the other hand, on occasion, a copy record includes an LC classification number, but not a Dewey number that we question. For example, the books *Maus I* and *Maus II* have been assigned the 741 Dewey number for graphic novels. We are not so sure we want to put the books in with

---

Summary of Number & Coded Fields in the MARC Record Discussed Thus Far

- **010: Library of Congress Control Number:** 12 character number that is unique to each item. Tag is not repeatable, both indicators are blank, data are entered without hyphens, and no closing punctuation.

- **020: International Standard Book Number:** a unique number applied to publishing houses. Tag is repeatable, both indicators are blank, data are entered without hyphens, and no closing punctuation. (Sister tags, 022 and 024.)

- **040: Cataloging Source:** three-letter code defining the cataloging agency. Tag is not repeatable, both indicators are blank, data are entered in $a or $d, and no closing punctuation.

- **041: Language Code:** three-letter codes to record the language of the item including multiple languages and translations. Tag is not repeatable, first indicator is 0 (not a translation) or 1 (is a translation), second indicator is blank, data are entered in subfields a, b, d, or h, and no closing punctuation.

- **043: Geographic Code:** 12-character alphabetic code used to define the geographic location of the topic of the item. Tag is not repeatable, both indicators are undefined, data is entered in $a, and no closing punctuation.

- **050: Library of Congress Classification Number:** classification number using the Library of Congress system. This tag will not be assigned by the school librarian unless the library uses that system, which is highly unlikely.

- **082: Dewey Decimal Classification Number:** classification number taken from DDC or DDC Abridged. Tag is repeatable, but multiple 082 tags in a school library media automation system will probably result in an invalid record. First indicator is 0 (full edition) or 1 (abridged edition); second indicator is blank, 0 (LC assigned), or 4 (assigned by another institution); $a includes the number; $2 includes the edition used to assign the number. (Sister tag may be the 092 that some systems use for locally assigned numbers.)

comic books, but we are not sure where to classify the books. A look at the 050 tag reveals that LC has assigned the books classifications under DS. DS is the LC classification for history. This tells us that, even though it looks like these are works of fiction, LC has classified them as fact, as historical fact, and that helps us select the 940 Dewey number. LC classification is complicated and extensive; we refer you to an online outline available at http://www.loc.gov/catdir/cpso/lcco/lcco.html for a review of each classification.

As we have already seen in chapter five, the Dewey classification number is located in the 082 tag. We won't go into detail here as this topic has already been covered. However, as we are working our way down the MARC record, it is important for us to include tags already discussed within the context of the entire MARC record.

Area 1: Title and Statement of Responsibility – Tags 245 & 246

The next part of the MARC record is probably better approached from perspective of the Areas of Description. Area 1 corresponds to the information recorded in tags 245, 246, 1XX, and 7XX. This information includes title information (24X tags) and name information for the person(s) or corporate bodies involved with the intellectual content of the work, that is authors, illustrators, editors, etc. (1XX and 7XX tags). Although we're going to jump back and forth a little bit in the MARC record, because so many tags depend on what is entered into the 245 tag, we feel it's best to take up that tag first and forego the numerical order of the tags for a little while, so bear with us as we go directly to the 245 tag.

245 Tag: It is useful when just learning how to catalog to begin with the 245 tag. This is the tag for the title of the work and the statement of responsibility. There are a few tags that work off of this tag, which is why it is helpful to begin with and work out from it. First it is important to note that there may be only one 245 tag in the surrogate record; the 245 tag is not repeatable. The 245 tag begins with the first part of the title and is followed by a statement on the type of item it is if the item is not a book (e.g., a video, cassette, DVD, etc.), more title information (subtitle), and names of people or corporate bodies responsible for the content of the item (author, illustrator, etc.). It is not necessary to have all of these elements in each 245 tag. Some items have a title but no subtitle; some items have an author but no illustrator. The point is that in describing an information package, this type of information needs to be recorded and the 245 tag is the place to do this recording.

The first indicator is coded to note if a 1XX tag exists in the record. We will describe later in this section on what qualifies as information for the 1XX field. The second indicator is used to note the number of spaces to skip for "filing" purposes. In the old days of card catalogs, librarians knew that one did not file a title beginning with the word "The" under the letter "T." Computers are not as smart as humans. When retrieving records, the computer needs to be told which words to look for and which ones to skip. In English, the initial articles "the," "a," and "an" are skipped in retrieving records. For example the book *The Talking Eggs* would be retrieved under the word "talking" not "the." The second indicator values, 0-9, correspond to the number of spaces the computer needs to skip in $a. The value equals one space for each letter plus one space for the space between the initial article and the next word in the title. In our example of *The Talking Eggs*, our second indicator would be 4; three spaces for t-h-e and one space for the space between "the" and "talking." This principle also works for non-English initial articles.

A common mistake of novice catalogers or catalogers new to electronic cataloging is to ignore the field indicators. In the 245 tag this can be a serious mistake because an incorrect value of the second indicator can lead to incorrect retrieval results. Library discussion lists often have the question, "Why can't I find my record for *The Talking Eggs* (for example) under a title search, but I can in a keyword search?" The answer of course is that the second indicator in the 245 tag is incorrect and must be changed to 4 in order to find it under a title search. It comes up in a keyword search because keyword searching is not limited to the placement of the words in the record.

There are 12 valid subfields in the 245 tag. Of those fields, we will discuss four: $a, $h, $b, $c, as they are the most commonly used subfields in this tag. The 245 tag always begins with the $a. Into this subfield one enters what *AACR* refers to as the "title proper." This is the first part of the title before the subtitle information, or the entire title if there is no subtitle information. The $a is followed by choices. If one is cataloging a non-book item, then one will enter a $h. If one is cataloging a book and there is a subtitle, one enters a $b. If one is cataloging a book and there is no

Figure 6.1. Flow Chart for the Structure of the 245 Tag

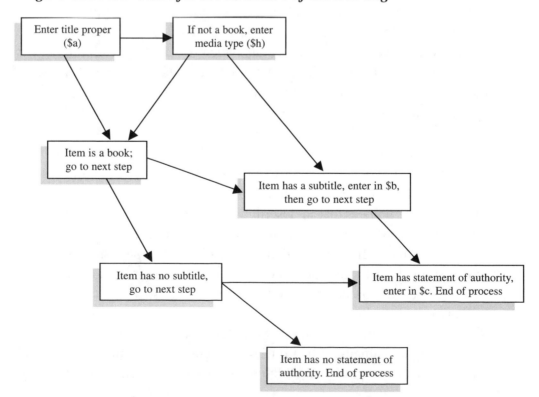

subtitle, one enters a $c. Finally, if one is cataloging a book and there is no subtitle and there is no named person or corporation responsible for the intellectual content of the item, then one enters a full stop, that is a period (.). A flow chart for deciding on the structure of the 245 tag is provided in Figure 6.1. All information entered in the 245 tag (except $h) comes from the chief source of information. Any information appearing in the 245 tag that is not from the chief source of information must be so noted by using brackets [ ].

The $h, as just noted, is used only for cataloging non-book materials. This subfield is referred to in *AACR* as the "general material designation" (GMD) and is an option available to the cataloger to make note right in the title area of what type of material is being cataloged. The advantage of utilizing the $h is in providing the user information to know right away that the item retrieved by the computer in response to a search is not a book. That can be terribly important to a user and we should train our library community members to take a good look at this part of the record. Having the $h appear right after the title proper should be like a red flag to the user saying, "Hey, this item is *not* a book it's a DVD!" In the box below, you see a list of terms available to use for this subfield. The list has been shortened based on the types of items normally found in a school library media collection. If the item type you are looking for is not in this list, you should find a copy of *AACR* and look under rule 1.1C1 for the full list. In recent years we have seen the increased use of the vernacular terms in the $h instead of the "approved" descriptors. While we still see "electronic resource" for CD-ROMs, it is not uncommon to see DVD instead of "electronic resource." This use of the vernacular may be in recognition of the fact that a DVD isn't necessarily bound to computer use as the term electronic resource was originally created to define. We prefer the use of electronic resource for computer software and videorecording or sound recording for DVDs and CD-ROMs whose primary function it is to show movies or play songs. Cleary this is an area of current controversy and, as with most cataloging choices, the answer is to do that which works best for information retrieval for your library community.

Partial list of General Material Designations (GMD)

Activity card
Braille
Cartographic material
Chart
Electronic resource (*Optional*: use specific material type, e.g. DVD or CD-ROM.)
Game
Kit
Motion picture
Music
Picture
Realia (Use this for things like LCD projectors.)
Sound recording
Videorecording (Note, this is one word.)

There are several punctuation rules for this tag. The $h (if there is one) is separated from the $a with a space. The $b is separated from $a (or $h if there is one) by a space and a colon. The $c is separated from the rest of the fields by a space and backward slash (/). Within $c, if there are a number of people listed and they have different jobs, e.g. an author and an illustrator, the jobs are separated by a space then a semicolon and then by another space. If there are two authors, they have the same job so are not separated by the semicolon. If the information on the title page does not include a connecting word, such as "and" or "with," the cataloger may supply this word but must do so by enclosing the word in brackets, otherwise the names can be separated by a comma and a space. This tag always ends in a full stop unless there is no $c and the title ends in some other kind of punctuation. If we use the circumflex (^) to show spaces, an example of the punctuation in the 245 would look something like this:

245 XX $aTitle^$h[GMD]^:$bother title^/$cauthor [and] second author^;^illustrator.

Notice in creating MARC tags, there are no spaces between the letter of the subfield and the word being entered. The computer understands that a subfield delimiter (a "$" in our case) and a letter immediately following the subfield delimiter have some meaning (depending on the tag and subfield) and that the information immediately following the delimiter and letter is the desired information.

Capitalization in this tag catches the new cataloger every time. We are so used to creating bibliographies where we capitalize each word in the title, and certainly the first word following a colon, that we are surprised by the rules of this tag. *AACR* tells us to "transcribe the title proper exactly as to wording, order, and spelling, but not necessarily as to punctuation and capitalization" (rule 1.1B1, p.1-7). This means that unless you have a proper noun within the title, only the first word is capitalized. Although this may seem odd at first, the rule harkens back to those old typewriters of the 1800s when that capital key was very hard to work and it just made more sense to capitalize only when absolutely necessary. Let's take a look at a few examples to see how the 245 tag works.

- On the item as:

Frog and Toad
Are Friends
by Arnold Lobel

- Typed into the record as:
  245 10 $aFrog and Toad are friends /$cby Arnold Lobel.
  - Notice the first indicator tells the computer that there will be a 1XX tag; the second indicator is a 0 and tells the computer to file this record under "f" for "frog;" this item only has a title proper and there is no subtitle; it is a book so there is no need for a $h; the statement of responsibility lies solely on the shoulders of Lobel; notice that "frog" and "toad" are both capitalized, as these are the characters' names.

- On the item as:

BARD OF AVON

The Story of William Shakespeare

DIANE STANLEY AND PETER VENNEMA

ILLUSTRATED BY DIANE STANLEY

- Typed into the record as:

  245 10 $aBard of Avon :$bthe story of William Shakespeare /$cDiane Stanley and Peter Vennema ; illustrated by Diane Stanley.

- Notice again the first indicator code that this record has a 1XX tag; notice that this title is filed directly under the letter b, and so the second indicator is a 0 telling the computer to skip zero spaces; despite the fact that nearly all information on the title page is in capital letters, we capitalize only the first word of the title, proper names (Avon, William, and Shakespeare), and the names of the responsible people; we do have a subtitle that is recorded in the $b, notice the colon before the $b; and we have multiple people in the $c, notice that Stanley and Vennema are listed together, as they appear on the item as the authors, Stanley is repeated again as the illustrator; notice the space semicolon and space (^;^) separating the authors and the illustrator; that notation (brought to us by ISBD) is used in the $c of the 245 tag to separate people with different jobs, Vennema is an author so he and Stanley are kept together, but Stanley also illustrated the text so she is listed again with the use of the semicolon.

- On item (title screen) as:

Strega Nona

- Typed into the record as:

  245 00 $aStrega Nona $h[videorecording] /$c[by Tomie dePaola]

- Notice the appearance of the $h to note that this is a videotape but in cataloging language we call it a videorecording; notice that the $c information is in brackets. We use the title screen as our chief source of information; dePaola's name is not on the title screen but the narrator says dePaola wrote the book and his name is on the case; therefore, we add the information, but put it in brackets.

- On the item as:

Eyewitness

THE VISUAL DICTIONARY of the UNIVERSE

- Typed into the record as:

  245 04 $aThe visual dictionary of the universe.

- Although this item is a book and therefore might seem to be an easy cataloging task, it has in fact a few anomalies that might trip up the novice cataloger. Skipping over the indicators for just a moment, look at the subfield information and notice that the 245 tag has only one subfield: subfield a. There is no statement of responsibility because none was given on the title page and none was given on the verso of the title page. Sometimes in works like these, one will find a statement on the verso of the title page that does assign responsibility, such as "Text by John Smith. Photographs by Jane Doe." But such is not the case with this item, so we must leave out the $c. Because there is no $c, we will also find that there is a 0 in the first indicator spot. A 0 means that this record will not have a 1XX tag. Notice too that the second indicator has a value of 4 telling the computer to skip the first four spaces (t-h-e and space) and to file and retrieve this record under "v" for "visual." Notice too that we have left out the word "Eyewitness." We did this because "Eyewitness" is really part of the series title: Eyewitness Visual Dictionaries. *AACR* rule 1.1B1 tells us that introductory words or phrases should not be included in the title proper (1-8). Motion pictures are replete with these kinds of statements, "Walt Disney presents," or "A WGBH production" and the like are examples of introductory phrases. We are treating "Eyewitness" in the same way. If we didn't know any better, we would have a lot of titles in our catalog beginning with the word "Eyewitness." Eventually we will want to make a note of "Eyewitness," but we won't do it here.

- On the title screen as:

  > NOODLEBUG
  > On the Move

  On the DVD disc as:

  > NOODLEBUG™
  > DVD Video
  > On the Move

  On the CD disc as:

  > NOODLEBUG™
  > Music CD
  > On the Move

  On the container as:

  > NOODLEBUG™
  > On the Move

  On the back of the container:

  > School Specialty
  > Children's Publishing
  > ©2003 Carus Publishing Company and Noodlebug
  > Productions LLC. All rights reserved. © 2005 Noodlebug
  > Productions LLC.

- Typed into the record as:

  245 00 $aNoodlebug $h[DVD] :$bon the move /$cCarus Publishing and Noodlebug Publications.

- This mixed media information package offers us all sorts of interesting problems. The title proper seems deceptively easy. Given our information, we might be tempted to write: $aNoodlebug on the move. However, our cataloger has put "on the move" into a $b. A look at the cataloging at other institutions shows that there seems to be many ways to enter this information from keeping it all in $a to using a subfield we'll not be exploring in this text, $p. It turns out (and we know this by looking at the parent's guide included with the set) that there are several different Noodlebug titles. Separating "on the move" from "Noodlebug" in either the $b or the $p shows that "Noodelbug" is the title proper and the other part is just that, "other title information." The $p in the 245 tag tells us that this item has two titles. The first title in $a probably covers more than one item. The second title in $p is the name that is special to this particular information package. In this case, we think the use of the $p may be more than necessary; use of $p is certainly uncommon in school library materials. Therefore, we are happy to stick with the $b for "other title information." For more information about $p, you can go to the Library of Congress MARC page: http://www.loc.gov/marc/bibliographic/ecbdtils.html#mrcb245. Notice the $h uses the vernacular term "DVD" instead of "electronic resource." We could have also opted for "videorecording" since that also describes what we have. However, we feel that DVD is going to be familiar to our students and therefore a more useful term. Now look at $c and note that we have included information that is not provided on the title screen. In our *Strega Nona* example, we included that kind of information in brackets. In mixed media, our chief source of information is the item itself plus any other accompanying material that best describes the item. Therefore, we are free to include the statement of authority without including it in brackets.

Bilingual materials require special attention in entering the information into the MARC record. *AACR* (rule 1.1D) tells us to record parallel titles using an equal sign (=) between the titles. The parallel title is the title in a different language. This differs from other title information that would be in the same language as the title proper. It sounds so simple, but it gets complicated very quickly. The problem is not in the *AACR* rule but in the MARC format. Here are the three ways of dealing with multiple languages; remember, this is assuming that all of this information is appearing on the chief source of information.

1. If all information on the chief source of information is given in more than one language, then the parallel title information follows the $c:

   1a. 245 10 $aMagic dogs of the volcanoes /$cby Manlio Argueta ; pictures by Elly Simmons ; English translation by Stacey Ross = Los perros magicos de los volcanoes / escrito por Manlio Argueta ; ilustrado por Elly Simmons ; traducido al ingles por Stacey Ross.

   1b. Notice how the structure of the information parallels that of the first part of the 245 tag including the use of the space semicolon space in recording the names in the statement of responsibility.

2. If there is no statement of responsibility, the parallel title follows other title information in the $b:

   2a. 245 00 $aLeyenda azteca :$bIztaccihuatl y Popocatepetl = Aztec legend : Iztaccihuatl and Popocatepetl.

2b. Since there is no $c, the parallel title immediately follows the other title information in $b.

---

245 Tag – Title and Statement of Responsibility

- The 245 is not repeatable.

- First indicator is coded 0 for no 1XX fields or 1 for 1XX fields.

- Second indicator is coded 0-9 for spaces to skip for filing characters.

- Most common subfields are $a title proper (must have); $h GMD (non-books only); $b other title information; and $c statement of responsibility.
  - If there is a $h it is always directly after the $a information and has no preceding punctuation; $b is usually preceded by a colon (:) but may also be preceded by an equal sign (=); $c is always preceded by a backward slash (/).

- Unless some other punctuation exists, this tag always ends in a full stop (.).

Examples:

> 245 14 $aThe cat in the hat /$cby Dr. Seuss.
> 245 12 $aA chocolate moose for dinner /$cwritten and illustrated by Fred Gwynne.
> 245 00 $aWe will never forget $h[DVD] /$cWGN productions ; produced by Bob Smith.

Exercises: put these titles in a 245 tag format and try to apply one subject heading and a Dewey classification number.

6.4. Title page: Body decoration
                        Jillian Powell.

{Powell is the author; the book is about the different ways people decorate their bodies including tattooing, cosmetics, and hair styles.}

6.5. Title page: WALTER DEAN MYERS
                        NOW IS YOUR TIME!
                        The African-American
                        Struggle for Freedom

{Myers is the author; the book is a history of the African-American struggle for freedom and equality, beginning with the capture of Africans in 1619, continuing through the American Revolution, the Civil War, and into contemporary times.}

6.6. Title page: Mermaid Tales From Around The World
                        Retold by Mary Pope Osborne
                        Illustrated by Troy Howell.

{Collection of 12 mermaid tales from around the world.}

6.7. Title on disc: The Sea of Trolls
                        by Nancy Farmer
                        read by Gerard Doyle

{12 CD recording of a fiction story involving Druids, Norse mythology, brothers and sisters, and Vikings.}

3. If all information except the title is given in only one language and there is no other title information, then the parallel title information is given in the $b. But unlike titles all in one language, the $b is immediately preceded not by a colon but by the equal sign (=).

   3a. 245 10 $aLittle Red Riding Hood =$bCaperucita roja /$cby the Brothers Grimm ; illustrated by Pau Estrada.

   3b. Notice the use of the equal sign instead of the colon before the $b. Notice also the form of the statement of responsibility "the Brothers Grimm." That's the way the name appears on the title page and so that is how we transcribe it as per the *AACR* rule discussed previously. It's a strange way to see the name, and so we point it out here as a good illustration of that rule.

246 Tag: Sometimes an item contains some subtitle information or proper title information that we need to retrieve as title information in its own right. The 246 tag, called Varying Form of Title, is used for this purpose; it is called *tracing for an alternate title*. In our example of *Bard of Avon*, we have the following subtitle: *The Story of William Shakespeare*. That subtitle is very descriptive of the book, and it would not be out of the realm of possibility that a student might enter a title search for "The Story of William Shakespeare." Therefore, we want to create a way so that the $b information can be retrieved through a title search. We do this by adding a 246 tag to the surrogate record. Prior to 1993, this information was recorded in the 740 tag and records for older items may still reflect that use of the 740 tag. In fact, vendors of automated systems for school libraries did not recognize the use of the 246 tag for book items right away (it was previously used just for periodical publications) and so even records beyond 1993 might have a 740 instead of a 246 tag. However, it is safe to say the school library media specialist can now use the 246 tag for added title information. Thus our example of *Bard of Avon* would also include a 246 tag:

246 3_ $aStory of William Shakespeare

Notice in this tag that the initial article "the" has been dropped from the title. In the 246 tag there is no indicator for non-filing characters, therefore the initial article is dropped. Notice too that the tag does not end in a full stop. There is no closing punctuation in the 246 tag unless specified on the item, as in a question or exclamation mark.

We would also use this tag for our bilingual items, to trace for the titles in the other languages thus:

- 245 10 $aMagic dogs of the volcanoes /$cstory by Manlio Argueta ; pictures by Elly Simmons ; English translation by Stacey Ross = Los perros magicos de los volcanoes / escrito por Manlio Argueta ; ilustrado por Elly Simmons ; traducido al ingles por Stacey Ross.

  • 246 3_ $aPerros magicos de los volcanoes

  • Notice here that the initial article "los" has been dropped from the title, just as we dropped the initial article "the" from the previous example.

- 245 00 $aLeyenda azteca :$bIztaccihuatl y Popocatepetl = Aztec legend : Iztaccihuatl and Popocatepetl.
  - 246 3_ $Aztec legend
  - Notice that we transcribed here only "Aztec legend." Technically speaking we could have added a $b and the rest of the English title, but the $b is so rarely used in the 246 tag that we have opted not to include that information.
- 245 10 $aLittle Red Riding Hood =$bCaperucita Roja /$cby the Brothers Grimm ; illustrated by Pau Estrada.
  - 246 3_ $aCaperucita Roja
  - Notice here and in the other examples, that we do not include any information from the $c, as that information is not transcribed in the 246 tag.

This tag is used if the title proper contains numbers or symbols that need to be written in alternative ways. We make these added entries if the numbers or symbols occur in the first five words of the title. Here are some examples:

- 245 10 $a10 ways to feel better /$cby Dr. Feelgood.
  - 246 3_ $aTen ways to feel better
- 245 14 $aThe 5 & 10 stores of yesteryear /$cby William Jennings.
  - 246 3_ $aFive and ten stores of yesteryear
  - 246 3_ $aFive & ten stores of yesteryear
  - 246 3_ $a5 and 10 stores of yesteryear
  - Notice how we created three 246 tags for this one title to account for both the numbers (5, 10) and the ampersand (&). We do this to try to think of the various ways a patron might search for the title, using numbers or symbols or not. There may even be more combinations, such as "five and dime," but how many tracings we make might be dependent on our users. The point is that in dealing with numbers, we need to try to account for as many variances in spelling as the librarian deems necessary for information retrieval.

Finally, we have the case of the title beginning with the name of a person or company. An example might be *Elvis Presley's Love Me Tender* or *Walt Disney's Aladdin*. In both cases, our title proper begins with the name of the person (Presley or Disney). The problem is that our students might be more likely to look for the title *Love Me Tender* or *Aladdin*. Therefore, we need to trace for what one might consider the "true" title. Here are the 245 and 246 tags for both of these examples:

- 245 10 $aElvis Presley's Love me tender /$clyrics by Elvis Presley and Vera Matson ; illustrated by Tom Browning.
  - 246 3_ $aLove me tender
  - Notice in our 245 tag that the word "Love" is capitalized. We capitalize that word because it is the first word in the title of the work.
- 245 00 $aWalt Disney's Aladdin $h[DVD] /$cWalt Disney Productions.
  - 246 3_ $aAladdin $h[DVD]

- Again we see that "Aladdin" is capitalized. Not only is Aladdin the title, but it is also the proper name of the character, thus his name is capitalized. Note too that we have the $h included in the tag, just as we see in the 245 tag.

Both of the indicators in the 246 tag have various meanings. We opt for defining only one meaning in each place; 3 for the first indicator and blank (_) for the second indicator. The first indicator is used to tell the computer if there is a note explaining this alternate title or not. Since we usually don't add an extra

---

246 Tag Summary

- The 246 tag is repeatable.

- First indicator for our purposes most commonly is coded 3 for no note/added entry; other values are 0 for note/no added entry, 1 for note/added entry, and 2 no note/no added entry.

- Second indicator for our purposes is most commonly coded as blank; there are nine other valid codes (0-8) for this tag that define the type of title information being entered, spine, caption, and so on.

- There are 11 valid subfields for this tag, most school library media specialists will use the $a and $h as needed only.

- There is no closing punctuation in the 246 tag unless specified on the item, as in a question or exclamation mark.

Example:

> 245 10 $aStateswoman to the world :$ba story about Eleanor Roosevelt /$cby Maryann N. Weidt ; illustrations by Lydia M. Anderson.
> 246 3_ $aStory about Eleanor Roosevelt

Exercises: Create 245 and 246 tags for the following (be sure to correct for capitalization):

6.8. The time we had together
The story of Richard Rogers and Oscar Hammerstein
By John Smith

6.9. The GREATEST *Puppy* ever
My dog Fluffy
written by Samuel Jackson and illustrated by Laura Smith

6.10. 24 girls in 7 days
ALEX BRADLEY

6.11. Extra credit: On title screen as:

Moon	Un lazo
Rope	a la
	Luna
A Peruvian	Una leyenda
Folktale	peruana
Lois Ehlert	translated into Spanish by Amy Prince

This is a bilingual item. Can you create a 041 tag for it?

This is a folktale. Can you create a classification and subject heading for it?

note, we opt for the indicator value of 3 to show there is no note, but there is an added title entry. The second indicator differs in the 246 from the 245 tag. In the 245 tag, the second indicator is used to note the number of spaces to skip for filing the title name. In the 246, this place is used to note the type of title being traced. In most cases, we don't need to make an extra note, that is, we're tracing for the other title information and not for a spine title, half title, cover title, or other kinds of bibliographic information that is important in some libraries, but usually not very important to note for school library media collections. Therefore we opt for the blank indicator, which is most often the default value in school library media automation systems.

Area 1 Continued: Main Entry Tags (1XX) & Added Entry Tags (7XX)

It is interesting that the Library of Congress chooses to use the phrase "main entry" for this tag area because, in this age of electronic cataloging, that concept is mostly moot. In times past, when catalog cards were typed by hand, the concept of main entry related to the fact that it was laborious and time consuming to type all the information about an item on every card that was produced. And so a single card, the main entry card, was created in which all the information about an item was included. All other cards included minimal amounts of information about the item and the user was referred to the main entry card for complete bibliographic information. The author of the work was usually the main point of access. The other main point of access was the title of the work if there was no author, more than three authors, or if the work was an edited volume. When libraries shifted to electronic access, this idea of a main entry card became less important. Camps developed in the library world between those who believed in the concept of main entry and those who believed that concept was now moot. For us, it is useful to look at the 1XX field simply as another access point even though LC still refers to it as main entry.

The 1XX tag tells us that this is the primary choice of access to this information package. In the school environment, we might think of this as the author statement as that is our most common use for it, although the 1XX fields include much more than just the name of the author. There are four possible tags in this area, but only one can be selected. That means, for example, that if there is a 100 tag, there can be no 130 tag. The tag numbers are 100, 110, 111, and 130 for personal name, corporate name, meeting name, and uniform title, respectively. The information for a name tag (100, 110, or 111) is usually taken from the 245 tag, which is why we talked about that tag first.

1XX and 7XX tags: Personal Name Entries: Tags 1XX and 7XX are access points in the surrogate record for the names of people and corporations responsible for the intellectual content of the work in hand. These tags may also be used to trace for conferences or meetings and other title information. We will not be discussing access for conferences as these types of materials seldom find their way into a school library collection.

Typically in school library collections, users want to be able to find materials based on the name of the author, illustrator, editor (usually confused as the author), or a corporate name (such as National Geographic). To do this we take information from the 245 $c. This information can also come from the 300 tag and 5XX tags as we will see later in this chapter. For now, let us focus on getting this information from the 245 $c. We have already discussed entering information in the $c of the 245 tag, but let us explore that information with a little more detail as it will affect what we do with the 1XX and 7XX tags. *AACR* directs us to enter information in this subfield that is shown prominently on the chief source of information in the form in which it appears with the following explanations:

- Omit titles of people unless the omission would result in some ambiguity, e.g. Dr. Seuss, Mrs. David Jones, the Prince of Wales, but *not* Tom Woods, Ph D., Dr. John Rice, Lady Jane Aster.

- A statement of responsibility that is connected to the title proper, e.g. *Sally Doe's Beauty Tips For Teens*, should stay with the title and need not be repeated in the $c, although Sally Doe will show up in the 100 tag.

- If three people are listed on the chief source of information, list all three; if more than three are listed, list the first or most prominently named person then three ellipses and "et al." in brackets, e.g. by Tom Jones … [et al.], unless they have different functions, see the next point.

- Use a semicolon (;) to separate different functions, e.g. written by Tom Jones ; illustrated by Jim Brown.

Once this information has been recorded in the 245 $c, we want to be able to access the record using that information. In many automated systems, the information in the $c can be accessed using a keyword search. However, if the student is entering a search by author (or personal name), this information will not be retrieved and the item will remain hidden to the student. So we need a place or places in the MARC record to put the information so it will be retrieved. In the old days of manual cataloging, this was known as *tracing*. Catalogers still talk today about tracing for names and titles, but it is a shorthand way of saying we need an access point for retrieval of the information by searching the name or corporation. The places in the MARC record for tracing names and corporations are the 1XX and 7XX tags.

The 1XX field is the place to trace for the name of a person or corporation related to the intellectual or artistic content of the item. The 1XX tag is not repeatable and only one name can appear in the tag. For other names, such as an illustrator name or joint author's name, we use the 7XX tag. In the computer world, the 1XX and 7XX tags serve very similar functions and there are those who say there should be no 1XX tag, only 7XX tags. We will let the experts argue this issue. For us, we think of the 1XX tag as the first person named in the 245 $c tag and the 7XX tag as the place to put other names associated with the intellectual content of the item. The structure of the 1XX and 7XX is similar, but the purpose is different.

There can be only one 100 tag with only one name in it. The 700 tag is used for other names and may be repeated. We will examine the two tags by looking at specific examples.

Let us go back to our 245 tag examples and see how the 100 and 700 tags work.

- Title page: Frog And Toad Are Friends by Arnold Lobel

- Typed into the record as:
  - 100 1_ $aLobel, Arnold.
  - 245 10 $aFrog and Toad are friends /$cby Arnold Lobel.
    - This is a good example to start with as it is very straightforward. There is only one person responsible for the intellectual content of the item, that's Lobel; his name is entered in the 100 tag.

- Title page: Bard of Avon The Story of William Shakespeare Diane Stanley and Peter Vennema Illustrated by Diane Stanley

- Typed into the record as:
  - 100 1_ $aStanley, Diane.
  - 245 10 $aBard of Avon :$bthe story of William Shakespeare /$cDiane Stanley and Peter Vennema ; illustrated by Diane Stanley.
  - 700 1_ $aVennema, Peter, $ejoint author.
    - This example is a little trickier than our first, but only because Stanley is mentioned twice in the 245 $c. If we remember that we're talking access and the computer searches both the 100 and 700 tags when conducting a name search, then we can see why we would enter Stanley in only one tag. It would be redundant and would do nothing for retrieval to list her both in a 100 tag and again in a 700 tag.
      - Notice the comma before the $e in the 700 tag and the fact that "joint author" is written out in full.

- Title page: MAGIC DOGS OF THE VOLCANOES LOS PERROS MAGICOS DE LOS VOLCANES Story by/Escrito por Manlio Argueta Pictures by/Ilustrado por Elly Simmons English translation by/Traducido al ingles por Stacey Ross

- Typed into the record as:
  - 100 1_ $aArgueta, Manlio.
  - 245 10 $aMagic dogs of the volcanoes /$cstory by Manlio Argueta ; pictures by Elly Simmons ; English translation by Stacey Ross = Los perros magicos de los volcanoes / escrito por Manlio Argueta ; ilustrado por Elly Simmons ; traducido al ingles por Stacey Ross.
  - 700 1_ $aSimmons, Elly, $eill.
  - 700 1_ $aRoss, Stacey, $etrans.
    - There is nothing overly exciting about the 100 tag; we've seen the same thing in our previous two examples. What we notice in this example is

the *relator* codes for the other two entries in the 700 tags. We use relator codes to show the relationship between the name and the contribution made to the item in hand. In our two examples we have "ill." and "tr." to show that Simmons is the illustrator of the work and Ross is the translator. This is purely an optional thing to do, but we suggest getting into the habit of doing so because it can provide useful information about the person. For example, using the relator "ill." serves to separate the works that Steven Kellogg wrote from the works that he only illustrated.

- Title page: George and Martha *Written and Illustrated by* James Marshall

- Typed into the record as:
  - 100 1_ $aMarshall, James, $d1942-1992.
  - 245 10 $aGeorge and Martha /$cwritten and illustrated by James Marshall.
    - In this example we have an author with birth and death dates. This record has been updated to include the author's death dates. Some older records may have only $d1942- . Should you encounter this, you might want to update the record yourself. In our previous examples, we see that not every person has dates associated with his or her name. The Library of Congress establishes dates if it is necessary and the established name is what you will see in the CIP data and in copy cataloging. If you are creating an original record or you are updating copy, don't feel that you need to investigate the life of an author to find birth and death dates. Accept what you have in front of you and move on; you have too many other things to do to spend your time looking up biographical data on an author!

- On the disc as: The Sea of Trolls by Nancy Farmer read by Gerard Doyle

- Typed into the record as:
  - 100 1_ $aFarmer, Nancy, $d1941-
  - 245 14 $aThe sea of trolls $h[sound recording] /$cby Nancy Farmer.
  - 700 1_ $aDoyle, Gerard, $enrt.
    - Notice here that we have an open date for Farmer as she is still alive (we found this date from the LC database). There is no full stop at the end of this tag as the hyphen accounts for the final punctuation. Notice that Doyle's name does not appear in the $c (as we saw in the previous set of exercises). Doyle is the narrator and his name will go in a note tag (defined later in this chapter). However, he still earns a tracing in the 700 tag.

The 100 and 700 tags share similar structure but are also different:

- There can only be one name in the 100 tag.

- The 100 tag is not repeatable.

- First indicator: usually will be coded 1 for entry by surname, but may also see code 0 for forename entry or 3 for family name entry.

- Second indicator: usually will be coded as blank.

- There are 31 valid subfields for these two tags; most common ones will be $a Personal name (must have a subfield a), and $d Birth and death dates; other less common but not infrequent subfields are $e Relator term (as in "ill." for illustrator, "ed." for editor, or "trans." for translator), $q Fuller form of name, and $c Titles associated with the name.

- Tag ends in a full stop, unless other punctuation is present.

Example:
100 1_ $aSmith, John F. $q(John Franklin), $d1898-1989.

- There can only be one name in the 700 tag.

- There can be more than one 700 tag, it is repeatable.

- First indicator is the same in the 700 tag as it is for the 100 tag using 1, 0, or 3 for type of name entry.

- The second indicator is slightly different in the 700 tag; usually it is blank (like the 100 tag), but there is also a "2" for an analytical entry (uncommon in school library media collections).

- The $e for "relator" is very common in the 700 tag, and used most often to note the name is for the illustrator (ill.), editor (ed.), or translator (trans.)

- Tag ends in a full stop, unless other punctuation is present.

Example:
700 1_ $aSmith, John F. $q(John Franklin), $d1898-1989, $eill.

Exercises
Take the information from the $c and put it into 100 or 700 tags as needed.
6.12. 245 10 $aOpposites /$cby Sandra Boynton.
6.13. 245 10 $aBooks and libraries /$cby Jack Knowlton ; pictures by Harriett Barton.
6.14. 245 10 $aElvis Presley's Love me tender /$clyrics by Elvis Presley and Vera Matson ; illustrated by Tom Browning.

110 and 710 tags: Corporate Name Entries: Sometimes it happens that the contributor to the intellectual content of the item is not a person but a "thing" or corporate body. This happens most often with non-book items. Computer programs, maps, and motion pictures are almost always created through the efforts of an organization and that organization deserves some credit for its contributions. To do this, we use the 110 or 710 fields. These fields have the same purpose as the 100 and 700 fields except we are now tracing for a corporate body rather than for a person. Like the 100 tag, the 110 tag is *not* repeatable; however, like the 700 tag, the 710 tag *is* repeatable. The first indicator for either 110 or 710 is defined according to the way the corporate body is entered into the tag. If the name of the corporate body is recorded in *inverted order* (sort of like last name first), then the first indicator value is 0. This is the least common way to enter corporate bodies. A more common way to enter a corporate body is called "jurisdiction order." *Jurisdiction order* is used most often for government bodies wherein the place name is given first and then the department name. Jurisdiction order is given the value 1. *Direct order* is the term used to refer to a body that is recorded in the order in which it is seen on the item and is given the value of 2. The second indicator is most often blank, although, again, like the 700 tag, the 710 tag can have the indicator 2 to show it is an analytic entry, but that is very rare in the school library media catalog. Of the 22 valid subfields for these tags, the most common one, besides the beginning $a, is the $b. This is used for corporate bodies entered in jurisdiction order. The $b is preceded by a full stop. Unless there is other punctuation, these tags both end in a full stop. Let's take a look at some examples to see these tags in action.

- Title from disc: Green Eggs and Ham by Dr. Seuss
  - 100 1_ $aSeuss, $cDr.
  - 245 10 $aGreen eggs and ham $h[electronic resource] /$cby Dr. Seuss.
  - 710 2_ $aLiving Books (Firm)
    - Notice the 100 tag and the fact that Seuss is only a last name and is followed by a comma and then the $c for his title, "Dr." Remember that an honorific like "Dr." or "Sir" is not included unless it is needed to identify the individual. In this case, we really need that "Dr." because that's our only identification for who this person is. We could also look the name up in the Library of Congress database and confirm our decision that it is important to include that "Dr."
    - Now look at the 710 tag. First of all we need to know from whence this information has come as it most certainly is not in the 245 $c! If we were to look at this program on the computer, we would see "Living Books" all over the introductory part before the title screen. We know then that even though we are not including this information in the 245 $c, it has to be traced. (We'll reference this corporate body later in the record in the 260 tag.) We see here an example of a tracing for a corporate body that is not mentioned in the 245 tag. Now look at the tag itself; we see the first indicator value "2" meaning that this corporate body is entered in direct order. But how do we know to use "Firm" in this entry? It isn't on the item itself, so how do we know to do this? We know because our copy cataloging shows it in this way. If we were to enter this record as an original and had no clue about how to create this name, we probably would not have that term "Firm" in the record. If we were creating an original record, we would probably look up Living Books on

the LC authority database to use as a guide for creating this tag. However, we're lucky, we have some good copy to use and it shows us how to cite this corporate body. Notice that because the word "Firm" is enclosed in parentheses, the closing parenthesis acts as our final punctuation and there is no full stop at the end of this tag.

- Title from the title screen: Strega Nona
  - 245 00 $aStrega Nona $h[videorecording] /$c[por Tomie De Paola]
  - 700 1_ $aDe Paola, Tomie
  - 710 2_ $aWeston Woods Studios.
  - 710 2_ $aScholastic Inc.
    - Notice that the first indicator in the 245 tag is 0 and that there is no 100 tag. We all know that Tomie De Paola is responsible for the intellectual content of the book, but what about the film? In films, there is seldom a personal or corporate name for the main entry (even Stanley Kubrick doesn't get a 100 main entry for his films). The reason for this is that so many people are involved in creating a film, or often any other non-book item, that it is impossible to select the one person for the main entry access point. So most motion pictures (including videotapes and DVDs) will be entered under the title (245 tag, first indicator 0) with other tracings for the people involved in the project as we see here in our example with Mr. De Paola entered in the 700 tag instead of the 100 tag.
    - It might be argued that school children will never look for an item given the name of the production company. Here we apply *AACR* rule 21.30E.1, "Make an added entry under the heading for a prominently named corporate body unless it functions solely as distributor or manufacturer" (21-48). This rule tells us that if a corporate body does more than simply publish an item, then it should be traced accordingly. (In MARC that is achieved through the 710 tag.) Both Scholastic and Weston Woods appear prominently immediately preceding the title screen; therefore, we make added entries for them in two separate 710 tags.
- Title page: The Visual Dictionary of the Universe
  - 245 04 $aThe visual dictionary of the universe.
  - 710 2_ $aDorling Kindersley Limited.
    - We don't normally trace for the names of publishers; however, Dorling Kindersley is so well known for its visual dictionaries and eyewitness books that it is quite likely a school student may run a name search for Dorling Kindersley and so, again, we want to be able to retrieve items by the company's name. Moreover, in this case DK has not given us the name of any person responsible for the intellectual content of the item, therefore we can only assume that it was created by the corporate body, and so we give it credit in the 710 tag. (We might even be tempted to create a 710 tag for "DK," as so many of us use that abbreviation with which to refer to this publisher.) However, because of the popularity of these publications, even if

a name was given on the item, we would probably still be tempted to trace for the publishers. We do this through the same rule, 21.30E.1, described in the previous example, which reads further, "Make an added entry under a prominently named publisher if the responsibility for the work extends beyond that of merely publishing the item being catalogued … In case of doubt, make an added entry [for the corporate body]" (21-48).

- Title on title screen: National Geographic The Human Body
  - 245 04 $aThe human body $h[electronic resource] /$cNational Geographic Educational Division.
  - 710 2_ $aNational Geographic Society (U.S.). $bEducational Division.
    - Again we rely on copy cataloging to tell us how we should enter the National Geographic Society, especially because it might not appear in its full form on the item (as is the case with our example). We see that even though the $a ends with information in parentheses, there is still the full stop before the $b information. We do this because ISBD tells us that subordinate units (in our case Educational Division) are preceded by a full stop regardless of other punctuation.[1]

---

110 and 710 tags share the following structure:

- The 110 tag is not repeatable but the 710 is.

- First indicator describes the format of the entry:
  - Value 0 means the entry is in inverted order (personal name inverted, not very common for slm collections), e.g. $aFranklin (Benjamin) Printing Press Incorporated.
  - Value 1 means the entry is in jurisdiction order, e.g. $aCanada. $bDept. of Agriculture.
  - Value 2 means the entry is in direct order, e.g. $aNational Geographic Society (U.S.). $bEducational Division.

- Second indicator will usually be blank, in 710 one may see a value 2 for analytical entry, but this is not very common.

- There are 22 valid subfields for these tags. Of these, the most common subfields are $a Corporate name or jurisdiction name and $b Subordinate unit.

Examples:
> 110 1_ $aDelaware. $bDept. of Education.
> 110 2_ $aNational Geographic Society (U.S.). $bCartographic Division.
> –for a work that emanates from one specific part of National Geographic.

Look further: Look on various library databases for the following and notice both the OPAC and MARC display:
> **6.15.** Weston Woods
> **6.16.** Scholastic (notice the variety of Scholastic entities)
> **6.17.** National Geographic
> **6.18.** Living Books

---

[1]For more information on ISBD punctuation of personal and corporate names, see *Guidelines for authority records and references* at http://www.ifla.org/VII/s13/garr/garr.pdf.

Summary of Area 1: Title and the statement of responsibility (1XX, 245, 246, 7XX)

- "Transcribe the title proper exactly as to wording, order, and spelling, but not necessarily as to punctuation and capitalization." (*AACR* 1.1B1, p.1-7)

- Chief source of information for a book is the title page itself. Chief source of information for non-book materials is usually the item itself first and then other label and container supplied information. If any information is given here that is not directly from the title page, it must be enclosed in brackets [ ].

- Record author names as given, omitting titles and abbreviations unless needed for identification (Miss Jane, Mrs. John Smith, Martin Luther King, Jr.) or if title of nobility (Sir Winston Churchill, Baroness Orczy, but not President John F. Kennedy). (*AACR* 1.1F7, p. 1-15)

- MARC tags included in this area are: 245, 246, 1XX, 7XX.

Generic example:

- 100 1_ $aLast name, First name, $ddates.

- 245 xx $aThis is the title of my work :$bit has a subtitle /$cit has an Author ; and an Illustrator. (A non-book item would also include a $h between $a and $b.)

- 246 3_ $aThis is part of the title that is important to trace (usually from 245 $b)

- 700 1_ $aLast name, First name, $ddates, $erelator. (as in ill. or ed.)

Specific examples:

- 100 1_ $aStubbolo, Garth, $d1952-

- 245 14 $aThe great waste mystery $h[kit] :$brecycling in Delaware /$cdeveloped and written by Garth Stubbolo and Teren Gordon in cooperation with the Delaware Solid Waste Authority.

- 246 3_ $aRecycling in Delaware

- 700 1_ $aGordon, Teren, $ejoint author.

- 710 2_ $aDelaware Solid Waste Authority.

Exercises: Apply 1XX, 245, 246, 6XX, 7XX, and 082 tags as necessary (check your answers against a library database):

6.19. This is a non-fiction book about frogs and toads. On the title page as:

> FROGS AND TOADS
> BY REBECCA K. O'CONNOR

6.20. This is a book on tape; it is fiction about a boy, Harry Potter, and the trouble he runs into in his second year at the wizardry school of Hogwarts. On the cassette tape as:

> HARRY POTTER AND THE CHAMBER OF SECRETS
> J.K. Rowling
> Read by Jim Dale

6.21. This videotape is a biography of the jazz pianist Duke Ellington based on the book of the same title. On the title screen as:

> Duke Ellington
> The Piano Prince and his Orchestra

Immediately preceding the title screen are credits for Scholastic and Weston Woods. The animated tape is based on the book by Andrea Davis Pinkney, illustrated by Brian Pinkney although those names show up only in the credits at the end of the movie.

The rest of the tags in this area are not commonly assigned by school library media specialists, but they do appear in records so it is helpful to at least know what they are even if you never assign them yourself.

- *111 & 711 Tag: Main Entry, Meeting Name.* Should you ever find yourself in the position of cataloging a conference proceeding wherein the name of the conference is the main entry, this is the tag in which you would enter that information.

- *130 Tag: Main Entry, Uniform Title. AND 240 Tag: Uniform title.* These are two tricky tags that may not be all that uncommon in a record especially if cataloging a translation or a folk tale. These two tags are used to record the authoritative title of the item. Enter information here only if you have it from a copy cataloging resource. If the surrogate record does not have a 100, 110, or 111 tag, then use the 130 tag to record the uniform title; if there is a 100, 110, or 111 tag, then use the 240 tag. Uniform title is the term used to refer to a single title that pulls together all derivations of that title together. For example, it might not be uncommon for records of different translations of *The Fisherman and His Wife* to include a 130 tag that looks like this: 130 0_ $aVon dem Fischer und seiner Frau. $lEnglish. But, one would only see that if the item in hand is truly a translation and not a loose adaptation. Unless you see this tag in copy cataloging, it's best to not try to create it.

Area 2: Edition – Tag 250

We come now to the part of the record that notes the edition statement and information about the publication of the information package. We have stopped jumping around the record and from here on out will pretty much just go in numerical order of the fields.

When there is edition information on the item, we enter that data in the 250 tag. To determine if you need a 250 tag in your record or not, look for keywords such as "edition," "revision," "complete," "abridged," "version," and similar words, but not "printing," which does not, in the publishing world, indicate a new edition. Likewise, a reprinted edition is recorded in a note rather than in this edition area. The 250 tag is not repeatable and both indicators are blank. There are four valid subfields in this tag, but most often the only subfield we will need to be concerned about is the $a into which all edition information is entered. This tag ends in a full stop. Here are some examples:

- On the item as: Second Edition
  - Typed into the record as: 250 __ $a2nd ed.

- On the item cover as: NEW EDITION   *and*

- On the title page as: FOURTH EDITION
  - Typed into the record as: 250 __ $a4th ed.
  - Note here that even though the cover has the words "new edition," the title page takes precedent as the chief source of information and therefore we record the edition statement as the "4th ed." rather than as "new ed."

- On the item as: MAC/Windows version
  - Typed into the record as: 250 __ $aMac/Windows version.
  - In cataloging for school library media collections, we must be vigilant about computer programs. The version of the program can determine on which type of computer the program will run. Most of the time, the version of the program is on the disc itself.
  - Note that the edition statement is recorded as it appears on the item without capitalizing all of the letters. The word "version" is not abbreviated; *AACR* directs us to abbreviate the words "edition" (ed.) and "revised" (rev.) but not "version." We suspect that it is only a matter of time before "version" is abbreviated as well.
- On the item as: First published in 2004
  - This is not a valid edition statement and is not recorded in this tag in the MARC record. It may be an important statement (depending on the item) and may be recorded in a note (5XX tag), but it is not recorded here in the 250 tag.

---

250 Tag: Edition statement: (Area 2)

- "Transcribe the edition statement as found on the item." (*AACR* 1.2B1, p. 1-19)

- Use abbreviations for numbers (1st, 2nd, 3rd, etc.) and for the words revision (rev.), edition (ed.), enlarged (enl.). Write out other edition words such as abridged, complete, unabridged, version.

- Chief source of information for books is the title page, verso title page, and colophon. Chief source of information for non-book materials is the item itself first and then the accompanying label and container information. Any other information supplied must be enclosed in brackets [ ].

- This area ends in a full stop unless other punctuation (e.g. brackets) is used.

- The 250 tag is not repeatable.

- Both indicators are blank.

- For our purposes, there is only the $a in this tag, although there are three other valid subfields.

Examples:
       250 __ $a1st American ed.
       250 __ $aVersion 1.01.

Librarians often ask if they have a paperback and hardback edition of the same title, must they create two records, one for each format. The answer is, "Maybe." One will find records that describe an item with several ISBNs: one for the hardback, one for the paperback, and one for the library-binding version. Technically, if the items are identical in every sense of the word, e.g. pagination, illustrations, copyright date, then one may include both "versions" in one bibliographic record. If, however, the items differ in any way, then more records must be created. If there are two books with the same title and all other parts are the same but one has emblazoned upon it, "25th Anniversary Edition" or "Reading Rainbow Edition" then, ridiculous as this may seem, a second record should be created. However, if the cover reads, "As Seen on Reading Rainbow!" then it is all right to put both copies on one record. The question of when one needs to create a new record is explored in more detail at the end of this chapter.

Area 3: Material Specific Details – Tag 255

Area 3 covers information for non-book items only. In this area, information regarding the scale of maps, the type of computer file, and musical format is recorded. Much of this information goes beyond the needs of the school library community. In this section we will consider recording map scale only. The information for computer format is increasingly being considered optional information; therefore, we will not cover it here. For information about cataloging music items (e.g. scores, librettos) one should refer to the Library of Congress MARC page (http://www.loc.gov/marc) and the resource page on cataloging from the Music Library Association (http://theme.music.indiana.edu/tech_s/mla/index. htm#cataloging). For our purposes, then, we will examine only the 255 tag, Cartographic Mathematical Data.

The 255 tag. This tag is used to note the scale of a map. Atlases, cataloged as books, are not included here. Simply stated, one should enter the information supplied on the map or globe. The information is typically stated in a ratio (1:XXXX). If scale information is not available, use the phrase *Scale not given* in this area and go on with your cataloging. This tag is repeatable, meaning, if you have a double-sided map with two different scales, both could be recorded in two separate 255 tags. The indicators are both blank. There are nine available subfields for this tag; however, we will focus only on the subfield used to state the scale, $a.

Tag 255: Material Specific Details for Maps Only (Area 3)

- Give the scale of a cartographic item as a representative fraction expressed as a ration (1:XX) (*AACR* 3.3B1, p. 3-11)
- Chief source of information is first the item itself, second any labels or container information.
- This area ends with a full stop.
- Both indicators are blank.
- For our purposes we use only $a.
- The 255 tag is repeatable if there is more than one scale on the map.

Examples:

       255 __ $aScale 1:90,000.
       255 __ $aScale not given.

Area 4: Publication, Distribution, Etc. – Tag 260

According to *AACR*, this area is used to note "information about the place, name, and date of all types of publishing, distributing, releasing, and issuing activities" (1.4B1, p. 1-22). Information in this area is also referred to as the imprint and includes publication information in the following order: place of publication, name of publisher, and date of publication. In some cases, there are multiple places and names given on the item.

The 260 tag. The tag for Area 4 is the 260 tag and both indicators are blank. According to the Library of Congress, this tag is repeatable; however, most school library media automated programs will not accept a second 260 tag and it is better to learn how to enter information about mixed publication data within a single 260 tag than it is to try to repeat the tag. There are eight valid subfields in this tag; we will focus on three of them: subfields a, b, and c. For book materials, the chief source of information for this tag is the title page. We know that children's materials often supply publication information on the verso of the title page or at the back of the book, perhaps an attempt to maintain the integrity of title page illustration. In this case, information may be taken from the verso and the back of the book without including this information in brackets. For non-book items, the chief source of information is that part of the item that appears to us most similar to a title page. This includes title screens for computer programs and videos, labels on the items for cassette tapes, disc surface for CD-ROMs and DVDs, and the item itself for maps.

The place of publication is recorded in the first subfield, $a. If a second $a is required, it is preceded by a semicolon (;). In cataloging children's materials, we often find multiple places of publication supplied by the publisher. We are directed by *AACR* to record the place that is most prominently placed on the item, and if that place is not in the country in which the item is being cataloged, then add a local place name if possible. Hence, a publishing company residing in both New York and Chicago with New York as the place listed first would simply be referred to in $a as New York. In this case, there is no need to reference Chicago. However, if the prominently named place was London and then New York was named second, we would be obliged to have two $a's—one for the first named place (London) and one for the named place in the United States (New York) (assuming we are cataloging in the United States). We are also directed to include the name of the state or country, if necessary, to clarify the place of publication. If there is no place named and it is impossible to determine even a country of publication, use the abbreviation S.l. to note this. (In our examples, we will assume we are cataloging in the United States.)

- On the item as: Westport, Connecticut * London
  - Typed into record as: 260 __ $aWestport, Conn.
    - Note here that Connecticut is abbreviated. *AACR* tells us to include the country, state, province if it appears on the item and if it is deemed necessary to distinguish that place from other places of the same name (*AACR* 1.4C3, p. 1-23). Not knowing how many other Westports there are, we opt to include the state name because it is included on the chief

source of information. We are also directed by *AACR* that it is all right to abbreviate names of states, provinces, and so forth using their approved list given in Appendix B of *AACR*. To our knowledge, that list is not available freely online and so we include the list of abbreviations for the United States in the box below.

- Note also that we do not include a second $a for London. Since London is mentioned second and we are not cataloging in England, we are not obligated to include that information in our record. If, however, we were cataloging in England, we would then have to include a second $a for London.

Abbreviations for U.S. states (taken from AACR, Appendix B, B.14 "Names of Certain Countries, States, Provinces, Territories, Etc.")

Alabama	Ala.	Nebraska	Neb.
Arizona	Ariz.	Nevada	Nev.
Arkansas	Ark.	New Hampshire	N.H.
California	Calif.	New Jersey	N.J.
Colorado	Colo.	New Mexico	N.M.
Connecticut	Conn.	New York	N.Y.
Delaware	Del.	North Carolina	N.C.
District of Columbia	D.C.	North Dakota	N.D.
Florida	Fla.	Oklahoma	Okla.
Georgia	Ga.	Oregon	Or.
Illinois	Ill.	Pennsylvania	Pa.
Indiana	Ind.	Rhode Island	R.I.
Kansas	Kan.	South Carolina	S.C.
Kentucky	Ky.	South Dakota	S.D.
Louisiana	La.	Tennessee	Tenn.
Maine	Me.	Texas	Tex.
Maryland	Md.	Vermont	Vt.
Massachusetts	Mass.	Virginia	Va.
Michigan	Mich.	Washington	Wash.
Minnesota	Minn.	West Virginia	W. Va.
Mississippi	Miss.	Wisconsin	Wis.
Missouri	Mo.	Wyoming	Wyo.

AACR instructs not to abbreviate any state not given in this list.

- On the item as: Published in Canada by Tundra Books, 481 University Avenue, Toronto, Ontario M5G 2E9 Published in the United States by Tundra Books of Northern New York, P.O. Box 1030, Plattsburgh, New York 12901
  - Typed into record as: 260 __ $aToronto, Ont. ;$aPlattsburgh, N.Y.
  - Because this is a Canadian publication and the Canadian information is given first in the item, we have to list both the Canadian and U.S. places of publication. Note the use of the space and the semicolon before the second $a and the abbreviations for Ontario and New York.

- On the item as: Allyn and Bacon Boston London Toronto Sydney Tokyo Singapore
  - Typed into the record as: 260 __ $aBoston
  - Notice that we don't much care about the other places of publication and that we did not further identify Boston by adding the state name, partly because it is not given on the item and partly because if one says "Boston" in the United States, one can be pretty sure the reference is to Boston, Massachusetts.

- On the item as: HarperFestival a division of HarperCollins Publishers
  - Typed into the record as: 260 __ $a[New York?]
  - Notice here that no place name has been given on the chief source of information. We looked up HarperCollins on the Internet and found their headquarters are in New York. We think that New York is the place of publication; however, we bracket the information because it is supplied by us, the catalogers, and was not found on the chief source of information. If we were really sure New York was the place, we would not have the question mark; it's included because we're really guessing here.

The name of the publisher is recorded in $b in the shortest recognizable form. The $b is preceded by a colon (:). Although *AACR* allows us to shorten the name of the publisher, school library media specialists should be careful shortening names of publishers beyond recognition. Remember, there are divisions of companies that need to be recorded so that they become differentiated from each other, for example, Scholastic, Scholastic Professional Books, and Scholastic Reference. As with place names, sometimes an item is published simultaneously by more than one publisher. (Dorling Kindersley books are a good example of this.) If there is more than one publisher, a second $b preceded by a colon is added.

- On the item as: Random House San Francisco, California
  - Typed into the record as: 260 __ $aSan Francisco, Calif. :$bRandom House
  - This is a straightforward example following the rules with no surprises.

- On the item as: HarperFestival a division of HarperCollins Publishers
  - 260 __ $a[New York?] :$bHarperFestival
  - Note that we use the name of the division and not the name of the larger publishing house in this example.

- On the item as: First published in 1983 Macdonald & Company (Publishers) Ltd … London © Macdonald & Company 1983 Adapted and published in the United States by Silver Burdett Company, Morristown, N.J.
  - Typed into record as: 260 __ $aLondon :$bMacdonald & Co. ;$aMorristown, N.J. :$bSilver Burdett Co.
  - Notice how we separated the information about each publishing house using the repetition of the $a and $b with the appropriate ISBD punctuation (;$a and :$b). However, we keep the place names with the publishers. In other words, we do not list first all of the places and then all of the publishers.
  - Notice the first place name is given only as "London." Although there are at least two cities of London that produce publications, England and Canada, the unwritten rule is that London alone refers to the city in England.

Finally, $c contains information on the date of publication. This subfield is immediately preceded by a comma (,); however, unlike the other two subfields, there is no space between the information in $b and the punctuation (comma) in $c. There may be some confusion in recording dates of items that are reissued in anniversary or paperback form. For example, is the date of publication for the 25th anniversary edition of *Roll of Thunder, Hear My Cry* 1976 or 2001? While the copyright for the text is 1976, this particular edition was published in 2001 and that is the date used in $c. Similarly, paperback editions will have the most recent date recorded in $c. Do not, however, confuse this with a printing date that is generally ignored by catalogers. The publication dates may be (but are not required to be) followed by the copyright date.

- On the item as: 2001 Libraries Unlimited, Inc. Englewood, Colorado
  - Typed into record as: 260 __ $aEnglewood, Colo. :$bLibraries Unlimited,$c2001.
  - Notice the abbreviation of Colorado and the abbreviation of Libraries Unlimited, Inc. to just Libraries Unlimited.

- On the item as: Hyperion Books For Children New York Text copyright © 2003
  - Typed into record as: 260 __ $aNew York :$bHyperion Books for Children,$cc2003.
  - Notice the $c, we see the subfield designation c, but we also see a second c. That second c denotes the date is a copyright date rather than a publication date.

- On the item as: Allyn and Bacon Boston London Toronto Sydney Tokyo Singapore Copyright © 2000, 1979, Allyn & Bacon
  - Typed into record as: 260 __ $aBoston :$bAllyn & Bacon,$cc2000.
  - Notice it is not necessary to include in this tag the date 1979. In this example, we have a new edition and can assume the text is different enough so that it really doesn't matter that the text was also copyrighted in 1979. However, with the republication of older stories, we may want to make a reference to the older date. See the next example.

- On the item as: Copyright ©1958 by Dr. Seuss. Copyright renewed 1986 by Theodor S. Geisel … Published in New York by Random House, Inc., and simultaneously in Toronto, Canada, by Random House of Canada, Limited. Educational edition published by Houghton Mifflin Company, Boston.
  - Typed into record as: 260 __ $aNew York :$bRandom House,$cc1986, c1958.
  - In this example, it behooves us to include the older date because of the nature of copyright laws and the history of Dr. Seuss books. The book was originally published in 1958 in a time when copyright had to be renewed after a certain length of time. Additionally, it is important to show that the book in hand is not a first edition publication. Therefore, we include both copyright dates to show that this is a more recent publication of the old text.

---

260 Tag: Publication, Distribution, etc. (Area 4)

- "In this area, record information about the place, name, and date of all types of publishing, distributing, releasing, and issuing activities." (*AACR*, 1.4B1, p.1-22)
- Chief source of information for books is the title page, verso title page, and colophon. Non-book materials use that part of the item that best resembles a title page.
- Record place named as given on item (San Francisco, Calif.) and add name of country or state to name of city of publication if needed for further identification. Multiple places are recorded thus: first named place, then add subsequent places if displayed prominently, also add a place in the United States if not the first named place (or prominent), and it is provided on the item. If no place is named, supply a guess in brackets or use the abbreviation for sine loco: [s.l.].
- Record publisher's name in the shortest recognizable form; if in doubt, write it out, but generally avoid words such as publisher, company, limited, incorporated. If no publisher is named, use the abbreviation for sine nomine in brackets: [s.n.].
- Record most recent date of publication, but avoid printing dates. Include guess of dates in brackets.
- Both indicators are blank.
- The tag is repeatable but for our purposes it is best not to do so. Subfields a and b within the tag may be repeated.
- This tag ends in a full stop.

Examples:

      260 __ $aBoston :$bLittle, Brown,$cc2004.
      260 __ $aNew York :$bAladdin Paperbacks,$c2001, c1999.

Exercises: Put this information into the proper 260 tag:

6.22. On the title page as:
      New York   Scholastic
On the verso of the title page as:
      © 2005 by the author

6.23. On the tape cassette as:
      New York London Franklin Watts 2003

6.24. On the end of the film as:
      National Geographic Productions © MCMXCVIII
(National Geographic is located in Washington, D.C., but the location isn't on the item, you have to supply it.)

Area 5: Physical Description – Tag 300

In this area, we record the physical extent of the items, e.g. number of pages, disks. The tag is 300 and both indicators are blank. In theory this tag is repeatable but some library systems will mark a record as invalid if there is more than one 300 tag. There are nine valid subfields, but we will limit our discussion to four subfields: a, b, c, and e. The chief source of information is the item itself. For the most part, because the item itself is the chief source of information, we don't have to worry about bracketing information. The exception to this is in pagination for books—see below.

In $a, we record the *extent* of the item. For books, it is the number of pages, for other materials it is the number of items and the running time if applicable. Children's picture books are notorious for not including any pagination. In past practice it has been the responsibility of the cataloger to count the number of pages and include that number in brackets. That practice still holds true for adult books, but for children's books, we have the option of recording only the number of volumes thus: 1 v. (unpaged). This option is a great timesaving device.

Examples:

- 300 __ $a32 p.
  - The last page of the item is numbered "32."

- 300 __ $a1 v. (unpaged)
  - This item is a children's book and the pages are unnumbered.

- 300 __ $axii, 300 p.
  - There are 12 pages numbered in Roman numerals and then 300 pages numbered in Arabic numerals. If the numbering continued from page xii to page 13, then we would not include the Roman numerals. If there were less than 10 pages with Roman numerals, we would ignore them.

- 300 __ $a[198] p.
  - The pages are unnumbered and since it is not a children's book, we had to count the pages (front and back are each one page) and enter them into the record using brackets.

- 300 __ $a1 videocassette (VHS) (68 min.)
  - We have the option on videotapes to show what kind of tape it is (Beta or VHS if applicable). These days, if we say videocassette we are really referring to the VHS type of tapes. The smaller tapes would not get the VHS designation, but the 8mm dimension will be recorded later in this tag. This is an option; it is nice to make the VHS designation here, but it is also information recorded in the notes area of the record.

- 300 __ $a2 sound cassettes (ca. 40 min.)
  - Because the running time is part of the physical extent of the item, it is recorded here in the $a. Note in this example we have an approximate running time and use the abbreviation "ca." to note this. Since there are two tapes here, the total running time is recorded here (which may account for

the approximation). In theory, one should preview the item with a stop-watch to record the exact running time. Most of us are content to take the time off of the container if it is supplied or we simply leave this information out if it is not supplied. If at all possible, the time should be recorded. This is especially true if it is an item that might be used for classroom instruction, as teachers need to know how long the item runs when planning out a lesson.

- 300 __ $a1 computer optical disc
  - The term "computer optical disc" covers a multitude of products including CD-ROMs, DVDs, and laser discs. We have the option to use the vernacular term here so that if you have a CD-ROM, you can use that term instead. It might well be more useful to your patrons to use the vernacular since many K-12 students (and classroom teachers) may not equate "computer optical disc" to a CD. We use the formal term here because, more likely than not, that is what you will see from a record from LC. However, should you choose to use the vernacular, the example may be rewritten as:
    - $a1 CD-ROM
                      or
    - $a1 DVD
  - Notice too the use of the term "disc" vs. "disk." According to the Library of Congress, "disk" refers to those 5 1/4 and 3 1/2 inch square "floppy" disks while "disc" refers to those round laser read items.

- 300 __ $a10 sound discs (10 hours)
  - We have seen a couple of ways that one can note recorded sound: as a cassette, computer optical disc and its related vernacular terms, and now as a sound disc. In referring to CD-ROMs, we recommend picking a term and sticking to it. In the school environment, we are probably most likely to be more comfortable with the vernacular "CD-ROM" than any of the other terms. You should, however, be familiar with the other terms as you will see them in copy and purchased cataloging.
  - Notice that we have the time stated in terms of hours rather than minutes. *AACR* allows us to use the time as stated on the item. While we can convert the time to minutes, it is much tidier to use the hour as a measure of the time. Shorter playing times, those generally less than three hours, will usually be seen in copy cataloging recorded in terms of minutes.

The next subfield, $b, refers to "*other physical details*" such as illustrations, sound, color, and other characteristics and is immediately preceded by a colon (:). Past practice dictated that catalogers list in detail the type of illustrative matter, for example, the number of color plates, maps, or forms when cataloging book materials. In the cataloging simplification program, catalogers are given the option of simply stating that the item has illustrations of some kind using the abbreviation "ill." Surrogate records will show a variety of types of illustrative matter including maps, portraits, and forms showing us the mix between past practices, detailed cataloging, and simplified cataloging. We may exercise the option, however, of simply using "ill." to show that the item contains some type of illustrations. This option is sometimes unsatisfying, as we may want to say more about the illustrations. We have the option of using other terms such as "col." for color illustrations, "b&w" for black and white illustrations, and "chiefly ill." for an item that is mostly illustrative. We can also use "photos" for items that have photographs as illustrative matter. This may be a critical aspect to note especially when looking at scientific works where photographic illustrations would be preferable to drawings. We always have the option to be more detailed in this subfield but for most of us it will be enough to say "ill." when cataloging book items. For non-book items we apply here as necessary the following: the type of recording (digital or analog), the presence of sound (sd.), the material composition (e.g. wood, plastic), or if the picture is black and white (b&w) or color (col.). Examples:

- 300 __ $a32 p. :$bcol. ill.
  - Here we have a 32 page book with color illustrations. Remember we could just use "ill." as we see in the next example. Notice the space and the colon before the $b.

- 300 __ $a1 v. (unpaged) :$bill.
  - Here we have an unpaged children's book with illustrations. We do not know if the illustrations are in color or not. These days we can probably assume they are in color.

- 300 __ $a1 videocassette (VHS) (68 min.) :$bsd., col.
  - Here we have a vhs videotape that runs 68 minutes, has a sound track, and is in color.

- 300 __ $a2 sound cassettes (ca. 40 min.) :$bdigital

- In the case of tapes we record the type of recording (digital or analog) here *if that information is readily available* (usually it is written on the item itself). If the information is not readily available, we will skip this subfield.

- 300 __ $a1 computer optical disc :$bsd., col.

- Here we have a computer disc of some kind. We don't know if it is a CD-ROM or a DVD, but we do know it has a soundtrack and the pictures or movies displayed are in color.

In the third subfield, $c, we record the *dimensions of the item*. This subfield is preceded by a space and a semicolon (;). Books are described by height in terms of centimeters measuring to the next centimeter, for example, a book measuring 23 1/2 centimeters is recorded as 24 centimeters. We use the abbreviation "cm." to note the measurement. If the book is wider than it is high, one also includes that measurement. Similarly, if the book is more than twice as high than it is wide, both measurements are given. This will account for the times in copy cataloging when one sees height and width measurements. Despite this rule, most non-catalogers will measure only the height and that seems to satisfy the requirements for $c. Record the dimensions of non-book materials thus:

- Tape cassettes have a standard measurement and so no $c is used.

- Videotapes must include the measurement, 1/2 in. unless the tape is the smaller size in which one uses 8mm.

- Measurements for computer disks are also given in inches; 3 1/2 in.

- CD-ROMs and DVDs are measured by diameter; 4 3/4 in.

- The dimensions of items in a container, as in a kit, are given in terms of the container in centimeters; "in box 12 x 4 x 24 cm."

Examples:

- 300 __ $a32 p. :$bcol. ill. ;$c23 cm.
  - This is by far the most common of the 300 tags; we see here very simply the number of pages, that there are color illustrations, and that the book is 23 centimeters high. Notice the punctuation, the space, and colon before $b and the space and semicolon before $c.

- 300 __ $a1 v. (unpaged) :$bill. ;$c15 x 32 cm.
  - Children's books are often short and long. In this example we see a book that is not as high as it is wide and so, following the rules (*AACR* 2.5D2, 2-18), we include both measurements here.

- 300 __ $a1 videocassette (vhs) (68 min.) :$bsd., col. ;$c1/2 in.
  - This is your standard videotape physical description tag with no surprises.

- 300 __ $a12 sound discs (240 min.) :$bdigital, stereo ;$c4 3/4 in.
  - "Books on tape" are now often found on compact discs; here we have 12 of them in stereo; as with all discs, they are measured in diameter; $4^3/_4$ inches.

- 300 __ $a2 sound cassettes (ca. 40 min.) :$bdigital.
  - This is not a typographical error. Keep in mind that tape cassettes are assumed to be of standard size and so there will be no $c for a standard tape cassette. If, however, one was to catalog one of those mini tapes, such as are found in small dictation machines, then we would record the size of the tape in centimeters thus, 3 x 5 cm.

- 300 __ $a1 computer optical disc :$bsd., col. ;$c4 3/4 in. *or*

- 300 __ $a1 DVD :$bsd., col. ;$c4 3/4 in.
  - In the second example we clearly see this is a DVD and we feel better knowing that our students will know exactly the kind of item they have retrieved.

- 300 __ $a14 sound discs :$bdigital ;$c4 3/4 in.
  - Notice that the sound disc is measured in the same way as a DVD.

- 300 __ $a1 globe :$bcol., on plastic stand ;$c23 cm. in diam. *or*

- 300 __ $a1 globe :$bcol., plastic coated paper gores over plastic core, mounted on spindle crowned by a plastic clockface, in a movable metal meridian circle, on plastic base ;$c23 cm. in diam.

- Many of us shy away from cataloging globes because we think they are so difficult to describe, but we can see here that this is not the case. We have a globe in color that is on a plastic stand and it measures 23 centimeters in diameter. Easy!

- The second example shows us that there can be much more to describing a globe! Both examples are correct. The first is closer to what we may do ourselves given that we are not professional catalogers. All of the information in the second example is critical to the scholar but may be unnecessary to the school-aged student (or K-12 classroom teacher for that matter). The question is, when does the school library media specialist need to include all that detail and when can he or she opt to condense it? The school library media specialist should always try to be as complete in cataloging as possible. Be complete, be correct, be careful, but don't be neurotic! Do the best you can do and then move on. The first example is accurate according to *AACR*.

The last subfield we will discuss for the 300 tag is $e, which describes *accompanying materials*. This is an important subfield in schools because so many of us have books with accompanying tapes. This subfield is immediately preceded by a space and a plus sign (+). Examples:

- 300 __ $a32 p. :$bcol. ill. ;$c23 cm. +$e1 sound cassette (30 min. : analog)

- Here we see a 32-page book with color illustrations with a tape cassette that runs 30 minutes. The 300 tag ends in a full stop unless there is some other punctuation. The parenthesis at the end of this line counts as that other punctuation.

- Notice the structure of the information in the $e and how it parallels that of the subfields a and b in this tag.

- 300 __ $a1 CD-ROM :$bsd., col. ;$c4 3/4 in. +$e1 user's manual + 1 book. *or*

- 300 __ $a1 CD-ROM :$bsd., col. ;$c4 3/4 in. +$e1 user's manual (13 p. ; 14 cm.) + 1 book (32p. : ill. ; 23 cm.)

- In this example, we have the computer program with a user's guide and an accompanying book. The way accompanying materials are described may vary. In these examples, we see a user's guide and a book. Technically both examples are correct, although the second example is a little "more" correct because it includes more information about the manual and the book. That extra information is helpful especially with respect to the manual as those small folded sheets that serve as both the disc cover and instructions. These may be referred to as "manuals" even though they are little more than folded sheets of paper. Compare the folded sheet of paper to a true manual of many pages and you can see why it would be helpful to have a more complete tag. However, if time is short, the first example will suffice.

- Again we point out the parallel structure of the parenthetical information and the fact that the close parenthesis serves as the ending punctuation for this tag.

300 Tag: Physical Description (Area 5)

- "Record the extent of the item by giving the number of physical units in Arabic numerals and the specific material designation as instructed in subrule .5B." (*AACR*, 1.5B1, p.1-13)
- MARC tag is 300. This tag is repeatable and both indicators are blank. This area ends in a full stop unless other punctuation is present.
- Chief source of information is the item itself.
- Books
  - Record pages in terms of the last numbered page. If preliminary pages are 10 or more, include that number (in Roman or Arabic numerals according to the item itself). If pages are not numbered and item is a children's book, give information as: 1 v. (unpaged); otherwise, count pages and state in brackets [ ].
  - Give "ill." for illustrative matter; may include b&w or col. for black and white or color illustrations respectively. May opt to further define type of illustrations in terms of maps, charts, forms, and so on.
  - Measure book in terms of centimeters; round up to the next centimeter if needed.
- Non-Books
  - Record the number of items being cataloged
  - Record the sound and illustrative aspects as applicable
  - Measure the item itself in inches or the container in centimeters

Examples:

Book:

    300 __ $a32 p. :$bcol. ill. ;$c25 cm.

Book with accompanying material:

    300 __ $a32 p. :$bill. ;$c23 cm. +$e1 sound cassette (ca. 30 min. : digital)

VHS with accompanying material:

    300 __ $a1 videocassette (VHS) (30 min.) :$bsd., col. ;$c1/2 in. +$e1 book (32 p. : col. ill. ; 18 cm.)

DVD:

    300 __ $a1 DVD (233 min.) :$bsd., col. ;$c4 3/4 in.

Exercises: Create 300 tags for the following:

6.25. Unpaged book for children with color illustrations that measures 23 1/2 centimeters.

6.26. A 164 page book for young adults with color photographs. It measures 14 centimeters high and 30 centimeters wide.

6.27. A DVD that runs 190 minutes, is in color, and has a soundtrack. It is the standard measurement; it comes with a book that is 64 pages with illustrations and measures 20$\frac{1}{2}$ centimeters.

Area 6: Series Statement – Tags 4XX

Area 6 is used to record any series titles connected with the item. A series may be numbered, such as Babysitter's Club, number 44, or unnumbered, such as Let's-Read-And-Find-Out Science Series. There is no hard and fast rule for knowing when a statement is truly a series statement or when it is simply a gimmick devised by the publisher. The inclusion of the word "series" is, obviously, a red flag. However, the absence of that word does not necessarily mean the statement is not a valid series statement. The chief source of information for books is the title page, verso of the title page, and the colophon. For non-book materials, the item itself, including title screens, labels attached to the item, and containers and external labels, forms the source for a series statement.

The tags involved in this area may be somewhat confusing. Time was that one would record series information in the 400, 410, 411, 440, 490, 800, 810, 811, 830, or 840 tags. If one used the 490 tag then it was accompanied by one of the 8XX tags. The rules have changed slightly with less use of the 490 and 8XX tags, although those tags can still be used. In terms of copy cataloging, one should take a good look at any 4XX tags. Some systems index only 440 tags. This means that users looking for series titles that are in the surrogate record in any 4XX or 8XX tag, except the 440, will get negative search results. Thus, in accepting copy for your cataloging, be watchful for 4XX tags other than the 440 tag.

For the purposes of this text, we will discuss only the 440 tag. This simplifies the discussion but still maintains technically correct cataloging practice. In the 440 tag, the first indicator is blank and the second indicator is used for non-filing characters. This second indicator is the same as the second indicator for the 245 tag. There are seven valid subfields in the 440 tag; we will discuss two of them: a and v. In $a, we enter the title of the series. If a series is numbered, that number will be recorded in $v. In $v, we will find the designation for issue number, "no." or volume number, "v." *There is no full stop in this tag.* The reason is that automated systems automatically enclose this information in parentheses ( ), which act as the final punctuation. If your system does not automatically add this punctuation, you must add it yourself because all series statements are enclosed in parentheses. Most items in school library collections have only one series statement if any at all. Should you find yourself with an item that has two or more series statements, include each series statement in its own 440 tag.

Examples:

- 440 _0 $aChoose your own adventure ;$vno. 58
  - Here we have number 58 in the Choose Your Own Adventure Series. Notice the use of the space and semicolon before the $v. Notice too the abbreviation of number (no.). If this was volume number 58, we would see $vv. 58.

- 440 _4 $aThe Asian American experience
  - This is an unnumbered series. Notice the capitalization of "Asian" and "American" but not "experience."

Note in these examples that the information looks very much like the 245 tag. First words and proper nouns only are capitalized, but unlike the 245, there is no final stop at the end of the tag.

It is worth mentioning here the relationship between the 4XX tags and some of the 8XX tags as those tags will be seen in older cataloging. In the past, it was the practice of catalogers to use the 490 tag to enter a kind of unofficial series statement and then use the 8XX tags to make a more official statement. The 490 tag usually had the name of the series as it appeared on the item and the 8XX tag would have the more authoritative form. A good example of that can be seen here for the Marc Brown Arthur chapter books. On the item, we see the series statement "A Marc Brown Arthur Chapter Book." So we wonder which of the following options would be the right one for our series statement.

1. 440 _2 $aA Marc Brown Arthur chapter book
2. 440 _0 $aMarc Brown Arthur chapter book
3. 440 _0 $aArthur chapter book

The Library of Congress uses the 490 and 800 tags to refer to this series:

490 1_ $aMarc Brown Arthur chapter book   *and*
800 1_ $aBrown, Marc Tolon. $tMarc Brown Arthur chapter book

Structuring the tags like this helps to put all of the series that have come from the original Arthur books together under the name of the creator, Brown, Marc. However, unless the system used is indexing the 490 and all of the 8XX tags, searchers will only be able to find this series by searching Brown, Marc Tolon (not a very likely search in the elementary school). Most systems have a way to establish that both the 4XX and 8XX tags will be indexed for series searching; however, we believe we are better off using multiple 440 tags. Using only a 440 tag (that can be repeated in the record) helps us to make sure that all forms of this series are available for searching by our patrons. So the answer to the question of which of those 440 tags (shown above) should be in the record is: two and three. Notice that examples one and two are the same with the exception of the inclusion of the word "A." The first example uses the non-filing characters in the second indicator; however, some systems are not recognizing that indicator and so we are much better off simply dropping the initial article and using a 0 in the second indicator spot as we have in that second example.

There appears to be a trend in children's literature to publish early readers based on characters of older favorite stories. One such example is Harold and the Purple Crayon. What was once a small picture book is now the heading for a beginning reader series. With our example we have the following: *Harold and the Purple Crayon Under the Sea.* Harold, Clifford, Arthur, and others appear in beginning readers that may or may not relate to their original works. Regardless, the books appear and we need to decide if we have a title or a series statement. In other words, is "Harold and the Purple Crayon" a series title or a title proper? Fortunately, we have other library databases to help us make this decision. For our example, we find that the Library of Congress has decided "Harold and the Purple Crayon" is indeed a series title and the title proper is "Under the Sea."

Area 7: Notes – Tags 5XX

This part of the MARC record is referred in general as the 500 tags or five-oh-oh tags. It refers to the part of the surrogate record where one supplies the user with some important facts about the item, such as awards, summaries, reading levels, and other aspects of the item about which users may be (or should be) interested. There are 48 different 5XX tags! Most systems offer help in using the 5XX tags for entering notes and these hints should be followed if possible. When in doubt, however, it is always possible to use the 500 (general notes) tag. We will limit our discussion to 12 of the 48 tags: 500, 504, 505, 508, 511, 520, 521, 526, 538, 546, 586, and 590. There is no chief source of information for this area. Information is recorded as needed and may or may not be part of the item itself. Therefore, brackets are not used here.

In this part of the MARC record, we get into something called "display" or "display constants." What this means is that there is a code given to the computer so that it will automatically display a word or phrase when the record is retrieved from the OPAC. Not every 5XX tag makes use of the display constants, but those that do save us lots of typing time. The display constant is defined in the indicators of some of the tags described below. Some systems seem to make use of the different displays by allowing the librarian to alter the indicators as needed, when in reality, no matter what indicators are used the display will always be the same thing (usually "Note"). This is not wrong but it becomes a waste of time to go through the exercise of using the proper indicator values if the system has only one default. If you have a system like this, you may be tempted to ignore the indicators; however, this is not a good idea. Having a record that is as correct and accurate as possible, even if the current system ignores some standard policies, will help in the long run. Chances are very good that the system will be upgraded and eventually will be following standardized practice or the library will migrate to a newer and better system. If the records are good, clean, and follow standardized rules and policies, the changes to upgraded or new systems is a much easier process. Therefore, in the sections following, we will describe the indicators to use to code for various display constants even if not all school library automation programs are up to (excuse the expression) code.

Tag 590 — Local Notes. We begin with the last named tag as it is often the first of the 5XX tags that new catalogers want to use. The 590 tag should be used with caution. Most systems do not index the 590 tag, therefore, information entered in that tag will not be retrievable via any kind of search. Using the 590 tag means that the data entered apply only to the specific item in hand. Even a note describing a specific variation of the item in hand, such as an autographed item or an item with missing pages, should be noted in the 500 tag. One could argue that notes dealing with the item within the specific library, such as "This item should be kept in the non-circulating section of the library," might be placed in the 590 tag; however, these are exceptional cases and this information could still be placed in the 500 tag. If you are going to use the 590 tag, the indicators are blank and the tag should end in a final stop. This tag is repeatable.

Tag 586 — Awards Note. Continuing in our backward motion, we come to the 586 tag. This tag is used to record any awards connected to the item such as Caldecott, Newbery, and the like. Up until very recently, many vendors did not index this tag and so school library media specialists included this information in the 500 tag. Old habits die hard and one will still find even very recent records with awards information in the 500 tag instead of the 586 tag. Before making use of this tag, check that your system indexes this tag. If it does not, then use the 500 tag. In the 586 tag, the indicators are blank. Information about the award is entered in $a, and no other subfields are needed. *This tag does not end in a full stop.* There is no formal format for this tag. We suggest that for ease of searching, the cataloger defines his or her own format for this tag as shown in the examples below.

Examples:

- 586 __ $aCaldecott medal winner, 1999
- 586 __ $aNewbery Honor Book award winner, 2000
- 586 __ $aAcademy award winner, best picture, 2001

Tag 546 — Language Note. This tag is used to make a text note about the language of the item. As we have already seen, the 041 tag is used to enter the code for the language of the item. However, this code does not show up in the public catalog, and, as of this printing, is not available for searching purposes in most school library automated systems. It should be noted in the surrogate record if the item is a translation or bilingual, or has some other linguistic features. We do this in the 546 tag. This tag is repeatable; the indicators are blank; all information is entered in the $a; and it ends in a full stop.

Examples:

- 546 __ $aBilingual text in English and Spanish.
  - Item includes both English and Spanish languages.
- 546 __ $aTranslated from the French, *Les Miserables*.
  - Item is an English translation of the French work, *Les Miserables*.
- 546 __ $aAll songs in French.
  - Item is a sound recording of French songs sung in French.
- 546 __ $aOpen signed in American Sign Language.
  - Item includes an open window with a signer using American Sign Language.
  - This could also be applied to items with closed or open captions.
- 546 __ $aIncludes soundtracks in English and Spanish.
  - Item has dual soundtracks in English and Spanish.

Tag 538 – System Requirements Note. Here one records information regarding the type of equipment needed for proper viewing of multimedia information packages. In the school library environment, this is most commonly applied to videotapes and computer programs. Typically, this tag is not indexed for keyword searching. The 538 tag is repeatable; both indicators are blank; and it ends in a full stop. Examples:

- 538 __ $aVHS.
  - The item is a video tape in vhs format.
- 538 __ $aSystem requirements: 66MHz 486DX or faster; 8MB RAM, 16MB recommended (16MB RAM for Windows 95/Windows 98); minimum 20MB hard disk space; Windows 3.1x or Windows 95/Windows 98; 640 x 480 display, 256 colors; High and True Color supported for Windows 95/Windows 98; Windows compatible sound device; video and sound cards compatible with DirectX for Windows 95/Windows 98; 2X CD-ROM drive or faster.
  - This information usually comes from the container. One may enter as much or as little information as deemed necessary for the user to understand the equipment needed to run the program. See next example.
- 538 __ $aSystem requirements: Windows 2000 or higher; DVD player.
  - Notice in this example and the previous one, information is separated by semicolons.

Tag 526 — Study Program Information Note. Here one records information about the item as it relates to school, classroom, or other curriculum standards. Notes such as, "For Mrs. Smith's Fall AP English class," can be entered here. Most often one will see data on reading program items, such as the Accelerated Reader and Reading Counts programs. As with all the specialized 5XX tags, before investing time and energy to this tag, check first to confirm that the system being used indexes information from this tag. The first indicator is marked 0 for a display constant "Reading program," or 8 for no computer-generated display. Some school library systems do not recognize the first indicators in which case you will need to enter the display constant information yourself (use 8 as the value). The second indicator is blank. This tag is repeatable and ends in a full stop. Tag 526 uses 10 subfields; we will describe the use of subfields a, b, c, d, and z. The first subfield, $a, is used to enter the name of the reading or study program, e.g. Accelerated Reader. Subfield b is used to enter the *interest* grade level of the item as assigned by the given program and may be expressed in terms of a range of grades. This information is added without explanatory text. For example, entering "5-10" means the interest grade levels are five through 10, that is, students in grades five through 10 would be *interested* in this item. This information isn't always expressed in grade numbers, but may also be seen in terms of more general ranges such as LG for "lower grades," MG for "middle grades," and UG for "upper grades." Subfield c is similar to $b except that it notes the *reading* grade level, again without explanatory text. Thus, entering 6.0 in $c would mean the item is for a student *reading* at the first semester of the sixth grade. Putting the two subfields together, one sees an item that is of interest to students in grades five through 10, reading at or above the sixth grade level. Subfield d is used to enter the point value of the item. These are not values to make up. The values will be supplied by the reading program, or will be on the item itself. Finally, $z is used to enter public notes such as, "This item may be used for credit in the Accelerated Reader program and Mrs. Smith's AP English class for Fall 2001." It is important to remember here that we are talking about standardized reading programs. If an item simply has a grade level attached some way, that information is recorded in the 521 tag (see page 143). You will notice in the examples that there is nothing to lead us to understand what all of this means; however, most systems have automatically assigned information to each of the subfields so the user will understand the information. In the examples, we show how the information is typed into the MARC record and how it displays in the OPAC. Examples:

- Typed into the record as: 526 8_ $zThis item may be used for Mrs. Smith's second period English class, Spring 2005.

- Appears in OPAC as: Notes: This item may be used for Mrs. Smith's second period English class, Spring 2005.
  - This is just a public note informing students that Mrs. Smith considers this item as proper reading for her second period English class during the Spring 2005 semester. (It will be up to Mrs. Smith to keep the librarian informed of the changes to her list.)

- 526 0_ $aReading Counts $b5-10 $c6.0 $d1.0.

- Appears in OPAC as:
  Study Program: Reading Counts
  Interest level: 5-10
  Reading level: 6.0
  Title point value: 1.0

- This reading program note says the item is of interest to fifth through 10th grades. It is at a sixth grade reading level and worth one point.

■ 526 0_ $aAccelerated Reader $bLG $c2.0 $d0.5.

■ Appears in OPAC as:
Study Program: Accelerated Reader
Interest level: LG
Reading level: 2.0
Title point value: 0.5

- This reading program note says the item of interest is for the lower grades reading interest level. It is written on the second grade reading level and is worth .5 points.

- Notice in both of these examples, the name of the reading program is capitalized because it is a proper noun.

Tag 521 — Target Audience Note. Often neglected or misused, the 521 tag designates the general audience level of the item. This may be expressed in terms of a broadly expressed audience level (e.g. for teen readers), a reading interest level (e.g. for reading interest grade levels four through eight), a reading grade level (e.g. for reading grade level 6.0), or a Lexile level (e.g. Lexile 450). This differs from the 526 tag because it does not refer to a formal study program, or even a local classroom level. It is a repeatable tag. The indicators are used to note the type of formatted information being supplied, or one may opt to use a free form of entry as will be explained later. School library media specialists should take a careful look at their systems to determine how this information will be entered. Some systems index this information only if it is in a specific format. Other systems do not index this information at all. In which case, one should enter the data in the correct field (521), but may also opt to enter the information in an indexed field, such as 520 or 500, to make sure the information is retrievable.

In this tag, the first indicator is used to define a display constant. There are seven choices in the display constants for this tag; we will concern ourselves with the five most common of them. The display constants in the first indicator place are defined as follows:

blank = Audience
0 = Reading grade level
1 = Interest age level
2 = Interest grade level
8 = no display generated

When applying these indicators, keep in mind that not all automated systems make use of all possible indicators. (This is true even up to the Library of Congress.) Before going through the trouble of applying a myriad of indicators, check your system and see how it displays the 521 field. You may only need to use the default (usually blank but sometimes 8) and fill in your own information in the a subfield. The second indicator is blank. This tag ends in a full stop.

Most of the time, reading interest, age, or grade level information is taken from the item itself. Publishers will sometimes note the reading or age level of an item using either standardized or in-house scales. This information in books is usually found on the verso of the title page or the back cover and is most often recorded in cryptic notation such as, RL: 1.5-2.3 (meaning reading grade levels 1.5-2.3) or 008-010 (meaning appropriate for children ages eight to 10). If the information is not on the item, it is all right to supply this information using other resources or your own best guess. Again, you are cautioned to check on the retrieval program of the automated system to be sure the information input in tag 521 is retrieved accurately. If all else fails, remember that using the 500 tag is a viable (if not completely correct) alternative to using the 521 tag. In doing this, however, information should also be recorded in the correct tag (521) as automated systems are constantly improving and we want to make sure that we don't have to go back to records to put information in the correct tag.

Here are some examples of the use of the 521 tag:

- First indicator blank
  - MARC entry: 521 __ $aAll grade levels.
  - OPAC display: Audience: All grade levels.
    - Note that the blank value of the first indicator makes the system automatically insert the word "Audience" into the display in the OPAC. This is the "display constant." The value of the first indicator dictates the display constant, which changes as the value changes as we see in our next examples.

- First indicator 0
  - MARC entry: 521 0_ $a3.1.
  - OPAC display: Reading grade level: 3.1.

- First indicator 1
  - MARC entry: 521 1_ $a008-010.
  - OPAC display: Interest age level: 008-012.
    - The information has been typed into the MARC record as it appeared on the item. The librarian may well have elected to type in "8-10" instead (leaving out all of those zeros) as a way of making this more readable for the user.

- First indicator 2
  - MARC entry: 521 2_ $a4-5.
  - OPAC display: Interest grade level: 4-5.

- First indicator 8
  - MARC entry: S21 8_ $aMPAA rating: PG-13.
  - OPAC display: MPAA rating: PG-13.
    - Note here that there is no prefatory word or phrase before the audience information. If you opt for the first indicator value 8, you need to be sure

that you have supplied enough information so that the tag makes sense to the user.

- In some systems, this is the default indicator. If this is true in your system, you will need to type in the phrase or word you want to see preceding this information.

Tag 520 — Summary, Etc. This tag is used to record a summary note for the item in hand. This is a very important part of the surrogate record. This tag is indexed for keyword searching; therefore, a good summary statement can be critical in retrieving just the right item. Summary statements also work hand in hand with subject headings to help clarify for the user the content of the item beyond the definitions of the subject headings. Summary statements should be short and succinct but should also include enough key words to be useful in the retrieval process. The Library of Congress creates summary statements that are as succinct as possible. Be aware, however, those succinct summaries may not get to the heart of the item. For example, the summary statement assigned by the Library of Congress for the book, *Hope Was Here*, reads: "When sixteen-year-old Hope and the aunt who has raised her move from Brooklyn to Mulhoney, Wisconsin, to work as waitress and cook in the Welcome Stairways diner, they become involved with the diner owner's political campaign to oust the town's corrupt mayor." While it may seem to do justice to the story, one can't help but wonder why there is the accompanying subject heading, "Cancer — Fiction." The summary of the book neglects a very important part of the book; the diner owner has leukemia and it is because of this that Hope and her aunt decide to help out. One may argue that the summary and the subject heading together are used to show all aspects of the content of the book in an efficient way without redundant information. For a school population, however, this may be unsatisfactory and we may feel the need to "doctor" the summary a bit to help out our students. Remember, Library of Congress records are not inviolate, and one may certainly change information to make the catalog record more useful for specific audiences.

The 520 tag is repeatable and ends in a full stop. There are six possible first indicators to define specific display constants. Most of us are using this tag to enter a summary statement, and therefore, it is suggested to go with the default of most systems, which is a blank value for the first indicator. Systems vary in the definition of a blank first indicator. In most cases, the display generated will be "Note(s)" or "Summary" either term is appropriate and therefore the various other first indicator values will not be discussed here. The second indicator is blank. There are five subfields in the 520 tag. Again, we will concern ourselves only with the first subfield, $a, as the other subfields add information that is not directly applicable in the school environment. Recall also that reading and interest grade levels may not be retrievable in a satisfactory manner in the 521 and 526 tags. Therefore, that information may be added in the 520 tag. In dealing with multimedia items, we find that it is extremely helpful to put in the front of the summary the type of material being described. This not only alerts the user to the type of item retrieved, but also serves to differentiate information packages with the same title. For example, here are three different summaries for Dr. Seuss' *Green Eggs and Ham*:

- 520 __ $aSam wants his friend to try a new taste treat in this story in rhyme.
  - Summary statement for the book.

- 520 __ $aIn this board game, for 2-4 players ages 4-6, players move from space to space to help Sam convince his friend to try a new taste treat.
  - Summary for the board game.

- 520 __ $aWindows or Macintosh CD-ROM computer program that allows the reader to follow along as Sam convinces his friend to try a new taste treat.
  - Summary for the computer program, with the emphasis that it is a CD-ROM.

Notice that in all three examples, the description of the content of the item is essentially the same. What differs is the helpful information right up front that tells the user if the item is or is not a book. Although this information is available in other parts of the record, we believe it is a very useful aide for users to have this information right up front in the summary statement.

Tag 511 — Participant or Performer Note. This tag is used for non-print visual materials that include an on-screen narrator or other presenters including performers. Also, performers for sound recordings are entered in this tag. This tag is repeatable and ends with a full stop. As with the 520, the cataloger is advised to use the default indicators provided in the cataloging program, most likely this will be a blank in both the first and second indicator places. Information about the item is entered in $a. There is no standard way of entering this information.

Examples:

- 511 __ $aPerformed by the American Ballet Theatre, featuring Mikahail Barishnikov and Gelsey Kirkland.
  - This is a film of the American Ballet Theatre. We emphasize here the stars of the production.

- 511 __ $aAnchor, Jon Stewart.
  - Stewart is mentioned here because we have a visual information package and he is on screen. If he was off screen, that is we could hear his voice but not see him, he would be entered in a 508 tag (see page 147).

- 511 __ $aNarrator, Raffi ; with voice characterizations by Robin Williams.
  - Here we have a sound recording where Raffi is doing the narration and Robin Williams is providing voices for different characters. It is important to note that this is a sound recording. If it was a videotape or other type of visual information package, and Raffi and Williams were off screen, they would be noted in the 508 tag.
  - Notice the use of the space, semicolon, space between the two different jobs of narrator and voice character, just as we saw in the $c of the 245 tag.

Tag 508 — Creation/Production Credits Note. Again, referring to non-print visual and sound materials, this tag is used to define the people involved in the production of such items. Producers, directors, off-screen narrators, program creators, and persons with similar responsibilities are entered in this tag. This tag is not repeatable, both indicators are undefined; and the tag ends in a full stop. Information for this tag is entered in $a. The amount of detail entered here depends on how much information is needed for the collection. Often in the school environment, only those names deemed "important" or "recognizable" by the cataloger are entered. However, even if not recognizable, one should, at the very least, enter the names of the producer and director. Examples:

- 508 __ $aExecutive producer, Steve Linden ; project director, Kris Moser ; programmers, Glenn Axworthy … [et al.] ; editorial consultant, Sharon Lerner.
  - As with the 511 tag, we see the separation of responsibilities by space semicolon space.
  - Notice the use of the ellipses after Glenn Axworthy. Computer programs often have an army of programmers responsible for the project. If more than three names are listed, list the first only followed by "et al."

- 508 __ $aProducer, Northern Lights Productions ; director, Ken Burns ; narrator, Tom Brokow.
  - Note that it may be desirable to search by name of the people or corporate bodies entered in tags 511 and 508. If the names are entered only in the 511 and 508 tags, this will be possible only in using a keyword search. To search by personal or corporate name (usually defined as author or name search in online systems), one must also enter the names in the 700 or 710 tags.

Tag 505 — Formatted Contents Note. This tag is used to enter full or partial contents information for the information package. It is a particularly useful note when cataloging anthologies that tend to fill the shelves of school library media centers. One would never list all of the stories included in such works, but one might opt to bring out those works connected to the school curriculum. For example, consider a collection of stories by Washington Irving that includes the *Legend of Sleepy Hollow*. Let's assume this story is read every year as part of the fifth grade English language arts curriculum. As the school library media specialist, you want students and teachers to know that this item includes the needed story. One way to do this is to enter the information in the 505 tag.

The 505 tag is repeatable; the second indicator is blank; and the tag ends in a full stop. There are four values for the first indicator defining various display constants: 0, 1, 2, and 8. The 0 indicator displays the constant "Contents:"; the 1 indicator displays the constant "Incomplete contents:"; the 2 indicator displays the constant "Partial contents:"; and the 8 indicator displays no constant at all. Before showing examples, we must first consider the difference between "Incomplete contents" and "Partial contents." To enter incomplete contents is to say that all the parts of a multipart item are not in the library. For example, the library has only part one of a two part video. In this case, the first indicator value would be entered a 1. Partial contents means that the entire item (or all parts) are in the library, but the cataloger chooses to enter only some of the contents information, as in the case of a large anthology where only some of the titles are important to the users.

Examples:

- First indicator value 0 (full contents)
  - MARC entry: 505 0_ $aWriting a paragraph -- Writing a short story -- Writing a novel.
  - OPAC display: Contents: Writing a paragraph -- Writing a short story -- Writing a novel.
    - Note how the different chapters of this book are separated by a space, double dash, space.
    - Note too how only the first word of each chapter title is capitalized, just as we have in the 245 tag.

- First indicator value 1 (incomplete contents)
  - MARC entry: 505 1_ $avol. 1. The early life of George Washington -- vol. 5. George Washington retires.
  - OPAC display: Incomplete contents: vol. 1. The early life of George Washington -- vol. 5. George Washington retires.
    - In this example, the library owns only volumes one and five of the multi-part set, and so we make a note of those titles but not to the other volumes which do not exist in this library.

- First indicator value 2 (partial contents)
  - MARC entry: 505 2_ $aLegend of Sleepy Hollow / Washington Irving -- Tell Tale Heart / Edgar Allan Poe.
  - OPAC display: Partial Contents: Legend of Sleepy Hollow / Washington Irving -- Tell Tale Heart / Edgar Allan Poe.
    - In this example we have a collection of short stories, but we are only naming the two stories that are important for retrieval in our library, those of Irving and Poe.
    - Note the repetition of the ISBD punctuation, that is, the space, slash, space between the title of the work and the author, just as we saw in the 245 tag.
    - Note also that in order to retrieve these titles by author or title searches, we need to create added entries; see 7XX earlier in this chapter.

- First indicator value 8 (no display constant)
  - MARC entry: 505 8_ $aSongs included on this CD are She Loves You and Yesterday.
  - OPAC display: Songs included on this CD are She Loves You and Yesterday.
  - Here we see the contents of a disc in an unformatted contents note.

Tag 504 — Bibliography, Etc. Note. This tag is used to note the presence of a reference section within or connected to an item including bibliographies, discographies, webliographies, filmographies, or any other reference materials associated with an information package. This tag is repeatable; both indicators are blank; and the tag ends in a full stop. Information for this tag is entered in $a. Catalogers can opt for the generic bibliography statement or include a note that is more specific (see examples). If an index is also included as part of the item, that information is added here. However, if there is only an index and no reference section, then the index information is recorded in the 500 note.

Examples:

- 504 __ $aIncludes bibliographical references. [Generic bibliography note]
- 504 __ $aIncludes bibliographical references and index. [Generic bibliography note with index]
- 504 __ $aBibliography: p. 238-250.
- 504 __ $aFilmography: p. 126-128.
- 504 __ $aDiscography: p. 130-132.

Tag 500 — General Note. This is the catchall place for information. Here one states source of title information for electronic resources, language of item if it is bilingual or not English, index information (see also tag 504), information supplied by cataloger, and other variances of the item. More often than not, if some information needs to be provided and it is unclear where or how the information should be entered, the 500 tag is the place. The 500 tag is repeatable, and both indicators are blank. The information is entered in the $a, and the tag ends in a full stop. There are no limits on the format of this tag. The only time this tag must appear in the record is in the cataloging of electronic resources. In this case, the cataloger must include a 500 tag to explain the source of the title proper. This rule is given because there are many sources for the title of electronic resources including the container, manuals, discs, or the title screens. It is the nature of electronic resources that the title may vary slightly on all of these sources; therefore, as a courtesy to other catalogers, the source of the title is given. Examples:

- 500 __ $aTitle taken from title screen.
  - Electronic resource wherein the cataloger actually loaded the program and took the title from the screen, versus simply using the title on the container or disc.
- 500 __ $aTitle taken from the cover.
  - Book that lacks a title page, for example a board book; recall that in books the chief source of information is the title page; if there is no title page, the source of the information must be explained in a 500 note.
- 500 __ $aTurtleback edition.
  - 500 __ $aReading Rainbow book.
  - Sometimes in children's publishing, statements are made that look like edition or series statements but are really publishing gimmicks. The statements,

"Reading Rainbow Book" or "Turtleback Book" are examples of this. You will want to make mention of these statements and this is the place to do so.

- 500 __ $aTitle supplied by cataloger.
  - Not a common occurrence in the school environment if one is talking about books, but as we make more and more attempts to catalog more unusual items such as Web pages, posters, and library equipment, we should see notes like this with increasing frequency.

Summary for 5XX Tags, Notes (Area 7)

- Take data recorded from any suitable source. (*AACR* 1.7A2, p. 1-38)
- Include information about variations in title, statements of responsibility, language, editions, and other information pertaining to the areas of description.
- Include information not accountable in the other areas, e.g. awards, audience interest level, and curriculum connections.
- Most 5XX tags are optional except in the case of electronic resources wherein one must explain the source of the title.
- Tags discussed include 504, 505, 508, 511, 520, 521, 526, 538, 546, 586, and 590, each with its own meaning. If all else fails, use the generic 500 tag.

Examples:

> 586 __ $aCaldecott award winner, 1999
> 546 __ $aBilingual text in English and Spanish.
> 538 __ $aSystem requirements: Windows 2000 or higher; DVD player.
> 526 0_ $aAccelerated Reader $bLG $c2.0 $d0.5.
> 521 2_ $a4-5.
> 520 __ $aWindows or Macintosh CD-ROM computer program that allows the reader to follow along as Sam convinces his friend to try a new taste treat.
> 511 __ $aNarrator, Raffi ; with voice characterizations by Robin Williams.
> 508 __ $aProducer, Northern Lights Productions ; director, Ken Burns ; narrator, Tom Brokow.
> 505 2_ $aLegend of Sleepy Hollow / Washington Irving -- Tell Tale Heart / Edgar Allan Poe.
> 504 __ $aIncludes bibliographical references and index.
> 500 __ $aIncludes index.

Exercises: Try to convert this information into the appropriate 5XX tag:

6.31. This book won the Caldecott Medal in 1995.

6.32. This film is closed captioned.

6.33. This CD-ROM requires the Windows 2000 or higher operating system, a printer, and a color monitor.

6.34. This book is for children at the reading grade levels three through five, and it has a bibliography and an index.

6.35. This book on disc is narrated by Gerard Doyle.

6.36. This DVD presents a performance of the actor Hal Holbrook portraying the author Mark Twain and was produced and directed by Ken Burns.

- 500 __ $aIncludes index.
  - As mentioned in the discussion of the 504 tag, if an item includes both a reference section (e.g. bibliography) and an index, then the note is made in the 504 tag. If there is an index only, then the note is here in the 500 tag.
- 500 __ $a"This tape is a school production for field testing with the Great Waste Mystery. It is not intended to be a final version." — videocassette.
  - This note is in quotes because it is text taken directly from the item. While we put this in quotation marks, a direct quote of a summary statement from the CIP data need not be enclosed in quotation marks.
- 500 __ $a"Written for families who have to deal with life-threatening diseases."
  - When a note is in quotation marks and there is no explanation as to the origin of the quote (as we see in the previous example), then we have a quote from the title page of a book. In this case, this statement is on the title page, but it is not information that belongs in the 245 tag. Since we need to account for it, we do so in the 500 tag.

5XX Tag Summary. There are a variety of uses for the 5XX tags; these are only some of them. All of the 5XX tags are listed with brief descriptions at the Library of Congress MARC page: http://www.loc.gov/marc/ under Bibliographic Formats. For the most part, all information in the 5XX tags is optional to the bibliographic record. Nevertheless, after reading this section, one can see how much fuller the record is when this kind of information is included. The librarian who skips the 5XX tags is doing a disservice to his or her community.

Tag 740

Before closing our discussion of the 5XX tags, we need to examine a problem in information retrieval. Most of these tags discussed above are searchable through a keyword search. However, titles and names of people and corporations will not be retrieved in a name or title search if they exist only in the 5XX tags. In order to retrieve names and titles given in the 5XX tags, we have to make use of the 7XX tags. We have already discussed how to use the 700 and 710 tags to trace for personal and corporate names found in the 245 tag. We can also apply this practice for personal and corporate names found in the 5XX tags. Thinking back to our examples, people like Tom Brokaw, Raffi, and Robin Williams who appear in our 508 and 511 tags will also get their own 700 tag in the record just as if the name appeared in the 245 $c tag. But how would we retrieve a title found in the 505 tag, such as *Legend of the Sleepy Hollow*? We do this by using a *740 tag*. The 740 tag is repeatable; the first indicator is for non-filing characters; the second indicator is blank; and the tag ends in a full stop. A word of caution; older records (prior to 1993) will have the 740 serve the purpose of added title entry for information from the 245 tag. If you see this, you must move this information to the 246 tag. The 740 tag is used for "uncontrolled" added title entries and serves to allow us to account for titles found in the 5XX part of the MARC record. Examples:

- If the Contents note looks like this:
  505 1_ $avol. 1. The early life of George Washington.

- Then the 740 tag will look like this:

    740 4_ $aThe early life of George Washington.

- *But* if our Contents note looks like this:

    505 2_ $aLegend of Sleepy Hollow / Washington Irving -- Tell Tale Heart / Edgar Allan Poe.

- Then we trace for the authors, not the titles, and we have this instead:

    700 1_ $aIrving, Washington. $tLegend of Sleepy Hollow.

    700 1_ $aPoe, Edgar Allan. $tTell tale heart.

    The library automation system should be set up to be able to retrieve the information in the $t of the 700 tag. If you check this and your title does not get retrieved, then you will also need to add a 740 for the title.

Additional Cataloging Considerations

There are three more questions that are often asked by new school library media specialists: When do I need to create a new record? Should I catalog my periodicals? How do I catalog my equipment? We will address those questions here.

Equipment

Yes, you should catalog your equipment. If you are responsible for knowing where each laptop, projector, and media cart is, then you need to catalog it. Some programs allow for cataloging an item and then "hiding" it from the general user. This is a matter of investigation of the system in your own library. Regardless of whether or not you can keep the equipment from displaying in your OPAC, it is to your benefit to catalog the equipment for which you are responsible and to check out anything that moves from your library into a classroom. Do not be afraid of cataloging these items. Control of your equipment is very important, and the following template should allow you to organize these items quickly and easily.

Leader: make sure you have entered the proper code for your item. In most cases you will want to change the monograph code "a" to "r" for realia or three-dimensional object. For those systems with iconic representation of material types, using the "r" code will change the book icon to some other icon. For example, the Follett system uses an arrowhead to represent a three-dimensional object. Most automation systems provide help in changing the Leader tag.

008 Tag: Again, depend on the system to help in fixing the information in this tag. Remember that, like the Leader, this tag is a series of codes. If your system does not offer good help in modifying this tag, contact the vendor. To help you out, recall that the 008 tag as a series of placeholders for material-specific information. Those spaces (spaces 18-34) in the line will have to be altered to define the piece of equipment. In general, you will be safe with these codes: nnn (no running time), r (for accompanying instructional materials if including a user's manual, otherwise leave this blank), r (material type is realia), and n (technique question is not applicable). Again, consult your system for the placement of these codes.

245 Tag: Use the best description for this item; consider how you and your users (classroom teachers) will refer to the item. Both indicators will have the value 0. Use "realia" in $h. Examples:

- 245 00 $aPanasonic LCD projector $h[realia]

- 245 00 $aDell Inspiron 4100 laptop computer $h[realia]

- 245 00 $aHitachi portable DVD player $h[realia]
  - Notice that there is no closing punctuation at the end of the tag as the brackets take the place of the full stop.
  - Notice that we did not enclose the title proper in brackets. Here is where we have bent the rules just a little. Try to use the title that is given to the item by the company. However, if that title is not descriptive of the item, modify it as little as possible to fit your needs.

260 Tag: Enter as completely as possible the place, name, and date of manufacture. Examples:

- 260 __ $aJapan :$bSony, $c2004.

- 260 __ $aSecaucus, New Jersey :$bPanasonic, $c[2004]

300 Tag: Enter the description of the item. Describe the individual item, not the number of copies of the item you have. If you have 10 tape recorders, describe the one item in the 300 tag and let the copy number or holdings area tell you how many of the item you have in your library. Examples:

- 300 __ $a1 camcorder +$e1 user's manual + 1 power cord + 1 battery pack.

- 300 __ $a1 camcorder +$e1 accessories pack.

- 500 __ $aAccessories include: 1 carrying case; 1 AC adapter with DC power cable; 1 battery pack; 1 shoulder strap; 1 lens cover; 1 vhs adapter; 1 digital photoshot disc; 1 memory card; 1 PC connection cable; 1 instruction manual.
  - Notice how the accessories to the item are given in $e (accompanying material). We have two examples. In the first, the cataloger lists all of the accessories in the $e. In the second example, the cataloger opts to list the accessories separately in a 500 note tag. Either is acceptable, although, technically, the first example is more correct.

5XX Tags: Enter notes as needed. We have seen where we might have a long list of accessories in our notes. We might also make a note of the location of the item(s), the access or use of the item(s), and a description of the item(s). Remember, these tags are optional and you should make use of them as they best suit your own needs. Examples:

- 520 __ $aVHS camcorder that is capable of direct playback on television or thru VCR with playpak adapter and also capable of digital photos that can be downloaded to a PC.

- 500 __ $aUses VHSc type cassette.

- 500 __ $aPATRON MUST SUPPLY TAPE.

- 082 14 $a[EQUIP SONYDVD 2005] $214

- 245 00 $aSony DVD player $h[realia]

- 260 __ $a[Japan] :$bSony Corporation, $c2005.

- 300 __ $a1 DVD player +$e1 user's manual + 1 power cord + 1 connector cord.

- 500 __ $aFor use in library media center only.

- 500 __ $aPlease ask at Circulation Desk for this item.

- 500 __ $aThis item requires four "C" batteries, not supplied by library.

- 500 __ $aMedia cart with LCD projector and wireless laptop kept in workroom and available for classroom project circulation only. Please see Mrs. Kaplan for availability.

Periodicals

Serials (or periodicals) cataloging is a field unto itself and there are catalogers who organize no other material types than serials. Most school library media specialists tend not to catalog their serials due in part to the ephemeral nature of the beast. Many school library media specialists do not hold on to back issues of popular magazines partly because they don't have the space to do so and partly because, for research purposes, students rely on databases rather than the printed copies of periodicals. Most of the time there is no problem in not cataloging serials as long as the serials do not circulate and it is not a problem if issues go missing. But if control is (pardon the expression) an issue, then cataloging is the answer.

Creating a serials record for temporary control and circulation is a relatively simple process. Like cataloging other materials, it is an easy job to find a record for a serials title. Creating an original record for a serials title can also be an easy process. Please note that the directions that follow are for the creation of a minimal record. At no other time in this text do we advocate for the creation of minimal records; catalog once, catalog completely is our motto. However, the nature of the use of periodicals in school libraries is such that all we really need is a minimal record. We really need only four to five tags for adequate retrieval and control of our periodicals. Minimally we include the following tags:

- 022 for the ISSN;

- 245 for the title;

- 082/092/900 for the call number; and

- 500 for a statement about the volumes in the collection.

Additionally we may want to have:

- 650 for a subject heading; and

- 520 for a contents note.

Notice we have omitted the publication data (260) and the physical description (300). Some systems require a 300 tag in the surrogate record. In this case, you could simply use "1 v." and be done with it.

Sample generic and specific minimal serials record (without the Leader or 008 tags)

Generic Record
022 __ $aenter ISSN here with hyphens.
245 00 $aEnter title here.
500 __ $aNote about how many volumes the library has.
520 __ $aSummary statement.
650 _0 $aSubject heading.
Classification number
Specific Record
022 __ $a0163-7061
245 00 $aNewsweek.
500 __ $aLibrary keeps current year only.
520 __ $aCurrent events magazine.
650 _0 $aCurrent events $vPeriodicals.
PER NSWK

Notice we did not put the call number in a MARC tag. Most programs have specific tags for the call number (e.g. 082, 092, 900) and so we have left the tag number out. What we did supply is an example of what a call number for a periodical might look like. We suggest preceding the number with "PER" to note the item is a periodical. We follow this, not with a true Dewey classification number (although you could do that), but rather with an abbreviation of the title of the periodical (in this case, Newsweek). In the record there will be a place for specific copy information. There you will add something specific for each issue, for example, 090105 for the Sept. 1, 2005, issue, or, Fall05 for the Fall 2005 issue. Playing around with this model in your own system will help you decide how you want to create control for your periodical titles. It really is not difficult and is worth the time to organize that part of your collection.

Creating New Records

As we promised in our discussion of the 250 tag, we will now discuss when it is necessary to create a new record. In adding new items to your collection, you will run into a situation where the item in hand is the same but different from the item already on the shelf with an existing surrogate record. Usually the difference is in an ISBN or publisher's statement. The question then arises as to when an item can be tacked on to an existing record and when a new surrogate record needs to be created.

Most of the time, a change in the ISBN is not enough to warrant the creation of a new record. The paperback and hardback printings of a book can be dealt with in the same record assuming that ISBN is the only difference between the works.

What then constitutes a reason for creating a new record? In some cases it is very easy to recognize when two copies of the same information package warrant two different surrogate records. However, sometimes it is difficult to tell if the item in hand is a different edition or if someone is playing fast and loose with publication data. This is especially evident in books with such statements as, "Book Fair Edition," or "Published by X with permission from Y for school book fairs."

AACR defines *edition* for books as: "All copies produced from essentially the same type image (whether by direct contact or by photographic or other methods) and issued by the same entity" (p. D-3). That "entity" word is important to us. Even if it appears to be a different edition, for example, "Reading Rainbow edition," if the publisher is the same as the original publication, then the information package in hand is *not* a new edition and can be added as a second copy to the existing surrogate record. We can say then that any time the publisher changes we have a new edition and should create a new surrogate record. However, *AACR* throws in something else to consider in defining edition for materials other than books and electronic resources stating, "All copies produced from essentially the same master copy and issued by the same entity. *A change in the identity of the distributor does not mean a change of edition*" (D-3, emphasis added). What then do we do with the book fair edition or the reprint edition, and does it really matter if we simply add a copy to the existing surrogate record?

The short answer is yes; it does matter if a copy is added to an existing record or if a new record is added. As more and more of us have our catalogs available for searching through the Internet, as more and more of us find ourselves contributing to district, county, or state union catalogs, and as more and more of us depend on the cataloging from other libraries, whether one elects to add to, change, or create a new record is a matter of importance. We must be cognizant of the rules and abide by them as best as we can and still be efficient in adding new information packages to our collections. The box on pages 157-158 offers checkpoints for deciding if the work in hand is a new edition or not.

Conclusion

This chapter was designed to illustrate the basic design of the MARC21 format as it relates to the physical description of information packages commonly found in school library media collections. The surrogate record was described in terms of the MARC tags and the eight areas of description. We have seen that there isn't really a way of sequentially creating a surrogate record and that cataloging requires quite a bit of judgment on the part of the person doing the cataloging.

Determining new editions by a careful examination of edition and publication statements:

1. The LCCN (010 tag) is the biggest determinate for making a new record or adding to an existing record. The LCCN (Library of Congress Control Number) tells us that the Library of Congress has decided that this is a new work. If your information package in hand has a different LCCN from that on the existing record, you have a different work and must create a new record.

2. If the publication statement reads that the information package is a reprint by permission of the original publisher, then you have a new edition. Catalog the item according to the new publisher; that is, make a new record, and make a note (534) about the publication history, thus, 534 __ $aReprint. Originally published New York : Dell, 1995.

3. If the edition statement reads the item is a special edition, as in "Yearling Book," "Reading Rainbow edition," or "Book Club edition," those statements alone are not enough to warrant a new record.

    3.1. If however, the statements are accompanied by a difference in publisher, other than a change in the division of the publishing house (see next item), then a new record is required.

4. If the publisher named on the existing surrogate record is a division of the publisher named in the information package in hand (or vice versa) and the publication dates are the same, then do not make a new record. Example: Aladdin Paperback versus Simon and Schuster.

    4.1. It is sometimes difficult to know if you have a division of a publishing house or a separate house. These days, publishers buy up each other on a frequent basis and where we once had two separate publishers, we now have a publisher and a division. Just take a look at Random House (http://www.randomhouse.com) to see the names of what were once separate publishing houses.

    4.2. If in doubt, treat a "published with permission" as a change in edition and create a new record; that's the safest, if not the most expedient approach.

5. Hardback editions of a paperback book, such as those produced by Permabound or Turtleback, are not new editions.

6. If the title page and verso title page read one publisher, e.g. Little, Brown, and the back of the book reads that it is a special edition for a different publisher, e.g. Special Scholastic edition, catalog for the original publisher; that is, add to the existing record, and make a 500 note for Scholastic.

    6.1. However, you will need to check the ISBNs. Often in this case, there is the ISBN for the original publication on the verso of the title page that is different from the ISBN on the back of the book. If this is the case, we still recommend cataloging for the original publication with the edition note and a 020 tag for the special edition ISBN with an explanation, e.g. 020 __ $a1234567890 (Scholastic book fair)

    6.2. In this case, you have an original publication and Scholastic is simply a change in distributor; therefore, there is no warrant for a new record.

Example:

- On the title page the publisher is listed as Aladdin Paperbacks. The verso of the title page reads, "First Aladdin Paperback Edition, September 2000." Text and illustrations are copyrighted 1997. Aladdin Paperbacks is an imprint of Simon & Schuster, Children's Publishing Division. The item is available in hardcover from Atheneum Books for Young Readers. Hardcover ISBN is 0689805268. Aladdin paperback edition ISBN is 0689838921. Notice the beginning of each ISBN is the same, identifying it as the same publishing house. The surrogate record you have is for the Atheneum hardcover edition. The information package you need to catalog is the Aladdin Paperback edition. You have the hardback edition on your shelf. Do you add to the existing surrogate record or create a new one?

- You create a new record. It's the dates that tell us the answer. A new publication date, even if we have the same copyright date, tells us we must make a new record.

■ On the title page, the publisher is Arthur A. Levine. On the verso is the statement, "Published for Scholastic Book Fairs with permission by Arthur A. Levine." There is also a Scholastic date of 1999 and a Levine copyright date of 1999. The LCCN is the same as the one on the existing surrogate record, but the ISBN for the Scholastic version is different than the one for the Levine version. Do you add to the existing surrogate record or create a new one?

- You add to the existing surrogate record and make this a second copy. In reality, your students don't care which edition they have and they will get confused if they see two records for the same title. But, speaking as a cataloger, you have an edition that was created with the same type image with just a change in distributor. Make a second 020 for the Scholastic ISBN and be done with it.

Chapter 7

The Future of Cataloging

Introduction

More and more electronic materials are creeping into the school library environment. Indeed, most school library media collections are already suffering from lack of organized access to electronic data. In this chapter, some of the latest trends in cataloging and how those trends will affect school library media collections are discussed.

Effects of the Internet and Metadata

When schools began to have access to information on the Internet, there should have been a shift in the way school library media specialists dealt with that kind of current, topical information. However, the information was treated in very much the same way it has always been dealt with. The information was placed in a kind of electronic vertical file via electronic bookmarks. As school library media specialists found helpful sites for school assignments, the sites would be added to the bookmarks file. If the number of bookmarks became unruly (as they quickly did) some of the more savvy library media specialists would create bookmark files, exactly like the vertical files of the past. This method of accessing appropriate Web sites is inefficient and does a disservice to the learning community.

Catalogers in larger public libraries and academic libraries quickly recognized the need to control the information on the Internet. In the 1990s the MARC format for electronic data took shape. The record looks very similar to any other MARC record; the main difference is the inclusion of the 856 tag. This tag is a direct link from the record to the Internet site. The wave of excitement about this tag did not really catch on in school library media centers, which at that time were in the throes of the automation process. It was hard enough to worry about moving from the card catalog to the OPAC without having to worry about cataloging Internet sites. Besides that, the automated systems for schools had no mechanism for connecting to the Internet and so it would have been a waste of time to even try to catalog electronic data. That main tag, the 856 tag, was simply not an active part of the surrogate record in most systems and it was beyond the interest and expertise of most school library media specialists to argue for the tag. Today, however, most automated programs now have the capability to link to the Internet directly from the catalog. Library media specialists owe it to their users to create those links.

One reason it is important that we find the time to make these links in the catalog is to respond to pushes by the government and our communities to put filters on our Internet access in order to protect our children from the evil sites available to them. If links are made through the library catalog, library media specialists can show the detractors that we are doing our best to provide current, accurate information, in a controlled manner, to our students.

Another reason for creating links from the OPAC to Internet information is to reduce useless "surfing" time and help to ensure that students are looking at quality sites that have been previously evaluated (much as books are evaluated before purchasing them). Finally, having Internet information in the catalog helps students find print materials in the school library media center itself. Students will look up a topic and find a link to an Internet site *and* reference to items that are on the bookshelves. Thus, students will see for themselves the connection between print and electronic information.

Perhaps the most popular argument for not including Internet links in the catalog is the one that states there is no time to constantly review and update dead links. It is true that maintaining a collection of electronic resources can be more time consuming than maintaining a book collection. Nevertheless, library media specialists must find ways to take care of this problem in order to provide students with the most current information possible. The most obvious solution to the problem is to catalog only those sites that are stable. In the early days of Internet information, sites came and went very quickly. Today the authoritative sites have settled down. Keeping to government and education sites that tend to be stable will cut down on dead links. Additionally, there are some vendors who offer monitoring programs for schools with sites on their catalogs. Programs such as Follett's "Monitor" allow the librarian to register sites with Follett. Follett then monitors the site and notifies the librarian of any URL changes.

Metadata (1)

When the formats for cataloging different material types were integrated into one MARC format, catalogers paid special attention to traditional cataloging methods as they were applied to controlling *metadata*. Metadata is, literally, data about data. In some libraries, we have been cataloging metadata for years. Creating a record for a part of a book, rather than the entire book itself, is cataloging metadata. The *Reader's Guide to Periodical Literature* is an example of metadata cataloging. The way we retrieve clip art for our PowerPoint presentations is also a result of metadata cataloging. In today's cataloging world, metadata is usually used to refer to electronically based information most specifically that which is found on the Internet, but it can be any digital information (e.g. clip art in a file). It is helpful to catalog, or in some way attempt to control, this information precisely because it is so seemingly uncontrollable. With declarations that *AACR* and MARC are too oriented to book cataloging and not flexible enough to deal with the idiosyncrasies of electronic information packages (2), information managers have worked hard to develop more flexible means of organizing electronic information. Standards, such as SGML (Standard Generalized Markup Language), XML (e-Xtensible Markup Language), and TEI DTD (Text Encoding Initiative Document Type Definitions) (3), have been developed to create a way for catalogers to transfer data about the information package into a syntax understood by computer programs for information retrieval purposes. Actually, MARC is an example of such a communication tool, however archaic it may appear to be to cataloging theoreticians today.

It is exciting to see the changes in cataloging theory, and it is quite possible that the new edition of *AACR* will focus more on the "work" rather than on the "manifestation" as described earlier in this text, resulting in a need to understand metadata in the not too distant future. However the practice of cataloging in school libraries is often dictated more by the behavior of the automated library systems than it is by theoretical advances. Therefore, in school libraries, at least for now, we are left to using the MARC format for information retrieval and *AACR* for information organization.

Cataloging Hints

Cataloging not just the parent site but also sites within the parent site is not a difficult matter. Most automated programs have a template option for electronic resources. What we need to do is focus on the positive aspects of making these resources available to our students from a single source (the catalog) rather than from multiple sources, such as bookmarks, subject pathfinders, or search engines.

A few caveats: Be reasonable about the sites you select to catalog just as you are reasonable about those you include in your bookmarks. Government and education sites tend to have more stable addresses than do commercial sites. If changing URLs is a concern, stick to sites you are fairly certain will maintain current sites and stable locations. Most library automation programs allow the cataloger to select the type of information package being described (see discussion on the Leader tag). Before beginning the cataloging process, be sure the record being created is for electronic resources.

Figure 7.1. NASA Home Web Page (Captured August 18, 2005)

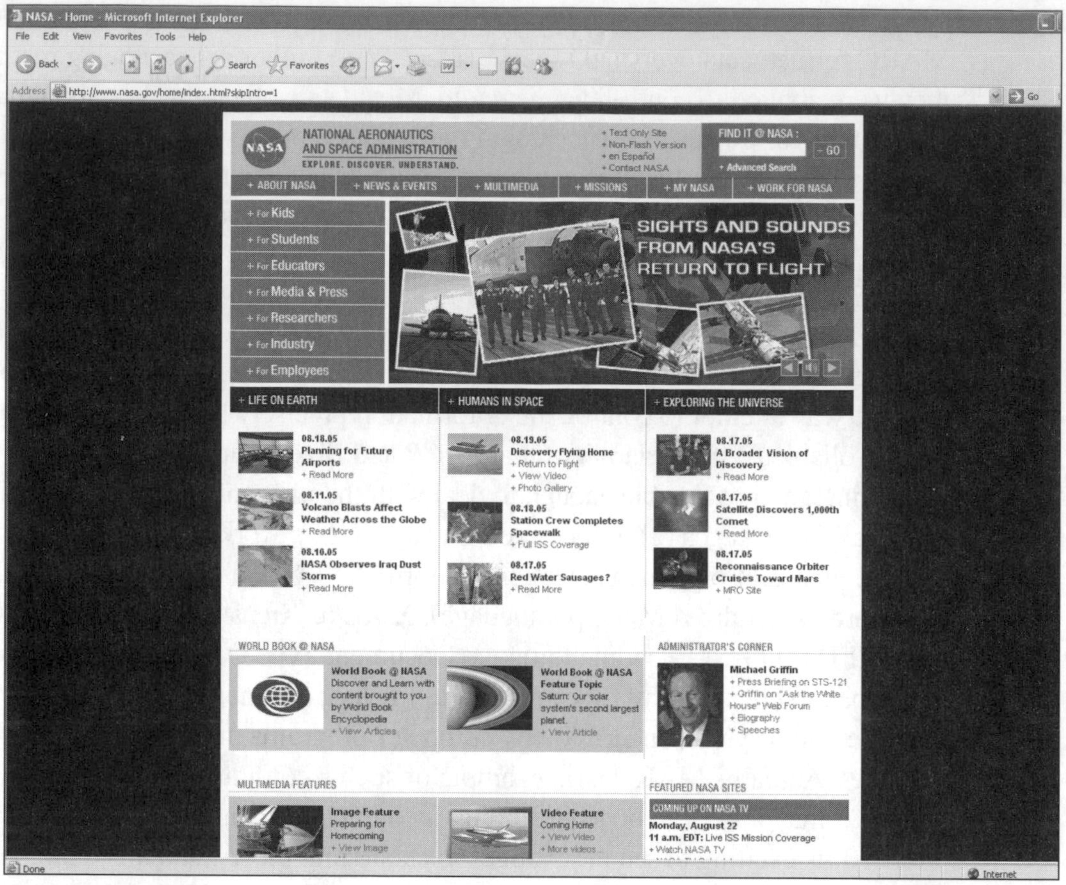

Let us use the NASA site as a template for cataloging metadata using the MARC communications format. Like a book, our surrogate record begins with the 245 tag. Consider the home page for NASA (see figure 7.1). Notice the prominence of the words, "National Aeronautics and Space Administration" with the NASA logo adjacent. We will take that as title. We might want to consider the NASA logo as other title information. Like most films, most Web sites will not have personal or corporate names for main entries. To include National Aeronautics and Space Administration as a statement of responsibility would be redundant. Thus our 245 will look like this:

- 245 00 $aNational Aeronautics and Space Administration $h[electronic resource] :$bNASA.

We will also want an additional title entry for NASA:

- 246 30 $aNASA

Moving down the MARC record, we need to describe the publication data. A small variation from book cataloging is the reference to date of publication. If it is clear (or known) when the site came online, include that information in the $c of the 260 tag. If not, the $c is left blank.

- 260 __ $aWashington, D.C. :$bNASA.

Since the information package does not exist physically anywhere, there is no 300 tag. In some school library automation programs, this may be a problem. Some programs require a 300 tag or the surrogate record cannot be saved. If this is the case, one might just add a descriptor such as "Web site" in the $a to take care of the problem, even though it is not technically correct.

There are several 5XX tags we can use to better describe our metadata. The first tag to enter is the 538 for access information. Because we are focused only on Internet sites, our entry is simple:

- 538 __ $aMode of access: Internet.

The second 5XX tag is a 500 for source of title. Included here is the screen used for deciding on a title and when that screen was accessed. We are picking out the most stable site we can, but even stable sites change their look now and then. Therefore, it is important to inform the user when the site was accessed just in case we may need to account for changes in site information. We also include the date the site was last updated. This can be very important information to the user. One wants to make sure the site is viable and wasn't just put up and forgotten. In our example site, we see that NASA is very good at keeping the site current.

- 500 __ $aTitle from home page (viewed on Oct. 13, 2004; last updated Oct. 13, 2004).

In cataloging Web sites, a summary statement is particularly important, especially if the site contains a variety of information. Many educational and government sites have descriptions of the objectives and goals of the site. These statements, often found in the "about us" links, can be copied and pasted into the 520 tag. One should look for keywords that will aid in the retrieval of the surrogate record. One might also include a 505 contents note that maps out the parts of the site:

- 520 __ $aOfficial site of NASA, with extensive links to NASA projects and information about the United States space program.
- 505 0_ $aLife on Earth -- Humans in space -- Exploring the universe.

The subject area is where we really see the benefits of cataloging parts of the site separate from each other. Imagine the number of subject headings one would need to cover even half of the content of all of the NASA pages put together. But, if the parts are cataloged separately, then a few broad headings are sufficient in describing the intellectual content of the parent page.

- 610 10 $aUnited States. $bNational Aeronautics and Space Administration.
- 650 _0 $aSpace flight $xHistory.
- 650 _0 $aSpace shuttles $zUnited States $xHistory.

The final part of the surrogate record is the 856 tag, Electronic Location and Access. As the title of the tag describes, this is where one enters the URL for the site. The first indicator will be 4, meaning that the information package being described is accessed through http. The second indicator is the relationship of the URL to the item as a whole. A value of 0 means that the item being described is the item at the URL. A value of 2 means the URL is for a related resource. If the second indicator is 2, there must be a corresponding $3 to explain the relationship. To avoid mistakes in the URL, whenever possible, one should use the copy and paste method to enter the URL information:

- 856 40 $uhttp://www.nasa.gov/home/index.html

- 856 42 $3Spanish version $uhttp://www.nasa.gov/about/highlights/En_Espanol.html

Figure 7.2. NASA Mars Web Page (captured August 18, 2005)

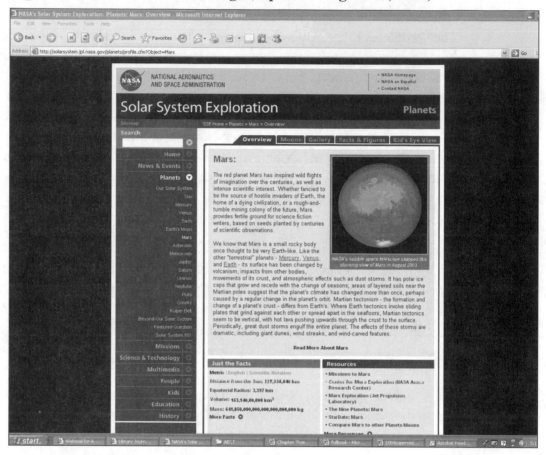

Let us look at one page of the NASA site and what that surrogate record would look like. Suppose that every year Mrs. Brown had her students investigate the planets. A site on the planet Mars would be particularly helpful, especially if the source was as authoritative as NASA. Figure 7.2 shows the front page of the Mars site and below is the full record. Notice the extended 245 tag. We must account for the parent site as well as the titles for the site itself. One of the problems with cataloging a part of a Web site is deciding how to deal with the separate title. This is easily accommodated by using a $p for the part of the title. Notice the full stops immediately preceding each $p. Notice too that a corporate entry has been added in the 710 tag for the Jet Propulsion Laboratory. Since JPL is part of the URL, the cataloger decided to make an entry for that entity.

245 00 $aNational Aeronautics and Space Administration $h[electronic resource] :$bsolar system exploration. $pPlanets. $pMars.

Cataloging hints for Internet sites

- Chief source of information is the title screen
  - The home screen if cataloging a parent site
  - The title of the sub-page if cataloging just a part of the site
- The 245 includes the following considerations:
  - The first indicator in the 245 tag is usually set to 0. If there is a need to trace a creator or organization, that information is recorded in the 7XX tags;
  - Add the $h[electronic resource] to the tag. (Remember, "electronic resource" is a relatively new term; do not be surprised to see "computer file" in this spot.)
  - If there is no recognizable title for the site, the cataloger must create one, remember created information is enclosed in brackets, [ ]
- If possible, try to add a 260 tag: 260 __ $a[Chicago, Ill. :$bs.n.],$c2000.
- There is no 300 tag.
  - Some systems require records to have a 300 tag; we suggest the following: 300 __ $aWeb site *or* 300 __ $aInternet site.
- Create notes (5XX) as needed to define source of the title, the nature of the site, last revision date, any other helpful information.
  - Include a 538 tag to describe the system requirements of the site. A simple note as follows is sufficient: 538 __ $aMode of access: World Wide Web.
- Include an 856 tag to show the URL.
  - Let both indicators be blank.
  - Use two of the available 28 subfields:
  - $z (public note) and $u (URL) thus:
    - 856 __ $zClick on the following address to access this site. $uhttp://www.oclc.org   *or*
    - 856 __ $zCopy the following URL and paste it into the locator bar of the school library home page. $uhttp://www.oclc.org
      (This example shows how to accommodate for the online catalog that does not provide direct access to the Internet.)
  - Note if the tag ends in a URL address, there is no closing punctuation.

246 30 $aSolar system exploration

246 30 $aPlanets

246 30 $aMars

260 __ $aWashington, D.C. :$bNASA.

538 __ $aMode of access: Internet.

500 __ $aTitle taken from home page (viewed Oct. 13, 2004; last updated Jan. 9, 2004).

520 1_ $aPart of the Planets section of the NASA Web site, this page focuses on the planet Mars with links to the Mars exploration and photographs.

505 0_ $aOverview -- Moons -- Gallery -- Facts and figures -- Kid's eye view -- Resources.

610 10 $aUnited States. $bNational Aeronautics and Space Administration.

```
650 _0 $aMars (Planet).
650 _0 $aPlanets.
650 _0 $aSolar system.
650 _0 $aAstronomy.
710 2_ $aJet Propulsion Laboratory (U.S.)
856 40 $uhttp://solarsystem.jpl.nasa.gov/planets/profile.cfm?Object=Mars
```

Conclusion

We have seen that it is not really so difficult to catalog a Web site. Indeed the benefits of having students rely mostly on the OPAC for information access truly outweighs the beginning difficulties of getting used to a new cataloging template. It would be great if one day a student could type in "Mars" and be lead to books, Internet sites, and database articles in one fell swoop. Until such a time, the least we can do is connect our books with good Internet sites. The way to do that is by cataloging the sites that we already have bookmarked. Whether one calls this cataloging metadata or cataloging Web sites, the point is that the job gets done and that we pull our students out of the Internet Ocean and back to the library catalog for one-stop information access.

References

1. This section is based on: Kaplan, Allison G. (2004) Meta-what?: Metadata and Information Management For School Library Media Collections. Presented at the 2004 Annual Convention of the Association for Educational Communications and Technology.

2. Tennant, R. (2004). *Building a New Bibliographic Infrastructure*. Library Journal. Accessed: 18 August 2005. Available at: http://www.libraryjournal.com/article/CA371079

3. To find out more about metadata, look at the following Web sites:

   Dublin Core: http://dublincore.org/
   LC: http:/www.loc.gov/marc/marcml.html
   GILS: http://www.gils.net/

Chapter 8

Processing Information Packages

Introduction

Many messages are sent to library discussion lists regarding the actual physical processing of library items. This chapter will present some recommendations about the physical processing of the item itself. There are no standards for physical processing. These ideas presented here are simply made based on years of experience in various libraries and many discussions with practicing librarians.

Labels

Barcodes work with automated circulation systems to keep track of library items, such as what is on the shelf, what has been checked out, what is overdue. Placement of the barcode is frequently a matter of debate and there is no one definitive answer. Where one positions the barcode depends very much on what one believes is the primary role of the barcode.

There are a variety of places to put the barcode and an equal number of reasons for putting them in those places. Most vendors that offer the service of putting the barcode on the book will give the librarian a choice of where the barcode will be located. Some librarians like to put the barcode on the inside of the front or back cover of a book because it's harder for the students to randomly tear the barcodes off when they are hidden. Others do not like putting them inside the covers because it is harder to discover if students have torn off the barcode. Some like to put the barcode on the front cover because it is easier to verify the title as the book is checked out. Others do not like the barcode on the front cover because it compromises the front cover artwork. Some librarians like to put the barcode on the back cover of the book so it does not interfere with the front cover artwork. Others don't like to put it on the back cover because it will cover up summaries that are often found on the back of the book.

We would like to suggest that one consider putting the barcode on the upper right hand corner of the back cover. One of the more onerous tasks in the library is that of taking inventory. In fact, before automated systems came along, that task was considered so onerous and so time consuming that often it was never done or it was done infrequently. With the barcodes on the upper right hand corner of the back cover, it is simple to partly pull the book from the shelf and scan the barcode. If the barcode is located anywhere else on the book, each book must be completely removed from the shelf before the barcode can be scanned into the system. This action can add hours to an already time consuming task.

Placement of barcodes on non-book items is a bit trickier. The cover of the item is the obvious place to put the barcode, assuming there is only one item to control, i.e. the item is not a multipart item. Some librarians like to put the barcode inside the cover so that the person who is doing the check out (the librarian or an assistant) is forced to make sure the item in the case is in fact the item that should be there. This is helpful, for example, for items like CD-ROMs, DVDs, videotapes, and tape cassettes. This may also hold true for kits, games, and other items that are in some sort of container. Having to open the container will ensure that the contents are verified before the item circulates. This saves on hassles later on if the item is returned with missing pieces.

As stated above, unlike cataloging rules, there are no standards upon which we can rely to make this decision. It rests on the librarian. We can, however, offer you one hard and fast rule: Decide where you want the barcode to be located and stick to that decision. It is terribly frustrating to have a group of children ready to check out books and have to rummage through each book to find where the elusive barcode is located.

Spine labels or call number labels are typically found on the bottom portion of the spine of the book. Some libraries with full cataloging staff insist that the label be located at a precise point on the spine so that all spine labels are at the same spot and look nice and neat on the shelf. We have seen places where processors actually use rules to measure where the spine label will go. This is not very realistic for the librarian who has to get the label on the item quickly. It is, however, some food for thought. When the spine label is on the same spot (or relatively same spot) for all books, it helps to give a uniform look to the bookshelves. For those items that are not wide enough for a spine label, as is the case with the ubiquitous 32-page picture book, labels are often put on the lower left corner of the front cover.

Non-book materials present a problem, as they are seldom uniform in their packaging. First one should label all parts of the item. This may be time consuming for items that have many parts, for example games and game pieces, but it is necessary. It is unfortunate and sometimes costly to have an unidentifiable piece that cannot be returned to its proper place. Call numbers on pieces can include the prefatory phrase "part of" to show that the item does not stand alone but is part of a bigger item. Library supply companies offer a variety of items to assist in the labeling process such as round labels with holes for CD-ROM or DVD discs, or special pens for writing on plastic. With respect to call number labels, one may find that several are needed on the tops and sides of boxes depending on how the item will be situated on the shelf.

Property stamps and pockets or date due slips must also be added to library items. Remember, these are items that will be used in and out of the library; they are not historical documents that must be free of extraneous matter. We want our items to be well marked so it cannot be mistaken to whom the items belong. For books, librarians often use a library property stamp (a stamp with the library and school name and sometimes the address) on the front cover, title page, and back page. Some libraries also stamp somewhere in the book itself. Librarians often talk about stamping on a certain page. Picking one page to stamp helps in the de-accessioning process wherein one must remove all library identification. It is easier to turn to a specific page than to leaf through the book page by page looking for the property stamp. Non-book materials must also have all pieces identified.

Pockets or due date slips may also be placed on the item. In the old days of manual circulation systems, librarians had cards with the due date placed in the pocket of the item to remind the user when to return the item. Due date cards are still used in some libraries while others have systems that will print out a receipt and need a place to put that receipt so it does not get lost. Some libraries use date stamps on due date sheets in the items. Which system is used is a matter of choice. It is useful, however, to have some system that will remind the students when they must return the items. For book materials, the pockets or due date slips are placed on the inside of the back cover (most frequently) or the front cover. For non-book materials, the inside of the box cover is the place of choice for the pocket or due date slip. For items that do not have nice box or container covers, the librarian is forced to find the best place to put the pocket or slip. One should avoid just floating the pocket or slip inside a container because they usually disappear or end up in another item.

Packaging

While not an issue for book materials, how one keeps non-book or multipart items together is very important. Original packaging, as in the case of computer programs, often is not substantial enough to survive the use demands of the school library. Librarians may find it better to dissect original packaging and put the items and relevant information into a more substantial container such as a zip-lock plastic bag or a plastic container that can be closed. These items are readily available in stores and from library supply companies. Again, be sure that all parts of the package, including the package itself, are well marked with the proper identification. Most importantly, keep multipart items together. Resist the temptation to put media in one place and the accompanying books in another. If two items come into the library packaged together, then keep them packaged together.

Placement on the Shelf

Packaging of non-book materials and where the materials will reside in the library are often ideas that should be discussed together. In the old days, librarians often disassembled non-book materials and kept like materials together. This is detrimental to the use of the item and compromises the purpose of the item. If a tape cassette is released with a book then the two items should be kept together; that is how they are intended to be used. So once the librarian has decided how these items can be packaged together, the next decision is where to put the items. Older school library collections are filled with special materials sections for filmstrips, records, and study prints. The decision to put materials in special places is often linked to space. Graphic materials, maps, globes, and prints, do not fit nicely on the shelves next to books. The decision is also linked to security; cassette tapes, videotapes, and computer disks walk out of the library with surprising ease.

We would like to argue that all items, when possible, should be inter-shelved with the books. This is to capitalize on the serendipity of finding the desired item by browsing. If a student is in the book stacks area, we want that student to find all the items on a particular subject, not just some of them. However, if security and space are an issue and it is imperative that non-book items be shelved away from the books, there should be some reference to the item on the bookshelf. This reference is called, for lack of a better term, a *dummy*. Made out of cardboard or Styrofoam, dummies have the same dimensions of books and can be set right next to a book in classification number order. The dummy is labeled to direct the user to the location of the item in need. Say, for example, that the library has a copy of the book and cassette tape of *Frog and Toad are Friends*. If the decision is made to put the cassette tape alone or the tape and book together in a separate place, a dummy for the tape (or the items together) is placed on the shelf in the proper order, next to the other Lobel books, to let the user know that there is a sound recording of this book located elsewhere in the library. The surrogate record should also include a directive 500 note, such as, "This item is located behind the circulation desk. Please ask for assistance." The use of dummies is a great way to keep the students informed of all the wonderful items in the library. Dummies are also prime targets for student mischief. Students seem to take great delight in moving the dummies around to the wrong places. We have no solution for this problem and stick to our recommendation of interfiling mixed materials.

Sometimes a library will have more than one copy of an item and, due to the nature of the item, simply cannot decide where on the shelves to place the item. This is particularly common with folktales that can either be classified in the Everybody section or in the 300s section. Sometimes librarians will fudge the data and will classify one copy under one number and one copy under another number.

This is not very good practice and should be avoided. It is confusing to look up a title and find it resides in two locations in the library. New catalogers are counseled to avoid this urge. Pick one number and put both copies there. It may be argued that this practice does not capitalize on serendipity that we so strongly encouraged previously. While this may be true, it does encourage students to learn the library classification system and to use the catalog as a finding tool.

Conclusion

This chapter has presented some nuts and bolts information about processing book and non-book items. This information has little to do with the MARC record but everything to do with getting the item on to the shelf. We recommend that barcodes be placed on the upper right hand corner of the back cover and that multipart items be kept together and, if at all possible, shelved with the books.

Appendix I: *Hint Sheet*

Below are the most commonly used MARC tags for cataloging book materials with a description of the tag and an illustrative example of the tag use.

010 - Library of Congress Control Number (LCCN)

Eight-digit number supplied by the Library of Congress. You do *not* make it up yourself! Not all items will have one, but those that do will be entered, thus:

> **010 __ $a766633**

with no closing punctuation and both indicators blank. Exceptions: You may see the number entered with a hyphen 76-6633 or with fillers to create the eight digits 76006633 or 76-006633. Do not use information from a $z in this tag, which is for discontinued numbers. This information is usually found around the CIP information in a book.

020 - International Standard Book Number (ISBN)

Ten-digit number assigned by the publisher to note a unique number for the item. If you have one number in the CIP data and a different number on the item (such as on the book cover), use the number on the item. This number is entered without hyphens, thus:

> **020 __ $a0491001304**

with no closing punctuation and both indicators are blank. You may also see a $c for cost of the item, thus:

> **020 __ $a0491001204$c$4.50**

Do not use information from a $z in this tag, which is for discontinued numbers. This tag is repeatable.

040 - Cataloging Source

Code to note from whence came the cataloging for the item in hand; indicators are blank, $a notes the original cataloging agency, usually DLC for Library of Congress, $c for agency that turned the record into MARC format, and $d for the agency that modified the record. For our purposes, you may use either $c or $d to identify you or your institution, thus:

> **040 __ $aDLC$cOCLC$dagk**

with no closing punctuation. This tag is not repeatable although the subfields are.

041 - Language Code

Use this tag to note if item is or contains a translation or if the item is in a language other than English. First indicator is 0 if the item is not or does not contain a translation (in some language besides English), or 1 if item is or includes a translation. Second indicator is blank; $a is the language of the item; $h is the original language. Examples: Item is in English, but was originally in French (a translation) would be

> **041 1_ enghfre**

Item is in English and Spanish would be

> **041 0_ $aengspa**

Item is in German would be

041 0_ $ager

All with no closing punctuation. Note the bilingual text is not considered a translation.

050 - Library of Congress Call Number

Call number as derived from the Library of Congress classification schedules. You will not be creating this number.

082 - Dewey Decimal Call Number

Call number as derived from the Dewey Decimal Classification schedules. The first indicator defines which schedule was used; 0 for unabridged edition or 1 for abridged; a 4 in the second indicator place notes the number was assigned by an agency other than the Library of Congress; $a includes the number itself; and $2 notes the edition used, thus:

082 14 $a914.3$213

with no closing punctuation. This tag is repeatable, although I can't think of a situation where there would be more than one 082. Note that the actual tag you use in your library will depend on the system you're using.

245 - Title and Statement of Responsibility

All records must have a title. The first indicator 1 shows record includes 1XX tag and 0 shows the record does not include 1XX tag; second indicator 0-9 for filing characteristics, that is, skip all spaces for initial articles, English language includes A (2), An (3), The (4). There is always a $a for the title proper, if necessary, add $b for remainder or other title information and $c for statement of responsibility. There are other subfields available for this tag, but these are the most common. Tag ends in full stop and is not repeatable, thus:

245 14 $aThe paper bag princess /$cby Robert N. Munsch ; illustrated by Michael Martchenko.

also

245 00 $aExcellent organizations :$bhow to develop and manage them /$cedited by James Lewis, Jr.

246 - Varying Form of Title

Use this tag to trace for other forms of the title proper (as in numbers) or to trace for other title information. This is a relatively recent use of the tag and records up to about 1993 will have this information in the 740 tag. Initial articles are dropped from the beginning of the title information. The first indicator can have a variety of values; however, the one you will use most often is 3 (no note, title added entry). The second indicator also has a number of values; the easiest way to go is to leave this indicator blank, thus:

245 04 $aThe 5 hats.

246 3_ $aFive hats (Notice the drop of the initial article.)

Information is entered in $a; however, that subfield may be preceded by a $i that is used to explain the 246 information thus:

245 00 $aCats and dogs playing together.

246 3_ $iSpine title:$aCats and dogs at play

This tag does *not* end with a full stop and is repeatable.

250 - Edition Statement

Note edition as given on the item; both indicators are blank; information is input to the $a although other subfields are available for this tag, thus:

250 __ $a1st ed.

or

250 __ $a1st HarperTrophy ed.

This tag ends in a full stop.

260 - Publication, Distribution, etc. (Imprint)

Imprint information; both indicators are blank; $a for place, $b for publisher, $c for date of publication. Although this tag is not repeatable, the subfields a and b, but not c, are, thus:

260 __ $aNew York :$bHarper Row,$c1996.

This tag ends in a full stop.

300 - Physical Description

Add information relating to the physical aspects of the item itself. Although technically repeatable, this tag is seldom repeated and some programs will not allow for repetition. Both indicators are blank, thus:

300 __ $a32 p. :$bill. ;$c23 cm. +$e1 puppet.

with full stop at end unless finishing with other punctuation (such as parentheses).

440 - Series Statement

If needed, add a series statement; older cataloging may also show 400, 410, 411, and 490 tags. The 490 tag is still used, but we prefer to use the 440 tag. First indicator is blank, second indicator is 0 (hold over from filing characteristics); use $v for volume number or sequential number of the series, thus:

440 _0 $aChoose your own adventure ;$vno. 18

with no closing punctuation. This tag is repeatable.

5XX - Notes

This area in the MARC record provides a variety of ways to bring out certain aspects of the item being cataloged; *generally all 5XX tags are repeatable and end in a full stop.* Indexing of these tags varies according to the system. Check with the vendor before using some of the more specific 5XX tags. Some of the more common 5XX tags are:

500 - General Notes

Both indicators are blank; include here such notes as origin of title information, translation information, previous edition titles, index, and other information from title or cover that is important to include in the record, thus:

500 __ $aIncludes index.

504 - Bibliography

If item includes a bibliography or references of some sort, make note of it here; you may also include reference to an index if both are in the item at hand, thus:

504 __ $aIncludes bibliographical references and indexes.

but, index alone is 500 tag.

520 - Summary

Summary statement of the item kept short and to the point; Library of Congress keeps both indicators blank, which works for me but check your own system, as there may be a use for the first indicator, thus:

> **520 __ $aThe story of a boy and his dog and how the boy learns to love again.**

521 - Audience

Refers to who might want to use the item. Such phrases as "For reading grade levels 4-6" or "For reading interest ages 8-12" are used here, but using the codes in the first indicator position, one can make use of display constants: Blank is no display constant; 0 is Reading grade level; 1 is Interest age level; 2 is Interest grade level, thus:

> **521 0_ $a2-3. or 521 1_ $a8-10. or 521 2_ $a2-4.**

586 – Awards

Use this tag to note awards connected with the item; both indicators are blank, thus:

> **586 __ $aCaldecott Award winner, 1999**

This tag does not end in a full stop unless needed for abbreviations.

650 - Topical Subject Headings

Record topics from standardized list; first indicator is blank, second indicator 0 is Library of Congress Subject Heading (*LCSH*); 1 is LC Children's Subject Heading (*LC/AC*), 4 is some other source not defined, and 7 is some other source defined at the end of the tag in $2. Subfields include $x for topical subdivisions, $y for chronological subdivisions, $z for geographical subdivisions, $v for form subdivisions. Use of the subdivisions is defined by the list you are using, thus:

> **650 _7 $aDragons$zGreat Britain$vFiction. $2sears**

with a full stop before the $2. This tag is repeatable.

651 - Geographic Subject Headings

Record names of places as subject headings here; indicators are the same as those used in 650 tag, thus:

> **651 _7 $aUnited States$xHistory$y1783-1809$vFiction. $2sears**

with a full stop before the $2. This tag is repeatable.

X00 - Personal Names, General Information (100, 600, 700)

Record personal names in inverted order as needed for main and added entries and as subject headings (remember the names of authors are not used in the subject areas); first indicator is 0 for forename, 1 for surname, or 3 for family name; second indicator for 100 and 700 is blank; second indicator for the 600 tag is the same as that of 650 tag; subfields include $a for name, $q for fuller form of name, $c for titles associated with name, $d for birth/death dates, $t title of work, and $e relator term (100 and 700 only), thus:

> **600 17 $aRoosevelt, Eleanor,$d1884-1962$xBiography. $2sears**

and

> **700 1_ $aChuchill, Winston,$cSir,$d1874-1965.$tThe great war.**

with full stop before the $2 and before the $t; 100 tag is not repeatable but 600 and 700 tags are.

Appendix II: MARC Template*

020	__	$a	(enter ISBN, no hyphens)
		^:$c	(optional to add price of item)
040	__	$a	(institution that originally cataloged item)
		$c	(institution that input the item in MARC format)
		$d	(institution that modified the record, your initials here)
082	14	$a	(Dewey # from abridged schedule)
		$2	(edition # of Dewey used)
100	1_	$a	(name of author of item)
		$q	(fuller form of name if available and necessary)
		,$d	(birth/death dates)
245	XX	$a	(title, indicators show 100 tag and filing characters)
		^:$b	(subtitle if needed)
		^/$c	(statement of responsibility)
246	3_	$i	(type of title, if needed)
		$a	(added title, to trace for numbers, abbreviations, and more.)
250	__	$a	(edition statement using ordinal number, e.g. 1st, 2nd)
260	__	$a	(place of publication, additional places use ;$a)
		^:$b	(name of publisher, additional names use :$b)
		,$c	(date of publication)
300	__	$a	(number of units, i.e. pages)
		^:$b	(illustrative matter)
		^;$c	(dimensions)
		^+$e	(accompanying materials)
440	_0	$a	(series title)
		.$n	(number of part/section)
		.$p	(name of part/section)
		;$v	(volume number - this is the subfield to use in most cases)
5XX	__	$a	(Notes to explain cataloging decisions and emphasize other aspects of the item, common tags are 500-general, 520-summary, 521-audience level)
600	17	$a	(personal name as subject heading)
650	_7	$a	(topical subject headings)
		$y	(order of subfields varies according to subject heading)
		$x	
		$z	
		$2	sears
651	_7	$a	(geographical subject headings, add other subfields as 650)
700	1_	$a	(added name entries, e.g. illustrator, editor)
		,$e	(subfields are same as those for 100 tag)

---

* Note the following punctuation is used: ^ is to mark a space before the subfield punctuation; _ is to mark a blank indicator place; X is to mark place holder in tag number.

Appendix III: *Automated Systems*

It is not really within the scope of a cataloging textbook to talk about automated library systems. Nevertheless, it is difficult to talk about cataloging without including a discussion on automated library systems. Therefore, we offer here a short discussion on some considerations for automating library services and migrating from one system to another.

By now it is safe to say that a majority of the public schools in the United States have automated systems in their school library media centers. However, the "majority" is not "all" and so we include here a list of considerations in automating a school library as well as a list of some of the major companies that offer programs for school libraries. This can also be useful information for those schools that have outgrown their current systems and need to migrate, or change, to another system.

Many school library media specialists think of automation only in terms of online public access computers (OPACs) that students and school personnel use to view the library media center's holdings. However, numerous other library procedures may be automated, such as circulation, cataloging, serials management, and acquisitions. One of the nice features of automated systems is that all of these functions can be monitored. Reporting on circulation statistics, the age of the collection, and the number of new items added to the collection as a whole or in a specific area are all ways of showing supportive documentation of the work done by school library media specialists.

An automated library contributes to an increase in overall productivity. It does not take away from tasks such as ordering books, circulation, or writing overdue notices; however, it can make such tasks simpler and easier to accomplish and track. You and your school library staff can assist students and classroom teachers rather than spending large amounts of time dealing with paperwork, taking inventory of the collection, and so forth. Additionally, an effective library automation system can reduce errors and redundancy; overdue, lost, or missing items can be accounted for more efficiently, assisting in the overall management of the school library collection.

Not only will productivity rise, but library automation systems can contribute to student learning outcomes, such as: 1) gaining skills and confidence in using technologies in real-life situations at the point of need; 2) developing information search skills using a relevant database; and 3) achieving greater success in locating resources to meet information needs in order to become independent learners. Schools with automated library systems provide their students equal opportunities to develop information and technology skills. Adequate information retrieval and experience in using technologies are two major assets of school library automation systems.

It is necessary to purchase an *integrated system* for the purposes of effectiveness and accuracy. An integrated system is an automated system in which all of the function modules (acquisitions, cataloging, circulation, serials, OPAC) share a common bibliographic database. An integrated system is superior in several ways to one that is not integrated: 1) errors may be reduced when records are entered only once and changes are automatically propagated throughout the system; 2) the duplication of effort to create and maintain multiple copies of bibliographic records is eliminated; and 3) library users may have access to all pertinent information at one location. The definition of an integrated system is beginning to shift from referring to a system that shares bibliographic records among local functions and modules to referring to a system that exchanges information with many other systems outside of the library.

As resources become scarcer and the demand for universal access to information increases, many public libraries are looking at integrated systems as ways of answering the demands of their public. At the same time, more and more systems for school libraries are adding the availability of Internet access to the school library database. Some school districts and public libraries are working together in purchasing a single integrated system that will allow access to all of the library catalogs. There is much to be said in favor of this arrangement. The increase in access to library information for school students can only be a positive factor. However, in entering such an agreement, school library media specialists should ask if they can maintain rights of unique circulation and cataloging requirements, if they can have the option of participating in interlibrary loan or not, and if the OPAC screens have the capability of iconic displays for younger children who have emerging literacy abilities and need the icons to help them with their searches. In other words, the OPAC screens must make information accessible to all users regardless of age and reading level.

In considering an integrated system (either your first one or migrating to a different one) be sure the system is predicated on *AACR* and MARC21 format. Today it is rare that a system would not include full MARC21 format, but since it was not so long ago that this was not the case, it always helps to ask this question. In fact, these days it would not be out of line to ask about the future of the system and its compatibility to FRBR. The system in question should have the ability to make the database accessible through the Z39.50 protocol so that your students and faculty can access the database outside of the school walls. The automated systems market is somewhat volatile. When choosing a system, take some time to investigate the vendor, or supplier, of the system. Look for vendors who have been around for a while and who are responsive to consumer input. Also be sure there is good technical support that includes service hours that match your work schedule, a toll-free phone number, timely responses to e-mail questions, and updates of the system program. You don't have time to be on hold when you have a technical problem. Asking the vendor about wait time before talking to technical support is not a rude question. Never skimp on the technical support agreement. Through company technical support you keep your system updated and have the ability to talk with a knowledgeable service person when something goes wrong. Understand that even with the best systems, something *will* go wrong, so make sure you have the insurance of a technical support agreement.

Finally, if your school or district has its own technical crew, you need to talk with them about mounting your automated system onto the school or district server. Many technical people are mistrustful of library programs and either refuse to load them onto a school server or drag their feet so long it is hardly worth the effort. Bring them on board so they feel like they are part of the process. Most programs are now very easy to load and update and, if the power is given, most school library media specialists can load the programs (or at least the updates) themselves. However, if the school or district computer folks are not on board with the idea of the automated system, then you will run into local problems that may be difficult to overcome.

Considerations in selecting an integrated library system:

- Functionality: cataloging, circulation, OPAC, Z39.50, reporting.
- Standards in cataloging: *AACR* and MARC21, accepts non-English alphabets and diacritics.
- Meets existing library operations and predictable future needs.
- Technical support services: "live" support, e-mail support, program updates, user group discussion lists.
- Ease of installation.
- School or district support: local technicians willing to work with the system.

Selected Integrated Library Systems

Numerous automation systems exist around the world today; each year leading systems are becoming more sophisticated and increasing their range of features. Web-based interfaces for OPACs are now the norm, as is the capability to catalog Web sites and to provide "hot links" from the OPACs to Internet resources. The following automation systems are merely examples that may be appropriate for school library media centers. Brief information follows each example, as does its Web site address for further details. These automation systems are given in alphabetical order with no endorsement. This list is by no means exhaustive.

CASPR. This company began in 1986 and since that time numerous updates have occurred, such as *LibraryCom* in 1999, which was the first library Web hosting and directory service. *LibraryWorld,* introduced in 1997, was first in offering searching capabilities with graphic icons. It's one of the few companies offering programs that work for both Windows and Mac computer operating systems simultaneously.

CASPR: http://www.caspr.com/index.html

COMPanion Co. Offering the integrated library system, *Alexandria*, since 1987, this program also links to Big6™ Turbo, a tool that assists students during their searches to help them refine searches and become more efficient users of information from the Big6™ research model (see http://big6.com).

Alexandria: http://www.goalexandria.com/

Follett Software Company. One of the largest providers of school library automation systems since 1985, this company offers *Circulation Plus,* which keeps circulation and inventory on the "right track;" *Catalog Plus*, in which MARC records searches more productively; *Destiny,* a fully integrated library system for district union catalogs; *WebCollections* Z39.50 protocol for Internet access to the library OPAC; *Alliance plus* for access to millions of MARC records with a special emphasis on school library collection needs; and many other features. Follett's processing packages and custom processing provide the options necessary for school library media center information access and organization needs.

Follett: http://www.fsc.follett.com/

Sagebrush. Another top provider of automated systems for school libraries, Sagebrush offers *Athena, Accent*, and *Spectrum*, which are all fully integrated library automation systems that combine circulation, catalog search (OPAC), cataloging, and inventory functions in a complete system that is easy to install and maintain. *Spectrum* is a cross platform program running on both Windows and Mac platforms. Sagebrush also offers *Pinpoint*, a program that allows students to search the library catalog, databases, and Web sites all at the same time.

Sagebrush: http://www.sagebrushcorp.com

SIRSI. Providing library automation programs since 1979, SIRSI and DRA merged in 2001 to create a company focusing on the technical needs of libraries worldwide. The *Unicorn* system, introduced in 2001, is the program most appropriate for the school library environment. It is designed to fill the needs of a wide variety of collection sizes, from single libraries to statewide consortia, making *Unicorn* a very flexible system with many options from which to choose. The *iBistro* system provides an "Amazon.com" look to the search screen, providing an image of the book cover, links to more information about the author, other titles by the author, other titles on the same subject, and suggested alternate subjects.

SIRSI: http://www.sirsi.com/Solutions/Markets/School/

Surpass. Since 1985, this company has been offering the *Surpass* integrated library system that fits the needs of schools from building to district-wide levels. Besides the usual cataloging, circulation, and OPAC modules, the program also offers *Surpass Serials*, a module for controlling serial publications and *Surpass Copycat*, a module that offers access to MARC records from a wide variety of library databases.

Surpass: http://www.surpasssoftware.com

Appendix IV: *Answers to the Exercises*

Chapter 4 Intellectual Access - Subject Headings

Personal Name Heading Exercises:

Try to create personal name subject headings and then use a copy cataloging source or the LC authorities file to find personal name subject headings for the following (watch out for information that is important to know but may not be entered into the tag itself).

4.1. Eleanor Roosevelt, former first lady and human rights advocate who lived from 1884 to 1962.

- Attempting to create the heading without looking her up, you should end up with something that looks like this:

- 600 10 $aRoosevelt, Eleanor, $d1884-1962.

- When we check the heading with the Library of Congress, we find our heading agrees with theirs.

- *Sears* doesn't have an entry for Mrs. Roosevelt, but we know by the structure for the key heading under Shakespeare (see p. xli) that we have structured the heading correctly.

- While it's interesting to know a little bit about Mrs. Roosevelt, the fact that she was a first lady and a human rights advocate means nothing when creating a name heading.

4.2. Bill Clinton, 42nd president of the United States, born 1946 as William Jefferson Clinton, to most of the world he is just plain Bill.

- Again, just using the information in front of us we get:

- 600 10 $aClinton, William Jefferson, $d1946-

- This one is deceptive. On our own, we use the fuller form of the name, but apparently, he's just "Bill" to the Library of Congress too as the correct heading is:

  - 600 10 $aClinton, Bill, $d1946-

- The fact that he was a U.S. president does not come into play in a name heading.

4.3. Dale Earnhardt, American racecar driver, born 1951, died in an accident during a race on Feb. 18, 2001.

- On our own we might create this heading:

  - 600 10 $aEarnhardt, Dale, $d1951-2001.

- LC disagrees with us. Even though the authority record was updated in 2001 after he died, the dates have not changed. You would be on firm ground if you included both birth and death dates, but LC uses only the birth date:

- 600 10 $aEarnhardt, Dale, $d1951-

4.4. Queen Elizabeth II, born 1926. Royalty presents all kinds of problems when setting up a personal name entry. Take a look at the entry established by the Library of Congress. Also, take a look at the entry for her husband, Prince Philip, and her son Prince Charles. Note that royalty is not entered under the person's last name but under the first name (note the use of the 0 in the first indicator space). This sometimes creates some confusion but is the answer to the question, "Why is the biography of Princess Diana filed between the biography of Johnny Depp and the biography of Celene Dion?"

- We have a lot of information, but we're really unsure about what to do with this woman. Here is our first attempt:

- 600 00 $aElizabeth, $bII, $d1926-

- But we're really unsure about this or any of the royal family, so we check LC:

  - 600 00 $aElizabeth $bII, $cQueen of Great Britain, $d1926-

- We weren't too far off and that makes us feel pretty good! Notice the title in the $c that she is given. Here are the name subject headings for Prince Philip, Prince Charles, and Princess Diana:

  - 600 00 $aPhilip, $cPrince, consort of Elizabeth II, Queen of Great Britain, $d1921-

  - 600 00 $aCharles, $cPrince of Wales, $d1948-

  - 600 00 $aDiana, $cPrincess of Wales, $d1961-

- You should notice a pattern, both with respect to royalty being entered under first names, and the use of $c for their titles. Notice too that, like Earnhardt, Diana has only a birth year attached to her name. Also, like Earnhardt, if you wanted to include her death date, you could just to show your students that you don't have an outdated catalog.

Topical Heading Exercises:

Using a copy cataloging source or the LC authorities database, try to find topical subject headings for the following (you may need more than one heading to cover the topic):

4.5. Care and feeding of pet tropical fish

- 650 _1 $aTropical fish.

- 650 _1 $aTropical fish $vHandbooks, manuals, etc.

- 650 _1 $aAquarium fishes.

- 650 _1 $aTropical fish $vHandbooks, manuals, etc.

  - Here we have examples of *LC/AC*. Notice the option one has of adding the subdivision "Handbooks, manuals, etc." According to *LC/AC* (and *LCSH*), this is a floating subdivision and can be applied as necessary to other subject headings.

- 650 _7 $aTropical fish. $2sears
- 650 _7 $aTropical fish $xCare. $2sears
  - This example from the *Sears* book is somehow a little bit more satisfying. There is something about that floating subdivision "Care" that seems to work better for our K-12 population than does the heading "Handbooks, manuals, etc."

4.6. Volcanoes and earthquakes around the world

- 650 _7 $aVolcanoes. $2sears
- 650 _7 $aEarthquakes. $2sears
- 650 _7 $aNatural disasters. $2sears
  - *Sears* gives us permission in all three cases to subdivide these headings by geographic location. As the item is about these disasters worldwide, that is unnecessary.
- 650 _1 $aVolcanoes.
- 650 _1 $aEarthquakes.
- 650 _1 $aNatural disasters.
  - The beauty of having the *Sears* book in front of us is that we find out that the subject headings can be subdivided geographically (even though it doesn't apply to this specific information package). Looking up the headings on the LC database does not provide us with that critical piece of information.

4.7. Italian cooking

- 650 _1 $aCookery, Italian.
  - This one was tricky because looking up "Italian cooking" in the LC database as a subject search will result in zero hits! It is not until we search "Italian cooking" as a keyword search that we find out the real subject heading.
- 650 _7 $aItalian cooking. $2sears
  - Even though this specific heading is not in the *Sears* book, if we look under "cooking," we see we have permission to add a phrase for regional cooking. The example given in the book (pg. 183) gives us the example, "French cooking," leaving us to add additional headings as needed.
  - *Sears* headings are so natural. The chances of a K-12 student looking up "Italian cooking" as a subject heading are probably much greater than those of the student looking up "Cookery, Italian."

4.8. Careers in dentistry

- 650 _0 $aDentistry.
- 650 _0 $aOccupations.
  - Here we have subject headings that are the same regardless of the vocabulary being consulted (LC or *Sears*). Although "occupations" is fairly broad, it is possible that a student might be interested in finding out about

some occupations, thus the subject heading leads the student from the general to the specific.

Geographic Heading Exercises:

Create geographic subject headings for the following. Use copy cataloging resources to check your answers (try to find both LCSH and Sears subject headings).

4.9. Item about the American Revolutionary War

- 651 _0 $aUnited States $xHistory $yRevolution, 1775-1783.
  - It might seem strange at first to have an event, like the American Revolutionary War, as a geographic heading rather than as a topical heading. Both *Sears* and LC usually deal with events in terms of places and history rather than as topics. You will see the same is true in our next problem.
  - Note the use of the topical subdivision (in $x) for history and the chronological subdivision ($y). These headings are given to us when we look up United States.
  - Just for fun, take a look at the subject heading for Great Britain during the same time period. What conclusions can you come to looking at this heading?
    651 _1 $aGreat Britain $xHistory $y1714-1837.

4.10. Item about the Russian Revolution

- 651 _1 $aSoviet Union $xHistory $y1917-1921.
- 651 _1 $aSoviet Union $xHistory $y1917-1936.
  - Notice that *LC/AC* allows us two different subject headings; one for the exact time period of the revolution and the other that goes beyond that time. Now look at the *Sears* heading:
- 651 _7 $aSoviet Union $xHistory $y1917-1921. $2sears
- 651 _7 $aSoviet Union $xHistory $y1917-1925. $2sears
  - Notice the time period is slightly different. We'd have to know more about the item we are cataloging to decide if we need the longer or shorter time period.
  - In both cases, we have the heading "Soviet Union." Even though that is an obsolete term, the revolution created the beginning of the Soviet Union and so that is the geographic term we use. Both *Sears* and LC (print form, not online) give us a note to help us with the decision. In *Sears* this note, under "Russia," reads, "Use for materials on Russia (including the Russian Empire) prior to 1917. Materials on the Union of Soviet Socialist Republics from its inception in 1917 until its dissolution in December 1991 are entered under Soviet Union" (p. 640).

4.11. Item about China in the 1920s

- 651 _7 $aChina $xHistory $y1912-1949. $2sears
  - *Sears* doesn't treat China the same way it treats the Soviet Union. There is no separate heading for The People's Republic of China; it's just plain China (p. 134).

- LC does the same as *Sears* but gives us more time periods to use instead of the one supplied in *Sears*. It would depend on the information package itself for us to determine which time period to use.

4.12. World War I and World War II present some interesting cataloging questions because neither *Sears* nor *LCSH* use those phrases as headings.

- How would you assign headings for a book about World War II in general? Because World War II took place all over, this is a topical heading instead of a geographic heading:
  - 650 _7 $aWorld War, 1939-1945. $2sears
  - 650 _0 $aWorld War, 1939-1945.
    - Subject headings for wars tend to follow a logic that escapes most K-12 students (and adults for that matter!). Make sure you include enough significant and descriptive keywords in your record so that it can be retrieved by the average person.
    - First, notice that the time period is not entered in the $y as we would think it should be. When the date is attached to the heading with the comma, as is the case here, it is part of the heading.

- What about an item that focused on the impact of the war in Germany only? Since we are talking about a specific place, the heading becomes a geographic heading:
  - 651 _0 $aGermany $xHistory $y1933-1945.
    - Notice the difference in the time period that coincides with the rise of Adolf Hitler to power.

Corporate Name Heading Exercises:

Create corporate subject headings for the following. Use copy cataloging resources to check your answers:

4.13. Buckingham Palace

- 610 20 $aBuckingham Palace (London, England)

4.14. The White House

- 610 20 $aWhite House (Washington, D.C.)
  - Notice in both of these examples, there is a place location in parentheses and that the close parenthesis acts as the final punctuation so there is no full stop.

4.15. Titanic (hint: a steamship, not a sailing ship)

- 610 20 $aTitanic (Steamship)
  - If you have a copy of *Sears* in hand, you'll notice that it was not helpful at all in finding headings for these three items. We don't get any hints within the body of the text to find out how to make headings like these. All we get are instructions, on page xl, that we need to make up these headings ourselves. It's a good thing we have access to the LC database to help us.

Chapter 5 Intellectual Access – Classification Exercises

First Summary Tables:

Use the first summary table (see first box in chapter five) to assign a general classification number for the following:

5.1. Information package on Hinduism: **200**

▪ Hinduism is a religion so we know we would classify this item in the 200 area.

5.2. Information package on the United States presidents: **900**

▪ This item might be equally at home in the 300 area for social sciences (that includes politics) or 900 under history. We'll choose the 900 area.

5.3. Information package on the civil rights movement in the United States: **300**

▪ Again we might have to make a choice here, depending on how we've classified our other materials. Most civil rights information packages will be classified in the 300 area for social sciences; however, there may also be some in 900 for historical discussions. We'll select the 300 area with the understanding for this problem and the previous one, that we need to have more information both about the classification numbers (we can't classifying based on 10 numbers) and the information package itself (remember it is the discipline and intent of the item that decides the classification number).

Numbers into MARC Format:

Put the following numbers into the MARC format; assume you are using the 14th edition of abridged Dewey and that the Library of Congress has assigned the number:

5.4. 796.81

082 10 $a796.81 $214

▪ The first indicator tells us that the abridged edition is being used to assign this number. The second indicator tells us that the Library of Congress assigned the number. The $2 tells us that the 14th edition of abridged Dewey was used to create the number.

5.5. 613.6

082 10 $a613.6 $214

5.6. 940.53

082 10 $a940.53 $214

Create Full Numbers:

Use *DDC14* or a copy cataloging resource to find numbers for the following (put the numbers in the MARC format):

5.7. African folktales

082 14 $a398.2096 $214

- Again, we have the first indicator telling us the abridged Dewey was used. The second indicator tells us that some institution besides LC has assigned the number.

- The number comes from the schedule for folktales, 398.2. At that number we are directed, on page 476, to use Table 2 to add the specific location of the folktales: "Add to the base number 398.209 notation 3—9 from Table 2, e.g. folk literature from France 398.20944…" If we go to Table 2, we see that 6 is the number for Africa. We add as follows:

$$398.2 \text{ (folk literature)}$$
$$+ \quad 09 \text{ (historical, geographic, persons treatment)}$$
$$+ \quad 6 \text{ (Africa, from Table 2)}$$
$$\overline{398.2096}$$

5.8. School nurses
082 14 $a371.7 $214

- In looking up school nurses in the Relative index, we find the classification is under the 371 for education. We're happy with that, after all we're talking about a member of the school faculty. However, it is just a little unnerving to find school nurses classified under the same number as cafeteria staff. The title of this number is "Student welfare" and the instructions tell us to class here "… student health programs … school social services …" so that works for us.

- Just for fun, go to the Relative index and look up school librarians. Notice that school library programs are classified, not under education, but rather under libraries (027.8). Just to pique your interest a little more, look at the next entry in the Relative index, "school library reading programs elementary education" and notice that that classification is back under (elementary) education, 372.42.

5.9. Soccer
082 14 $a796.334 $214

- Happily, this is a fairly straightforward number. It is the number we are given in the Relative index, but we still go to the schedules where we find the number is created as follows:

$$796 \text{ (athletic and outdoor sports and games)}$$
$$+ \quad .3 \text{ (ball games)}$$
$$+ \quad .33 \text{ (inflated ball driven by foot)}$$
$$+ \quad .334 \text{ (soccer)}$$
$$\overline{796.334}$$

Chapter 6 Physical Access Exercises

041 Tag (Language) Exercises

6.1. Bilingual dictionary in English and Spanish

- 041 0_ $aengspa

- We use the first indicator value 0 to show we do not have a translation.
- The $a tells us that the text is in two languages, English and Spanish.

6.2. Work in English, translated from the French

- 041 1_ $aeng$hfre

- This first indicator 1 tells us that we do have a translation.
  - The $a tells us that the language of the text is English and the $h tells us that the original language of the text was French.
  - Note how the two subfields are written together with no spaces.

6.3. Spanish language film with English subtitles

- 041 0_ $aspa$beng
  - Although we think we have a translation, this information package is one of our exceptions. Technically, there is no translation because the soundtrack has not been altered, and so we have the first indicator value 0.
  - We enter the language of the subtitles in $b.

245 Tag Exercises

Put these titles in a 245 tag format and try to apply one subject heading and a Dewey classification number.

6.4. Title page: Body decoration
  Jillian Powell.

{Powell is the author, and the book is about the different ways people decorate their bodies including tattooing, cosmetics, and hairstyles.}

- 082 14 $a391.6 $214
  - 391 is the classification number for Costume and personal appearance; under that number we find two possibilities, 391.5 (hairstyles) and 391.6 (personal appearance including tattooing and use of cosmetics). Although 391.5 comes first in the schedule, we follow the rule supplied in *DDC14*, page xxvii, that instructs us to use the number for the subject receiving fuller treatment. Since 391.6 includes two of our three content areas, we use that number.

- 245 10 $aBody decoration /$cJillian Powell.
  - This is a straightforward example of a title and author statement. There is no initial article in the title so the second indicator is 0. The first indicator is 1 because we have a clear author statement.

- 650 _1 $aCosmetics.

- 650 _1 $aTattooing.

- 650 _1 $aHairstyles.
  - It is just chance that these subject headings are the same as the words in our summary statement. These are the most specific subject headings we can apply. We might also try for something more general, e.g. 650 _7 $aPersonal appearance. $2sears

6.5. Title page: WALTER DEAN MYERS
NOW IS YOUR TIME!
The African-American
Struggle for Freedom

{Myers is the author; the book is a history of the African-American struggle for freedom and equality, beginning with the capture of Africans in 1619, continuing through the American Revolution, the Civil War, and into contemporary times.}

- 082 14 $a973 $214

  • Recall in the Dewey exercises, we said civil rights may be classed in the 300s or 900s. Here we have an example of where the location (United States) is more important then the discipline (civil rights).

- 245 10 $aNow is your time! :$bthe African-American struggle for freedom /$cWalter Dean Myers.

  • We transpose the title according to the title page but not necessarily according to layout. In our example, we have lots of capital letters, but don't be seduced by them; only the first word of the title need be capitalized except for proper nouns. So we see in $b the capitalization of African-American even though it is not the first word of the title. However, we do maintain the exclamation mark in $a.

- 650 0 $aAfrican Americans$xHistory$vJuvenile literature.

- 650 1 $aAfrican Americans$xHistory.

  • Notice we have two nearly identical subject headings; the difference is in the $v of the first subject heading. We have that designation because it is from *LCSH*, which, you recall, uses a designation (Juvenile literature) to show that the item is a nonfiction work for children. Our second subject heading does not do this because it is an *LC/AC* heading.

6.6. Title page: Mermaid Tales From Around The World
Retold by Mary Pope Osborne
Illustrated by Troy Howell.

{Collection of 12 mermaid tales from around the world.}

- 082 14 $a398.21 $214

  • By now we should recognize the 398.2 classification number. The .21 classification includes semi-human forms, such as mermaids, hence the number.

- 245 10 $aMermaid tales from around the world /$cretold by Mary Pope Osborne ; illustrated by Troy Howell.

  • We might be a little unsure of the "retold" word, but it is considered part of the author statement so it is included in the $c area. Notice the space, semicolon, space before the name of the illustrator.

- 650 _7 $aMermaids and mermen. $2sears

- 650 _1 $aMermaids.

  • Notice the difference in subject headings between the *Sears* and *LC/AC* headings.

6.7. Title on disc: The Sea of Trolls
     by Nancy Farmer
     read by Gerard Doyle

{12 CD recording of a fiction story involving Druids, Norse mythology, brothers and sisters, and Vikings}

- 082 14 $a[FIC] $214
  - As we've seen before, "fiction" does not fit in Dewey's classification system, so we use "FIC" to note this. We put it in brackets because it is not really a Dewey number. How you would enter this into your own catalog would depend on the organization of your automated system.
- 245 14 $aThe sea of trolls $h[sound recording] /$cby Nancy Farmer.
  - This is just an ordinary 245 tag. The exercise is included here to demonstrate that creating records for recordings is not a scary problem.
  - Having said that, we notice that Doyle is not mentioned in the 245 $c. This is the tricky part of the exercise. We will see later in this chapter how to deal with Doyle.
- 650 _1 $aBrothers and sisters $vFiction.
- 650 _1 $aVikings $vFiction.
- 650 _1 $aMythology, Norse.
- 650 _7 $aNorse mythology. $2sears
  - In this set of subject headings, we can really see how nice *Sears* is to our users. The first mythology heading is *LC/AC* and is an example of an inverted heading with the noun (mythology) before the adjective (Norse). But *Sears* is an example of direct entry and makes so much more sense when we think of how our users would look up mythical tales.

246 Tag Exercises

Create 245 and 246 tags for the following (be sure to correct for capitalization):

6.8. The time we had together
     The story of Richard Rogers and Oscar Hammerstein
     By John Smith

- 245 14 $aThe time we had together :$bthe story of Richard Rogers and Oscar Hammerstein /$cby John Smith.
  - Note the use of the 4 in the second indicator place.
- 246 3_ $aStory of Richard Rogers and Oscar Hammerstein
  - Note that we dropped the initial article "the" before entering the title under the word "story." This is no more than what we would have done had we typed out a catalog card and filed the card under "s" instead of under "t," but it does look a little strange.
  - Notice too there is no final stop at the end of this tag.

6.9. The GREATEST *Puppy* ever

My dog Fluffy

written by Samuel Jackson and illustrated by Laura Smith

- 245 14 $aThe greatest puppy ever :$bmy dog Fluffy /$cwritten by Samuel Jackson ; and illustrated by Laura Smith.
- 246 3_ $aMy dog Fluffy
  - Notice that "Fluffy" is capitalized because it is the name of the dog.

6.10. 24 girls in 7 days

ALEX BRADLEY

- 245 10 $a24 girls in 7 days /$cAlex Bradley.
- 246 3_ $aTwenty-four girls in seven days
  - Notice the way we wrote out the numbers 24 and 7.

6.11. Extra credit: On title screen as:

Moon	Un lazo
Rope	a la
	Luna
A Peruvian	Una leyenda
Folktale	peruana
Lois Ehlert	translated into Spanish by Amy Prince

This is a bilingual item; can you create a 041 tag for it?

This is a folktale, can you create a classification and subject heading for it?

- 041 0_ $aengspa
  - Notice that even though the words "translated by" appear on the title page, we still treat this as a bilingual item and not as a translation because the text is in both languages.
- 082 14 $a398.20985 $214
- 245 10 $aMoon rope :$ba Peruvian folktale = un lazo a la luna : una leyenda peruana /$cLois Ehlert ; translated into Spanish by Amy Prince.
  - Because there is only one statement of responsibility, we have the Spanish language title in the $b area.
- 246 3_ $aLazo a la luna
  - Although $b information can be included as $b in the 246 tag, we opt not to include it as it does not affect information retrieval.
  - Also tracing for "Peruvian folktale" may or may not be needed. We have opted not to, but if you did, this is how the tag would look:
    - 246 3_ $aPeruvian folktale

100 and 700 Tag Exercises

Take the information from the $c and put it into 100 or 700 tags as needed.

6.12. 245 10 $aOpposites /$cby Sandra Boynton.

- 100 1_ $aBoynton, Sandra.
  - No tricks to this problem, even looking it up on the LC database shows us that Sandra is just that, no titles, dates, or other distinguishing characteristics.

6.13. 245 10 $aBooks and libraries /$cby Jack Knowlton ; pictures by Harriett Barton.

- 100 1_ $aKnowlton, Jack.
- 700 1_ $aBarton, Harriett, $eill.
  - Again, this is fairly straightforward; note that we have one name in the 100 and one in the 700. New catalogers sometimes try to put two names into one tag, which cannot be done.

6.14. 245 10 $aElvis Presley's Love me tender /$clyrics by Elvis Presley and Vera Matson ; illustrated by Tom Browning.

- 100 1_ $aPresley, Elvis, $d1935-1977.
- 700 1_ $aMatson, Vera.
  - Note that Matson has ended up in a 700 tag even though she is also responsible for the text. Be careful not to confuse the purpose of the 700 tag which is to just trace for another person's name regardless of that person's contribution to the intellectual content of the item.
  - Note too that we did not add a relator subfield to Matson. We could have, by adding "$ejoint author," but for us the relator is most important for people who do things other than write, making writing the default for the name. If you opted for the relator, this is how your tag should look:
    - 700 1_ $aMatson, Vera $ejoint author.
- 700 1_ $aBrowning, Tom, $d1949- $eill.
  - Notice Browning has both a date and relator subfield. We can see how it was put together by checking the LC database. In general, the tag is structured with the date first ($d) and the relator second ($e).
  - We obtained our dates for all of the entries from the LC authority database.

110 and 710 Practice

Look on various library databases for the following and notice both the OPAC and MARC display:

6.15. Weston Woods

- As per LC: 710 2_ $aWeston Woods Studios.
- Typical OPAC display: Added Entry: Weston Woods Studios

6.16. Scholastic (notice the variety of Scholastic entities from the databases)

- As per LC: 710 2_ $aScholastic, Inc.

- Typical OPAC display: Added Entry: Scholastic, Inc.

- Most of the time we can ignore "Inc.," but this time, because there are so many incarnations of Scholastic, we need to keep it in the heading.

6.17. National Geographic

- As per LC: 710 2_ $aNational Geographic Society (U.S.)

- Typical OPAC display: Added Entry: National Geographic Society (US)

- Here, as with Scholastic, it is important to seek a higher authority on the creation of a tag for this corporate body.

6.18. Living Books

- As per LC: 710 2_ $aLiving Books (Firm)

- Typical OPAC display: Added Entry: Living Books (Firm)

- As with our other problems, we only know the authoritative way of entering a corporate body by checking the authority file for Library of Congress.

Area 1 Summary Exercises

Apply 1XX, 245, 246, 6XX, 7XX, and 082 tags as necessary (check your answers against a library database):

6.19. This is a work of non-fiction about a toad as it catches something to eat. On the title page as:

> FROGS AND TOADS
> BY REBECCA K. O'CONNOR

- 082 14 $a597.8 $214
  - This is a fairly easy number to find. If you have the Dewey book, you can easily look in the index under frogs or toads. Checking a database for this title also yields this number, but be aware if the number you find on the database is the abridged or unabridged number.

- 100 1_ $aO'Connor, Rebecca.
  - Even though O'Connor uses her middle initial on this item, looking up the name in the LC database, you will see that the middle initial is dropped. If you were creating an original record, you might include the initial; however, be aware that any other items you add to your collection must also include that initial.

- 245 10 $aFrogs and toads /$cby Rebecca K. O'Connor.
  - Nothing special in this tag except that the capitalization has been corrected.

- 650 _1 $aToads.

- 650 _1 $aFrogs.

- 650 _1 $aAmphibians.

- The addition of the broader subject term "amphibians" is optional. If your collection is such that you don't need the broader term, then feel free to leave it out.

- There is no need in this record for extra tracings in the 246 and 700 tags.

6.20. This is a book on tape; it is fiction about a boy, Harry Potter, and the trouble he runs into in his second year at the wizardry school of Hogwarts. On the cassette tape as:

> HARRY POTTER AND THE CHAMBER OF SECRETS
> J.K. Rowling
> Read by Jim Dale

- 082 14 $a[FIC] $214

- 100 1_ $aRowling, J. K.

- 245 10 $aHarry Potter and the chamber of secrets $h[sound recording] /$cJ.K. Rowling.

  - Because this is a non-book item, we have to have a $h.

  - Notice in the 100 tag there is a space between the "J" and the "K," but in the 245 there is no space. That is because the 100 tag is used for retrieval purposes but the 245 $c is not.

  - As with our Farmer example in the text, we see that Dale has not been included in the $c information. One may see records with Dale in the 245 $c; however, the answer given here is technically more correct.

- 651 _1 $aEngland $vFiction.

- 650 _1 $aWizards $vFiction.

- 650 _1 $aMagic $vFiction.

- 650 _1 $aSchools $vFiction.

- 700 1_ $aDale, Jim, $d1948- $enrt.

  - Notice the relator abbreviation. If you think "nrt" will be meaningless to your users, it is all right to use the word written out in full, "narrator."

6.21. This videotape is a biography of the jazz pianist Duke Ellington based on the book of the same title. On the title screen as:

> Duke Ellington
> The Piano Prince and his Orchestra

Immediately preceding the title screen are credits for Scholastic and Weston Woods. The animated tape is based on the book by Andrea Davis Pinkney, illustrated by Brian Pinkney, although those names show up only in the credits at the end of the tape.

- 082 14 $a[B] $214

  - We have opted here for the "B" designation for this item. For more information about biographies, see the discussion in chapter five.

- 245 00 $aDuke Ellington $h[videorecording] :$bthe piano prince and his orchestra.

- Unlike our *Strega Nona* example, this tape does not say the names of the author and illustrator at the title screen, therefore we do not include them here in the 245 tag. We will include them elsewhere in the record (in a 5XX tag) but not here.

■ 246 3_ $aPiano prince and his orchestra $h[videorecording]
- It is probably not very likely that anyone is going to search for this item by the subtitle, but we include it as a matter of practice.

■ 600 10 $aEllington, Duke, $d1899-1974.

■ 650 _1 $aAfrican Americans $vBiography.

■ 650 _0 $aJazz musicians $zUnited States $vBiography $vJuvenile literature.

■ 650 _1 $aMusicians.
- As we have seen, LC tends to allow us more detail than does *LC/AC* and so we include both the heading for Jazz musicians as well as that for Musicians.

■ 700 1_ $aPinkney, Andrea Davis.

■ 700 1_ $aPinkney, J. Brian, $eill.

■ 710 2_ $aWeston Woods Studios.

■ 710 2_ $aScholastic, Inc.
- If you are uncomfortable with tracing Scholastic and Weston Woods, it is all right to not include them here. However, consider the positive retrieval aspects if a classroom teacher could search under Weston Woods or other producers of educational media.

260 Tag Exercises

Put this information into the proper 260 tag.

6.22. On the title page as:

New York   Scholastic

On the verso of the title page as:

© 2005 by the author

■ 260 __ $aNew York :$bScholastic,$cc2005.
- Even though we have seen Scholastic in the 700 tag as "Scholastic, Inc.," it is not necessary to include the "Inc." in the 260 tag.
- Notice the second "c" in the $c. Remember not to be confused by the name of the subfield and other copyright designations.

6.23. On the tape cassette as:

New York London Franklin Watts 2003

■ 260 __ $aNew York :$bF. Watts,$c2003.
- We are assuming we are cataloging in the United States, therefore we don't need to reference the London location. If we were cataloging in another country, Canada for example, our tag would look like this:

260 __ $aNew York ; $aLondon :$bF. Watts,$c2003.

- We have abbreviated "Franklin Watts" as F. Watts. This is perfectly all right to do as long as we maintain enough of the name to keep this Watts separate from any other Watts publisher that there may be.

6.24. On the end of the film as:
National Geographic Productions © MCMXCVIII

(National Geographic is located in Washington, D.C. but the location isn't on the item, you have to supply it.)

- 260 __ $a[Washington, D.C.] :$bNational Geographic Productions, $c1998.
  - Notice the insertion of the brackets to show we are supplying the information about the place of publication.

300 Tag Exercises

Create 300 tags for the following:

6.25. Unpaged book for children with color illustrations that measures 23 1/2 centimeters.

- 300 __ $a1 v. (unpaged) :$bcol. ill. ;$c24 cm.
  - We're happy to have a children's book so we don't have to count the page numbers.
  - Remember to round up to the next whole centimeter when measuring a book.

6.26. A 164 page book for young adults with color photographs, it measures 14 centimeters high and 30 centimeters wide.

- 300 __ $a164 p. :$bcol. photos. ;$c14 x 30 cm.
- 300 __ $a164 p. :$bcol. ill. ;$c14 x 30 cm.
  - Both of these tags are correct. It is a matter of choice if we want to be explicit in saying we have photographs instead of just some kind of illustrations.
  - Because the book is more than twice as wide as it is high, we have to include both measurements.

6.27. A DVD that runs 190 minutes, is in color and has a soundtrack, is the standard measurement, comes with a book that is 64 pages with illustrations, and measures 20½ centimeters.

- 300 __ $a1 DVD (190 min.) :$bcol., sd. ;$c4 1/4 in. +$e1 book (64 p. : ill. ; 21 cm.)

440 Tag Exercises

Put the following information into 440 tags:

6.28. A New True Book

- 440 _0 $aNew true book
- 440 _2 $aA new true book
  - We offer two options here, both are correct, because some systems will make use of the second indicator, non-filing characteristics and others will

not. You need to check with your system to see which one is correct for you.

6.29. Magic Tree House #34

- 440 _0 $aMagic tree house ;$vno. 34
  - Notice we have changed the number sign (#) to the abbreviation for number (no.). We are obligated to do that. Using symbols within the text of the surrogate record can confuse the system.

6.30. My FIRST Chapter book #10

- 440 _0 $aMy first chapter book ;$vno. 10
  - This is a trick question to make sure you were not seduced by the capitalization of the word "first."

5XX Tags Exercises

Try to convert this information into the appropriate 5XX tag:

6.31. This book won the Caldecott Medal in 1995.

- 586 __ $aCaldecott Medal winner, 1995
  - Remember, this tag does not end in a full stop.

6.32. This film is closed-captioned.

- 546 __ $aClosed-captioned.

- 546 __ $aClosed-captioned for the hearing impaired.
  - Either form of this note is acceptable.

6.33. This CD-ROM requires the Windows 2000 or higher operating system, a printer, and a color monitor.

- 538 __ $aSystem requirements: Windows 98 or higher; printer; color monitor.
  - We have noted that this item is a CD-ROM elsewhere in the record so we don't include it here. This is just a systems requirements note.

6.34. This book is for children at the reading grade levels three through five and it has a bibliography and an index.

- 504 __ $aIncludes bibliographic references and index.

- 521 0_ $a3-5.
  - We need two different notes fields to enter this information into the record: the 504 for the bibliographic note and the 521 for the reading level.
  - Remember that the way the 521 tag is displayed can be dependent on the system itself, so be sure to check this in making the decision of how you will enter the information both for the indicators and within the tag itself.

6.35. This book on disc is narrated by Gerard Doyle.

- 511 __ $aGerard Doyle, narrator.
  - Recall that the information about Doyle is on the disc itself and that we could not enter this information in the 245 tag. We enter that information in

the 511 tag, but we will also want to create a 700 tag to be able to find Doyle under a name search.

6.36. This DVD presents a performance of the actor Hal Holbrook portraying the author Mark Twain and was produced and directed by Ken Burns.

- 511 __ $aHal Holbrook (Mark Twain) ; producer and director, Ken Burns.
  - The credits note tag allows us to enter the names of actors as well as those responsible for the intellectual content of the information package.
  - Alternatively, the producer and director may be included in the 245 tag if prominently displayed on the title screen. In that case, the 511 tag would only have the reference to Holbrook.

Glossary

AACR: *Anglo-American Cataloguing Rules.* The standard in the US, Canada, and UK for cataloging. The current edition is the second edition, 2002 revision, 2004 update.

Access Point: A name, term, code, and so forth under which a bibliographic record may be searched and identified. See also *Heading*.

Added Entry: An entry, additional to the main entry, by which an item is represented in a catalog, a secondary entry. See also *Main Entry*.

Alternative Title: The second part of a title proper that consists of two parts, each of which is a title, the parts are joined by "or," or its equivalent in another language (e.g. *The Enchanted Island*).

Area: A major section of the surrogate record, comprising data of a particular category or set of categories. There are eight areas of description in the surrogate record. See also *Title & Statement of Responsibility; Edition; Material Specific Details; Publication, Distribution, Etc.; Physical Description; Series; Notes;* and *Standard Numbers*.

Author: See *Personal Author.*

Authority Control: A method to control the multiple headings an entry could appear under in the library catalog. Multiple entries are cross-referred to a single entry, using authority control. Entries that may require authority control include subject headings and author entries.

Authority File: A file containing the official forms of names, uniform titles, series titles, and/or subject headings used as access points in a library catalog, and citations to sources used to establish them, as well as cross-references to variant forms not used as access points.

Automation: Automatic, as opposed to human, operation or control of a process, equipment or a system; or the techniques and equipment used to achieve this. In the library world, automation usually refers to the process of automating routing and special library functions, such as circulation, cataloging, or collection development.

Barcode: A printed horizontal strip of vertical bars of varying widths, groups of which represent decimal digits and are used for identifying commercial products or parts. A barcode reader reads barcodes and the code is interpreted either through a software or a hardware decoder. In libraries, barcodes are usually affixed to the book covers to assist in easier circulation and collection control.

Bibliographic Level: One of three standard styles of description prescribed by *AACR*, each containing varying amounts of bibliographic information from the least (level 1) to the most (level 3).

Bibliographic Record: The organized description of an information package; originally applied to the description of books, the phrase is now associated with such records of all material types. See also *Surrogate Record*.

Call Number: The shelf address of an item, made up of its classification number and shelf marks.

Catalog: 1) A list of library materials contained in a collection, a library, or a group of libraries, arranged according to some definite plan; 2) in a wider sense, a list of materials prepared for a particular purpose.

Chief Source of Information: The source of data to be given preference as the source from which a surrogate record (or portion thereof) is prepared.

Colophon: A page at the end of a printed item on which bibliographic information is given.

Control Field: A field in the MARC format identified by a tag beginning with the number zero. Control fields contain information such as a call number and ISBN.

Controlled Vocabulary: A list of terms authorized for indexing, such as a subject heading listing thesaurus.

Copy Cataloging: The act of taking one or more surrogate records from one library database and copying the record(s) into another library database; the surrogate records of another database, also known as copy.

Corporate Body: An organization or group of persons that is identified by a particular name and that acts, or may act, as an entity. Typical examples of corporate bodies are associations, institutions, business firms, nonprofit enterprises, governments, government agencies, religious bodies, local churches, and conferences.

Cross-reference: A message in the catalog that links two or more related access points (for example, a message at *Clemens, Samuel Langhorne* referring searchers to *Twain, Mark*).

Database: One or more large structured sets of persistent data, usually associated with software to update and query the data. A simple database might be a single file containing many records, each of which contains the same set of fields where each field is a certain fixed width.

Delimiter: In the MARC format, a symbol identifying the start of a subfield. Delimiters print variously as a double dagger, $, or |.

Direct Entry: An access point in which the desired name or word is the first part of the heading, without naming a larger unit of which it is a part; for example, the heading is *Ohio*, not *United States—Ohio*.

Edition: Area 2 (250 tag) of the surrogate record wherein the cataloger records the version of the item being cataloged most often identified on the item with the terms "edition" and "version" but not "printing."

Editor: One who prepares for publication an item not his or her own. The editorial work may be limited to the preparation of the item for the manufacturer, or it may include supervision of the manufacturing, revision, or elucidation of the content of the item, and the addition of an introduction, notes, and other critical matter.

Entry: A record of an item in a catalog. See also *Heading*.

Entry Word: The word by which an entry is arranged in the catalog, usually the first word (other than an article) of the heading.

Field: One part of a MARC record corresponding to one area of description, one subject heading, one call number, and so forth; also known as Tag.

Fixed Field: A field containing data of a specific length and format (e.g. ISBN).

Format: In its widest sense, a particular physical presentation of an information package.

General Material Designation: A term indicating the broad class of material to which an information package belongs (e.g. sound recording).

Heading: A name, word, or phrase placed at the head of a catalog entry to provide an access point. See also *Access Point*.

Indicators: In MARC format are numeric codes for the computer that define the process for dealing with the information in the tag subfields. Each tag has two indicators, even if one or both are blank.

Indirect Entry: An access point (usually a geographic or corporate body name) in which the desired name is not the first part of the heading; for example, the desired name is *Boston*, but the heading is *Massachusetts—Boston*.

Information Package: The item being cataloged, whether it is a book, DVD, or LCD multimedia projector. Term used to refer to all types of materials being cataloged in a generic form rather than describing a list of item types.

Intellectual Description: The part of the surrogate record that describes the topic or discipline of which the information package is about, usually recorded in the subject (6XX) and classification (08X) tags.

ISBD: International Standard Bibliographic Description. International standard that defines the punctuation found in the surrogate record.

ISBN: International Standard Book Number. This is a system of unique numerical 10- or 13-digit identifiers for published titles. It helps to ensure more efficient ordering, inventory control, and accounting.

ISSN: International Standard Serial Number. The standard number publishers assign to serial publications; most often refers to periodicals, journals, or magazines, but may also be assigned to monographic serial publications.

Joint Author: A person who collaborates with one or more other persons to produce a work in relation to which the collaborators perform the same function.

Key Heading: In *Sears List of Subject Headings*, a set of subdivisions for one term that may be applied to all terms of its type.

Keyword: A searchable word, such as a significant word in a title or one of the words in a multiword subject heading.

Main Entry: The complete catalog record of an item, presented in the form by which the entity is to be uniformly identified and cited. The main entry may include the tracing(s).

MARC: MAchine Readable Cataloging. A group of identifying codes used to communicate information about an information package using computers, originally developed by and for the catalogers at the Library of Congress.

Material Specific Details: Area 3 (255 tag) of the surrogate record that describes the scale equivalents for maps and the data specifics for electronic resources.

Minimum Level Cataloging: Catalog records containing less information than the minimum required by currently accepted standard rules.

Mixed Responsibility: An information package created by contributions of more than one responsible party, such as a book having an author, an editor, and an illustrator.

Modules/Application Module: A module is a software segment that performs a specific library function, such as cataloging or inter-library loans. Automation system vendors typically sell modules separately (with the exception of circulation and cataloging), and libraries need not purchase them all at once. Circulation and cataloging modules are usually sold together, with "add-on" modules as possible extra purchases.

Monograph: An information package published/produced in full within a finite time period, originally synonymous with the term "book" may now refer to any finite information package.

Multimedia: A multipart information package in which the parts belong to more than one medium and no one part predominates.

Notation: In a classification, the system of alpha or numeric symbols used to represent subjects.

Notes: Area 7 (5XX tags) of the surrogate record that includes either the physical description or intellectual content of the information package that is not explained elsewhere in the surrogate record.

OCLC: Online Computer Library Center. Formerly the Ohio College Library Center, a bibliographic utility headquartered in Dublin, Ohio.

OPAC: Online Public Access Catalog The electronic form of the library catalog.

Parallel Title: The title of an item in a language other than the primary language of the text.

Personal Author: The person chiefly responsible for the creation of the intellectual or artistic content of an information package.

Physical Description: Area 5 (300 tag) of the surrogate record that includes a description of the information package itself rather than its intellectual content. Also the description of the information package that includes all parts of the surrogate record except for subject headings and classification numbers.

Preliminaries: Pages in a book up to and including the verso of the title page, and its cover.

Protocol: A protocol, in the information world, is an electronic standard by which government, business, and organizations conduct their flow of information. For example, the Z39.50 protocol is a standard by which libraries can share their MARC records.

Publication, Distribution, Etc.: Area 4 (260 tag) of the surrogate record that includes a description of when, where, and by whom the information package was published.

Qualifier: A word or phrase that removes ambiguity from an access point, usually given in parentheses, such as Cambridge (Eng.).

Query: A user's request for information, generally as a formal request to a database or search engine. Queries are the search string entered by patrons when searching for a particular library item or subject in the library automation system.

Reference: A direction from one heading or entry to another.

Retrospective Conversion: This is the process by which libraries convert the shelf list into a searchable, computerized database of library holdings. This database can then be used as the backbone of an automation system.

Search Key: In computer systems, it is a combination of characters from parts of access points. Search keys are used in place of full access points to minimize the size of indexes needed by the computer system as well as to minimize the number of characters searchers must enter.

Serial: An information package published/produced in parts intended to go on without end; in successive parts bearing numeric or chronological designations and intended to be continued indefinitely.

Series: Area 6 (440 tag) of the surrogate record that describes the publication connection between the information package and the series; group of discrete items having, in addition to their own titles, a common title identifying them as parts of the series.

Shared Responsibility: Applies when an information package is created by more than one responsible party sharing the same type of contribution (e.g. a book with two authors).

Shelflist: A catalog of items owned by a library, arranged by call number.

Standard Numbers: Area 8 (tags 02X) of the surrogate record that includes internationally, nationally, or locally recognized numbers specific to the information package being described, most often associated with ISBN and ISSN.

Statement of Responsibility: Part of the first area of description naming those with overall responsibility for the creation of the information package, usually recorded in the 1XX, 245, and 7XX tags.

Subfield: Part of a field in the MARC format.

Subject Heading: A word or phrase identifying the content of an item being cataloged and used as an access point; a term from an authorized list of terms to be used as access points, called a Descriptor.

Surrogate Record: The result of taking physical and intellectual data about an information package and arranging that data according to standard cataloging rules (*AACR*); library databases are comprised of surrogate records. *See also Bibliographic Record.*

Tag: The three-digit code identifying a line in the MARC format, also known as Field.

Title & Statement of Responsibility: Area 1 of the surrogate record wherein the cataloger records the title proper, additional title information, and the statement of the person(s) or corporate body responsible for the intellectual content of the information package. Corresponds to MARC tags 1XX, 24X, and 7XX.

Title Proper: The main title of an item.

Trace or Tracing: Recording information in the surrogate record so that it will be indexed and retrieved by the automated system when a query is entered by the user; tracings in the surrogate record include, but are not limited to, author, title, series, and subject.

Uncontrolled Vocabulary: Indexing in which any terms, not just those on an authorized list, may be used for retrieval, such as a title keyword index.

Uniform Title (Field): A title/field used to collocate editions and versions of a work that appear under different titles proper. The uniform title assigned to an item may be the title by which it is commonly known (e.g., *Alice in Wonderland*, not *Alice's Adventures in Wonderland*).

USMARC: United States MAchine Readable Cataloging.

Variable Field: A field in the MARC format containing data that vary in length and format.

Vendor: A vendor is the manufacturer, distributor and seller of a library automation system.

Z39.50: A standard for information retrieval that makes it possible for any library that uses automated library systems conforming to the standard to tap remote library collections or other libraries to tap local collections.

Index

title proper 104-110, 112, 115, 122, 138-139, 149, 153, 174, 200, 204

Town Mouse and the Country Mouse, The 28-29, 33-34, 36

tracing 111, 114-115, 117-119, 192, 196, 202, 204

translation (s) 4, 27, 99-102, 109, 111, 116, 123, 140-141, 173-175, 189, 192

transparencies 24

trilingual 100

typography 28

U

Under the Sea 138

union catalog(s) 10, 18-19, 156, 181

United States MAchine Readable Cataloging 205

University of Delaware Project Coast list 8

unpaged 131, 133-134, 136, 197

URL(s) 160-161, 163-165

user's guide 25, 135

USMARC 205

V

tvariable control fields 92

variable field(s) 28, 31-32, 205

vendor(s) 21-22, 30, 32, 44, 46-47, 49, 57, 68, 88, 96, 111, 140, 152, 160, 167, 175, 179, 203, 205

Vennema, Peter vii, 39, 107, 116

videorecording(s) 24, 26, 31, 105, 107, 109, 120, 195-196

videotapes vi, 17, 24, 89, 120, 131, 134, 141, 168, 170

Visual Dictionary of the Universe 78, 107, 120

vocabulary, controlled 42, 44-45, 55-57, 70, 201, 204

vocabulary, uncontrolled 42, 204

W

Walt Disney's Aladdin 112

Web pages 150

Web site(s) v, vi, 5-7, 11-12, 20, 26, 28, 30-31, 42, 48, 68, 92, 95-96, 99, 102, 159, 162-166, 180-181

Weidt, Maryann N. 113

Weigand, Wayne A. 89

What is FRBR? 14

World Cat 20

X

XML 12, 161

Z

Z39.50 16-17, 179-181, 203, 205